MILLENNIAL FEMINISM AT WORK

MILLENNIAL FEMINISM AT WORK

Bridging Theory and Practice

Edited by Jane Juffer

ILR PRESS

AN IMPRINT OF CORNELL UNIVERSITY PRESS   ITHACA AND LONDON

First published 2021 by Cornell University Press

Library of Congress Cataloging-in-Publication Data

Names: Juffer, Jane, 1962– editor.
Title: Millennial feminism at work : bridging theory and practice / edited by Jane Juffer.
Description: Ithaca [New York] : ILR Press, an imprint of Cornell University Press, 2021. | Includes bibliographical references and index.
Identifiers: LCCN 2021018916 (print) | LCCN 2021018917 (ebook) | ISBN 9781501760273 (hardcover) | ISBN 9781501760280 (paperback) | ISBN 9781501760297 (epub) | ISBN 9781501760303 (pdf)
Subjects: LCSH: Women employees—Social conditions—21st century. | Sex role in the work environment. | Gender identity in the workplace. | Feminism. | Feminist theory. | Queer theory.
Classification: LCC HD6053 .M498 2021 (print) | LCC HD6053 (ebook) | DDC 305.42—dc23
LC record available at https://lccn.loc.gov/2021018916
LC ebook record available at https://lccn.loc.gov/2021018917

Contents

Acknowledgments   vii

Introduction: Feminist Studies and the Millennial Workforce   1
Jane Juffer

Part 1   **NONPROFIT ORGANIZATIONS**

    1. Affective Exertions at the Humanitarian Frontlines:
Engendering Recognition of Gendered Labor
and Mutuality through Feminist and Queer Theory   19
Kate Poor

    2. Subjugated Knowledge: Listening to LGBTQ
Homeless Youth   43
Sassafras Lowrey

    3. The Patriarchal Roots of Philanthropy   49
Lauren Danzig

Part 2   **THE BUSINESS WORLD**

    4. "Woman, You Are the One Doing It Wrong":
A Decolonial Conceptualization of Colombian
Working-Class Femininity   59
Laura Ramos-Jaimes

    5. How to Market Anticapitalist Feminism:
The Making of an Online Socialist Agenda   73
Alissa Medina

    6. The Perils of Perfection Feminism   79
Stephanie Newman

    7. Circuitous Paths from University to Work,
and Finding Feminist Willfulness along the Way   87
Jael Goldfine

Part 3 **PEDAGOGY**

8. Letter to a White Supremacist   105
Addie Tsai

9. Praise to Our School We Love So Dear—or Maybe Not:
Status Quo and Safe Spaces in High School   117
Hayley Zablotsky

10. Love the Killjoy   124
Justine Parkin

Part 4 **HEALTH AND MEDICINE**

11. Acts of Defiance: The Power of Anger and Sadness
in the Workplace   133
Rose Al Abosy

12. #MyBirthToo: The Patriarchy of the Modern
Obstetric System   139
Savannah Medley Taylor

13. Navigating Feminism and Vulnerability in the
Medical Workplace   147
Lily Pierce

Part 5 **MEDIA**

14. Where Are the Queer Politics? #MeToo, Robin Wright,
and Celebrity PR Work   157
Samuel Naimi

15. The Immanence of Social Media Labor? The Struggle
to Find a Feminist Dwelling   167
Sadaf Ferdowsi

16. Finding "the Trouble with Normal" in Journalism   176
Rachel Cromidas

17. "No Place to Be, Except with Each Other": How Women's
Studies Taught Me to Be Unionized   183
Reina Gattuso

List of Contributors   189
Index   193

Acknowledgments

This book would not have materialized had the following seven graduates of the Feminist, Gender, and Sexuality Studies (FGSS) Program at Cornell University not taken the time to return to campus to reflect on their experiences using feminist theory in their various jobs: Sarah Asman, Jael Goldfine, Samuel Naimi, Nevena Pilipovic-Wengler, Kate Poor, Alex Thomas, and Alane Trafford. Their "Feminist at Work" forum in March 2019 inspired undergraduate students to pursue feminist and queer studies and instructed faculty on how to better bridge theory and practice in the classroom. Their commitment to social justice while in the workplace embodies feminist praxis.

On a more personal note, these students and many others I have had the privilege of teaching during my twelve years in the FGSS Program at Cornell have kept me awake many nights—and I mean that in the best possible sense—awake contemplating their provocations, made from both inside and outside the classroom. I cannot begin to name all these students, but I want to give a special mention here to a handful whose engagements with me in the past several years have influenced this collection: Helena Brittain, Karla Maria Castillo Barrera, Emma DiGiovanni, Bailey Dineen, Nikita Forrester, Alyssa Kamath, Prameela Kottapalli, Andrea Maghacot, Bianca Murillo, Anuli Ononye, Nina Pingon, Jocelyn Vega, and Yujue Wang.

At the time of the "Feminist at Work" forum and in the subsequent year, Professor Durba Ghosh was director of FGSS, and her three years at the helm of our program revitalized my belief in institutional activism. Her sense of humor, deep commitment to ethical decision-making, and careful attention to students' needs created a nourishing community for which I will be forever grateful. Thanks also to my other faculty colleagues in FGSS, Tao Leigh Goffe, Saida Hodžić, Kate McCullough, Juno Parreñas, Lucinda Ramberg, and Sara Warner, and to the FGSS staff (who really run the program!), Aidan Kelly and Maria Montesano. In my other institutional space, Caroline Levine, as chair of the English Department, has supported my work and been an inspirational administrator. Frances Benson, my editor at ILR Press, believed in this project from the start and gave me invaluable advice; furthermore, she found a truly amazing reader, Abigail Brooks, whose thoughtful and comprehensive suggestions greatly improved each essay.

Finally, the contributors to this book have made the work of editing a true pleasure. Across the board, they responded quickly to my suggestions and came up with more of their own. Although many of us have not met, we did manage to form a virtual collective through group emails. Most, if not all, of these writers are managing precarious work situations yet believed in this project so much they were willing to devote their time, energy, intellect, and passion to demonstrate the power of feminist and queer theory. May we all get together someday soon— perhaps at a book launch!

MILLENNIAL FEMINISM AT WORK

INTRODUCTION

Feminist Studies and the Millennial Workforce

Jane Juffer

I am writing this introduction in the midst of the coronavirus pandemic, a time in which it seems as if nothing else really matters. Yet the pandemic has also made these essays even more timely, insofar as it has become all too clear how precarious are the jobs of so many people in the United States. The questions that set this book in motion in the summer of 2019 now seem even more urgent: How does one live with the constant threat of losing one's job? Or the constant pressure of cobbling together enough freelance writing jobs to pay the rent? How does one make sense of the gap between the relative ease of college life and the hardscrabble world of work?

This book gathers the voices of seventeen millennials who have been grappling with these issues from a feminist angle; all of them earned variations of feminist studies degrees in their undergraduate education. I solicited these essays after organizing a public event in March 2019 at Cornell University called "Feminism at Work," featuring seven alumni recently graduated with majors in our Feminist, Gender, and Sexuality Studies (FGSS) Program. They came from a variety of fields and places—director of housing for a refugee shelter in Texas, medical student beginning her residency in North Carolina, culture writer in New York City, fund-raiser for Planned Parenthood in New York City, publicity person for celebrities in Los Angeles, and graduate students in urban planning and communications in Boston and Maryland. They spoke movingly about the ways in which feminist studies had inspired and nurtured them through difficult times, informing their job decisions and coworker relationships and motivating them to seek work that changed the world. They also described how difficult it is to be an outspoken feminist in a world that valorizes professionalism over radical politics. They described how feminist theory helps them understand and critique these work conditions but also how difficult it is to change them.

How does one bring together theory and practice—the mantra of so much feminist work, both inside and outside the academy? Must that binary of inside and outside remain when, ideally, feminist studies should prepare students to enter the work world? These are questions that I constantly ask myself—as director of undergraduate studies for the better part of a decade and now, as I am about to become FGSS director. Too often, I fear, we as professors do not adequately consider both the connections and the gaps between the classroom and the workplace—especially the theory classroom. We can feel exhilarated by the power of theory, and these essays do demonstrate its ongoing power in many locations. However, they also demonstrate theory's limitations when it remains in the realm of the theoretical. While we certainly cannot hold theory solely responsible for its limits, we can ask—as all of these essays do—how to connect it more clearly to material change on the job.

To frame the book and articulate my call for papers as I expanded beyond the Cornell group, I turned to Sara Ahmed's 2017 *Living a Feminist Life*. My call for essays, distributed across social media sites, featured her question of what it means to "live a feminist life," postgraduation, when the support structures of college life are less present. In her book—which Ahmed was finishing even as she decided to leave academia in response to various frustrations with its intransigence—she defines feminist theory as "something we do at home" (7). "To bring feminist theory home," she says, "is to make feminism work in the places we live, the places we work" (10). *Feminism at Work* demonstrates the efforts of these seventeen writers to make feminist theory work at the places they work. There is no universal answer here, no singular definition of feminism. Rather, feminist theory offers strategies for analyzing the power imbalances of any particular site. Ahmed's definition of feminism is apt: "Feminism: how we survive the consequences of what we come up against by offering new ways of understanding what we come up against" (22). Theory at its best offers these "new ways of understanding."

What these millennials have come up against in the workplace is formidable and exhausting. Some people might consider these contributors to be relatively privileged workers—no one is working in the minimum-wage service industry, for example. Indeed, privilege is a consideration in all of these essays, as the writers grapple with the privilege of having gone to university and engaged in feminist theory. Yet in socioeconomic terms, none of these writers holds a privileged position. Most of them have struggled to make ends meet, have changed jobs at least once, or have deliberated about whether to continue working for nonprofits that minimize risks to their workers' mental and emotional health.

These precarious economic conditions are exacerbated by other vulnerabilities related to race, gender, and sexuality. They are also shaped by particular geographical conditions. For example, Addie Tsai, a community college teacher in Texas, describes the harassment she experienced by a white supremacist student and the vulnerability she felt as a queer Asian nonbinary person at a workplace governed by Texas Senate Bill 11, which permits handgun license holders to carry a concealed handgun on campus. Samuel Naimi, working in Hollywood public relations for Robin Wright, relates how his voice was ignored when Wright's co-actor on *House of Cards*, Kevin Spacey, came out as gay at the same time he seemed to acknowledge sexual assault allegations. This was particularly problematic because the Me Too movement was at its zenith, yet it was also largely ignoring sexual violence against LGBTQ people. Laura Ramos-Jaimes, returning to work in Colombia after earning her degree in economics and gender studies in London, relates her experiences with racism there and describes the manner in which racism is imbricated in the country's colonial history.

Across these heterogeneous essays, two powerful and interrelated themes emerge: the devaluation of affective labor and the pressure to not be too angry or "emotional." As I describe later, these themes have been the focus of feminist critique and activism for many years. Jobs connected to nurturing and caring remain on the low end of the pay scale; as Emma Goldberg of the *Washington Post* reported in a 2019 article on the ongoing gender pay gap, "Underlying the shorted pay slips is a culture of gendered stereotypes that pushes women toward lower-paying, care-focused work—and then pays less because those jobs are identified as women's work. . . . Embedded in the very DNA of Americans' understanding of work is a devaluation of women's time and skills."[1]

This devaluation of work that involves nurturing and caring is closely connected to the denigration of the very expression of emotions, which is still all too often tied to practices deemed to be "unprofessional." Numerous contributors in this book describe situations in which it was made clear that they should follow the rules at the risk of being perceived as too angry, too sensitive, or too demanding. The constant self-questioning about how to respond to and counter this silencing is exhausting, writes Rose Al Abosy. Describing her time as a research technician in a lab at the Dana-Farber Cancer Institute, she says, "Being angry all the time was exhausting. My job was already hard. Unpacking each event with extended conversation was time consuming, distracted me from my work, and made it difficult to collaborate with people on projects. At some point, I could no longer tell whether my goal was educating others about their problematic behavior or working toward making my environment marginally more hospitable."

"Theory in the Flesh"

One might consider each of these essays a personal testimony, as they are grounded in intimate experiences. However, they also engage the feminist tradition of connecting the personal to the political. Feminist theory arises from experiences of "pain and struggle," says bell hooks—experiences that then become the basis for "contesting interlocking systems of violence" (1984, 58). Similarly, Cherríe Moraga and Gloria Anzaldúa coined the concept "theory in the flesh" to capture the idea that theory emerges from embodied experience, in a reciprocal and constant relationship. As they write in *This Bridge Called Our Back: Writings by Radical Women of Color*, "A theory in the flesh means one where the physical realities of our lives— our skin color, the land or concrete we grew up on, our sexual longings—all fuse to create a politic born out of necessity" (2002, 21). There is no binary between mind and body, intellect and corporeality, but rather an intertwined articulation of the experiences of embodiment.

"Theory in the flesh" is oppositional to dominant forms of knowledge in part because it embraces the realm of the emotional as an affective, embodied, experiential kind of knowledge, thus rejecting the normative view that emotions are irrational and antithetical to reason and logic. As Alison Jaggar writes in "Love and Knowledge," "Reason has been associated with members of dominant political, social, and cultural groups, and emotion with members of subordinate groups," including women and people of color (2016, 385). Furthermore, when marginalized groups express themselves forcefully, they are discredited on the basis of their anger, and "the alleged epistemic authority of the dominant groups then justifies their political authority" (385).

Yet it is precisely this justified anger and the other feelings generated by subordination that lead to keen insights, says Jaggar, as our feelings prompt us to investigate why something feels wrong, which in turn leads to analysis and problem solving. As she says, "Conventionally inexplicable emotions, particularly though not exclusively those experienced by women, may lead us to make subversive observations that challenge dominant conceptions of the status quo" (1989, 387). As Audre Lorde succinctly notes, "Anger is loaded with information and energy" (1984, 127).

Lorde's collection of essays *Sister Outsider* is the second most cited source in the book. Initially, that surprised me, since these writers belong to a younger generation of feminists. I had expected them to rely on Sara Ahmed (especially given the wording in my call for papers), and indeed many of them did (her work is the most frequently cited). Yet I was also gratified to realize their training included a strong grounding in the history of feminist thinkers, especially someone so powerful as Lorde. I myself have welcomed this opportunity to reread Lorde as I am writing this introduction in 2020, when protesters across the United States and even the world are expressing their outrage at the death of George Floyd and other African Americans at the hands of police. In no uncertain terms, Lorde links feminism to anger at racism and other forms of oppression: "Every woman has a well-stocked arsenal of anger potentially useful against those oppressions, personal and institutional, which brought that anger into being. Focused with precision it can become a powerful source of energy serving progress and change. . . . I am speaking of basic and radical alterations in those assumptions underlining our lives" (1984, 127).

This idea of critiquing the "assumptions underlining our lives" is an apt way to define the theory that informs this book, since every essay explores and reflects on the assumptions that inform their workplaces—assumptions that usually go unexamined. Theory is often a preliminary step to action, as one must first understand what needs to be changed and why. Or perhaps we could deconstruct the distinction between thought and action, recognizing the hard work of thinking and the ongoing reflection required in organizing. We thus arrive at a definition of praxis, which incorporates reflection and a grappling with the complexities of power as one tries to figure out one's complicity as well as the potential for subversion or perhaps outright rebellion.

In addition to Ahmed and Lorde, a range of feminist and queer theorists are cited throughout these essays, with a significant amount of overlap, indicating a kind of common feminist vernacular for this generation. This "canon" includes Judith Butler, Kimberle Crenshaw, Patricia Hill Collins, Adrienne Rich, Donna Haraway, Gayle Rubin, Michael Warner, Zillah Eisenstein, bell hooks, James Baldwin, and Simone de Beauvoir. Some of the writers connect "old" theorists to new fields; for example, Sadaf Ferdowsi uses de Beauvoir's distinction between "transcendence" and "immanence" to analyze the labor of social media. Hayley Zablotsky uses Butler's theory of gender performativity to explicate gendered performances of high school students. Key concepts such as intersectionality also recur frequently as these writers deploy all the tools from their undergraduate toolbox to deconstruct the workplace. Understanding how power works does not, however, mean one is in a position to actually shift the power flows, given the nature of capitalism.

The Forces of Neoliberal Capital

It is crucial for feminist studies programs and departments—even or perhaps especially those with a humanities bent—to fully acknowledge and address the precarious work world in which most of our students will find themselves.

Undoubtedly, many programs around the United States and elsewhere in the world already do this, in various ways, and I do not purport to be providing an overview of gender studies programs in this introduction.

Nevertheless, there are also many programs that could do more to help students confront and navigate the so-called gig economy. As feminist scholar Angela McRobbie, writing from the United Kingdom and the field of cultural and media studies, says, "It is incumbent upon us social scientists and cultural studies academics to develop a vocabulary and a methodology for tracing freelance pathways in the cultural sector. We need to be able to understand at the level of experience how this terrain is negotiated. There remains a chasm of difference between middle-aged academics for whom the university sector has provided a single sourced income more or less since graduation and young people whose portfolio careers increasingly mean not serial jobs but multi-tasking" (2016, 26). Developing "a vocabulary and a methodology" requires us, I would argue, to offer courses that focus on this precarious economy, both critiquing it and providing tools for navigation and resistance. We must also connect these courses to real-world experience, in the form of internships and job training experiences. Goldsmiths, University of London, for example, where McRobbie works with first-year master's degree students in communications, offers such practical tracks as "brand development" and "cultural and creative entrepreneurship," along with "gender, media and culture." McRobbie's book *Be Creative* is full of anecdotes from former students who are now negotiating the realm of creative work in fashion, media, and various DIY fields, drawing on their cultural studies training to bring a critical edge to for-profit work.

Ideally, students would have the opportunity while still in college to "try out" theory in a workplace, so that there is time to return to the classroom and consider how the engagement redefines the theory. Many universities enable such realizations in the form of engaged community work and internships. At Cornell, for example, our FGSS Program for the past two years has received grant money from the Engaged Cornell initiative, whose mission is to have every Cornell undergraduate do some kind of community project before they graduate. In conjunction with my class on the injustices of immigrant detention in the United States, FGSS partnered with the Buffalo, New York–based group Justice for Migrant Families, whose focus is the Buffalo Federal Detention Center, which holds hundreds of immigrants in intolerable conditions. Our students visit people being held, providing the support of friendship, legal connections, and documentation of abuses and helping raise bond money and provide housing for those who are released. These visitations allow us to think through the important feminist question of how one advocates for others without appropriating their voices. This is a thorny theoretical issue—think Gayatri Spivak's essay "Can the Subaltern

Speak?"—and putting it into practice can both clarify and complicate the question of representation. Some of these students are already working this summer in related internships, and several others are on their way to law school and plan to focus on immigration law.

Engagement compels us to ask the inevitable questions about complicity—with the very arenas we are critiquing, whether that be immigration control, corporations, or nonprofit organizations. Even more, engagement requires us to go beyond complicity and proactively help student prepare for jobs in which they will need to know how to do things such as negotiate for a salary increase and work within environments that are more focused on individual success than collaboration. In other words, how does one move from a classroom in which we advocate for community and social justice to an environment that advocates teamwork for the good of the bottom line? While critiquing the lack of social support for young creatives, McRobbie nevertheless does not dismiss the possibilities created under neoliberalism—namely, the proliferation of new jobs for "creatives." As she says, the "micro-economies of culture and the arts find themselves the subject of commercial interest" (2016, 18). Furthermore, the very definition of what counts as creative work has expanded to include not only the usual jobs such as "writer, artist, film director or fashion designer" but also those of hairdresser and cook and, of course, those in the vast and rapidly expanding realm of social media. This is the world described by Brooke Duffy in her work on young people, mainly women, engaged in social media production; as she says, "The internet has also given rise to markedly gendered—and unabashedly commercial—genres of content production, fashion blogging, beauty vlogging, mommy blogging, and DIY design, among others" (2017, 42).

More work like McRobbie's and Duffy's is necessary, for too often, we in the academy posit creativity and capitalism as counterposing forces, and left-leaning students in our classes grow accustomed to the automatic critique of anything smacking of profit. It is time we discourage this dismissal and rather focus on helping them navigate the world they will quickly enter. I will never forget the first time I spoke to a student of mine—one of the best writers I have ever taught—about her realizations upon entering the freelance writing world after graduating with high honors and a stellar thesis on Taylor Swift fans. "I have had to learn how to monetize my time," she said, describing how every story idea she pitched was accompanied by an assessment of the time needed to complete it and the money ultimately earned. This was a negotiation she had never contemplated in college, where she spent long hours fine-tuning her thesis without needing to contemplate a cost-benefit analysis. As McRobbie aptly puts it, "The meaning of professionalism for art students is now also understood in terms of entrepreneurialism. This is seen as an accompaniment to imagination or inspiration. It also marks out the economization of imagination, the marketization of creativity. It does not just supplement the already existing capacities of the subject but drives them, steering the artistic subject in particular directions that are conducive to commercial success" (2016, 76).

These young people engage in their creative endeavors without the support and community that they had (most of them) as undergraduates, something that became painfully clear to me as I read the seventeen essays gathered in this book. Also, they do so without the social or state support of previous eras, when government—more so in McRobbie's context of the United Kingdom than in the United States—offered some support for a public arts sector. As Duffy says, "the rapid growth of independent employment" is "symptomatic of what scholars and labor advocates understand as a 'political economy of insecurity'" (2017, 10). As does McRobbie, Duffy describes both the downside and the potential implicit in this so-called gig economy, as young people feel "free" to pursue their passions. She defines aspirational labor as

> a mode of (mostly) uncompensated, independent work that is propelled by the much-venerated ideal of *getting paid to do what you love*. As both a practice and a worker ideology, aspirational labor shifts content creators' focus from the present to the future, dangling the prospect of a career where labor and leisure coexist. Indeed, aspirational laborers expect that they will one day be compensated for their productivity—be it through material rewards or social capital. But in the meantime, they remain suspended in the consumption and production of branded commodities. (2017, 5–6)

This "suspension" encourages improvisation, requires constant vigilance for opportunities, and entails a creative cobbling together of jobs in order to make ends meet. While sometimes exciting, this "lifestyle" is also exhausting and stressful.

This juggling act marks the experiences of most of the contributors to this book, many of whom, even a few years after graduation, have held several jobs simultaneously or changed jobs and career paths. For example, one of our contributors, Sadaf Ferdowsi, described to me in an introductory email exchange her career trajectory since graduating with a gender studies degree from the University of Chicago in 2013: "Since then, I have worked in retail, real estate, higher ed., film, tech, and currently I'm a writer for a marketing firm. I also took a year off working to be a caregiver for my father. I am now 28 and have been reflecting on how this wide range of work/caregiving experience impacts and shapes how I understand 'living a feminist life.'" In a similar vein, at the Cornell alumni panel, Jael Goldfine advised audience members to "divest from the moral value of a linear career. Conditions today make that statistically unlikely but also not necessarily the best option." Several essays address this theme, concluding that it's OK to quit a job when you discover you cannot tolerate the disjuncture between your politics and the work you're doing. Is that a sign of privilege? That, in fact, is the ongoing question for many of these writers: the recognition of a certain kind of cultural capital, but one that does not translate into financial security.

From Hartmann to Hardt

Many feminist scholars have recognized the need to locate their work in a critical if not oppositional relationship to capitalism. In her influential 1979 essay "The Unhappy Marriage of Marxism and Feminism: Towards a More Progressive Union," Heidi Hartmann argues that the Marxist critique of capitalism is inadequate because it does not account for gender, and that the radical feminist critique of patriarchy falls short because it is insufficiently historical and materialist. As she puts it, "Capitalist development creates the places for a hierarchy of workers, but traditional Marxist categories cannot tell us who will fill which places. Gender and racial hierarchies determine who fills the empty places. *Patriarchy is not simply hierarchical organization*, but hierarchy in which *particular* people fill *particular* places" ([1979] 1997, 103).

While Marxist analysis does address women's positions, it does so only in relation to their role as workers, either as waged workers or as performing the housework that facilitates capitalism. "Most Marxist analyses of women's position take as their question the relationship of women to the economic system, rather than that of women to men, apparently assuming the latter will be explained in their discussion of the former" (Hartmann [1979] 1997, 98). Furthermore, Marxist criticism gestures at but does not go far enough in theorizing the denigration of values associated with the domestic sphere, and here is where feminism's critique of patriarchy figures prominently: "The sexual division of labor places women in low-paying jobs, and in tasks thought to be appropriate to women's role. Women are teachers, welfare workers, and the great majority of workers in the health fields. The nurturant roles that women play in these jobs are of low status because capitalism emphasizes personal independence and the ability of private enterprise to meet social needs, emphases contradicted by the need for collectively provided social services" (Hartmann [1979] 1997, 111). Capitalism depends on these gendered roles.

Yet capitalism is also flexible, writes Hartmann, which prompts us to ask, some forty years later, is capitalism so flexible that it—more or less—has incorporated and diluted feminism? Or does the new form that capitalism has taken—namely, in its reliance on a precarious, flexible labor force—allow for a more sustained, albeit not radical, expression of feminism? For example, since Hartmann wrote her essay, much has changed in terms of the nuclear family formation that supported capitalism. The "social structures that enable men to control women's labor" (Hartmann [1979] 1997, 101) are less explicit, though obviously still present to some degree. Feminist and queer activism have facilitated a weakening of binary gender roles in a manner that has influenced, to varying degrees, the workplace. Femininity is no longer as firmly attached to biologically female-identified bodies. The very occupations and values that Hartmann identifies as gendered feminine, such as those in the service economy, are held by people of varying genders. Similarly, occupations and values deemed masculine are held and practiced by people who identify as women.

This de-essentializing of gender does not automatically signal progress, of course. It could, in fact, signal an intensified exploitation of all workers in the growing service economy. Yet there is potential in the delinking of so-called feminine values from biology—potential to address the devaluing of emotional labor that I described earlier that appears in many of this book's essays. This potential is addressed by Michael Hardt and Antonio Negri in their analysis in *Multitude* of a precarious labor force, which they say is composed of two types of labor—immaterial and affective—both of which encompass even as they rearticulate the kinds of feminized labor that Hartmann describes. Immaterial labor incorporates the realm of communication; it "produces ideas, symbols, codes, texts, linguistic figures, images, and other such products" (2004, 108). Affective labor incorporates mind and body, often with the goal of exploiting both:

> In fact, affects, such as joy and sadness, reveal the present state of life in the entire organism, expressing a certain state of the body along with a certain mode of thinking. Affective labor, then, is labor that produces or manipulates affects such as a feeling of ease, well-being, satisfaction, excitement, or passion. One can recognize affective labor, for example, in the work of legal assistants, flight attendants, and fast food workers (service with a smile). One indication of the rising importance of affective labor, at least in the dominant countries, is the tendency for employers to highlight education, attitude, character, and "prosocial" behavior as the primary skills employees need. A worker with a good attitude and social skills is another way of saying a worker adept at affective labor. (Hardt and Negri 2004, 108)

Both forms of labor are alienating in the Marxist sense, say Hardt and Negri, as conveyed in the sentiment, "I am selling my ability to make human relationships, something extremely intimate, at the command of the client and the boss" (111). Yet this alienation is different from that which occurred under Fordist capitalism, insofar as it depends less on the "expropriation of value measured by individual or collective labor time" and more on the "capture of value that is produced by cooperative labor and that becomes increasingly common through its circulation in social networks" (113). The products of both immaterial and affective labor are social, and within this reliance on connections—what Hardt and Negri term "the common"—is also the potential for a kind of solidarity that exceeds and therefore potentially resists alienation. In this view as well, there is no necessary link between affect and gender: the common has the potential to transcend the gender binary, in part because affective and material labor themselves are not inherently gendered.

This potential will seem too optimistic or even naïve to some feminist critics, such as McRobbie, who says, "Hardt comments that increasingly forms of labour entail elements of care, or emotion, and that these labour practices have the capacity to produce 'collective subjectivities' that could contest the formidable power of contemporary capitalism" (2016, 104). By contrast, she sees little evidence that "the manipulation of affect" in a "mostly female workforce" is producing a "new radical politics" (104). Rather, she argues, "capitalism makes a seductive offer to young women with the promise of pleasure in work, while at the same time this work is nowadays bound to be precarious and insecure and lacking the protection of conventional employment" (105). Similarly, Duffy argues that affective labor today differs little from the devalued feminized work of the past: "The labor of aspiration has conceptual similarities to traditional forms of 'women's work' (domestic labor, reproductive labor, care labor), which have remained invisible despite their central role in servicing the engines of capitalism" (2017, 9). Both McRobbie and Duffy suggest that capitalist rationality and individualism continue to overpower any sense of communality or valorization of caring in the workplace, whether that be for-profit, where we might expect this denigration of caring, or nonprofit, where we might hope for a nurturing environment. Caring labor is still gendered feminine.

Several essays in this book generally support this conclusion: the gendered binary is alive and well in the work world, including nonprofits. Unfortunately and paradoxically, the emphasis on caring for others often coincides with a lack of care for the health and well-being of the employees. In her essay in this volume, Kate Poor describes the situation at a shelter for refugees in Austin, Texas, where she works as the director of housing and regularly struggles with workplace hazards and burnout produced, in part, by the nonprofit's devaluation of worker well-being. At the same time as workers specialized in these femme forms of caretaking are considered unskilled and thus, are undercompensated, many of these organizations require feminine bodies to undertake great workplace risks, which are justified by the pursuit of care and justice for clients. This contradiction between politics and practices prompted Sassafras Lowrey to ultimately leave her job as director of an LGBTQ homeless drop-in program, where cisgender white male staff had difficulty seeing the importance of incorporating youth in decisions about how the shelter would function. A similar devaluation of affective labor occurs in the social media world, where, as Duffy has written and Sadaf Ferdowsi describes in her essay, a mainly female workforce performs the taxing affective labor of constant connection: "There was always a status to update, an article to share, or an influencer to research. The work never seemed to end."

Yet there is also, in many of these essays, a nod to Hardt's argument: both insofar as it is only from within capitalism that resistance will be mounted and because this resistance can derive from the very reliance on affective labor's attention to relationships. Workers at the refugee shelter, for example, form close bonds with each other and with some of their clients that provide a counter to the alienating effects of immigration policy. In her essay on working in mental health at a veterans' facility, Lily Pierce describes how she finds herself connecting with older white men in a manner that at times transcends identity categories. Justine Parkin finds inspiration for teaching her high school students in bell hooks's *All about Love*, writing, "What hooks means, I think, is that love is an ethic that must motivate a feminist's actions." Each of these three jobs represents a site of traditionally defined affective labor, yet all three writers see potential for transforming care into a non-gendered and valued practice. This transformation is much more likely to happen in an environment of care and support than in a workplace where one feels isolated.

Community is more difficult to form postgraduation than at college, many of these writers say. It was palpable to me as I spent time with the seven alumni who returned to the Cornell campus. Because they had graduated in different years, only a few of them knew each other, some well, but often not so well. Yet they almost immediately formed a close-knit cadre, wandering from one event and meal to the next—chatting, reminiscing, critiquing, and strategizing. The spatial and temporal conditions lent themselves to an almost seamless (re)formation of feminist community. They talked about how hard it had been to find a new community after graduation and how lonely they felt in their workplaces as they searched for politically like-minded coworkers. They also told the undergraduate students who attended their panel that the most critical thing to do upon getting a job is to begin the hard work of community building.

Furthermore, one must go beyond community to think about organizing as workers. One of the Cornell alum, Nevena Pilopovic-Wengler, began her presentation with a useful phrase as a supplement to the feminist mantra "The personal is political": "The logistical is political," she said. Ask the following questions of your workplace, she urged: "How is the workplace organized? Who is getting paid and how are they getting paid? Step back and prioritize other people." She said she was too willing to accept "below poverty wages" in her first job as a community organizer with Americorp/Vista: "I really wish I had advocated for myself as a worker. Networking was really painful for me—because it felt really steeped in racist, misogynist, capitalist practices." However, she said, she soon realized that networking was another form of the activism in which she had always engaged and a way to ask the question, "What does it mean to reach out to people you might want to stay in touch with for the rest of your life?"

When I thought about Pilopovic-Wengler's advice as I read through these essays, it struck me that most of the contributors who had stayed in their jobs were those who had found some kind of community or who had organized in the workplace. In her essay, Reina Gattuso describes how getting her master's degree at New Delhi's Jawaharlal Nehru University made her realize the importance of unionizing, as she experienced "an educational space with a robust leftist tradition, where student politics were omnipresent and even setting classroom deadlines was an act of collective bargaining." It was there, Gattuso says, that she began to see herself as a worker, and she carried that lesson with her back to New York City, where she is now an active member of the Industrial Workers of the World's Freelance Journalists Union.

Organization of the Book

While each of these essays demonstrates the necessity and the power of bringing together theory and practice, each writer does that in a different fashion. The essays vary in length, tone, style, and theoretical approaches. Some are intensely personal, revealing intimate feelings and experiences. Some are barely personal, choosing instead to focus on the way the writers are positioned within a particular work situation. This heterogeneity is to be expected in a book that speaks from the first-person point of view, even as it situates these variegated experiences within a common capitalist structure. In fact, two of my goals as editor were to avoid homogenizing millennial experiences and to create a space for the expression of whatever feelings and emotions are evoked within labor conditions at this time.

The book is organized into five sections—nonprofit organizations, the business world, pedagogy, health and medicine, and media—with the goal of foregrounding both similarities and differences within each field. In the nonprofit section, for example, while all three essays testify to the persistent devaluation of feminized labor and the hierarchies of power, each writer takes a different approach to this devaluation, given the particularities of her workplace. Poor finds solidarity with her coworkers, while Lowrey eventually decides not to continue the battle against the top-down hierarchy and turns to writing as a career. Lauren Danzig analyzes the patriarchal structure of philanthropy, showing how the world of fund-raising for nonprofits is thoroughly embedded in gendered binaries. Drawing on Judith Butler's theory of performativity, Danzig considers how these binaries can be subverted from within in order to raise more money for causes in which she believes.

While all of the work experiences described in this book take place within the ambit of capitalism, the four essays in the second section directly address capitalism at its most explicit—the business world. How might one be a feminist within this world? Writing from Colombia after graduating from the London School of Economics, Laura Ramos-Jaimes critiques the "canon" of US feminist can-do texts such as Sheryl Sandberg's *Lean In: Women, Work, and the Will to Lead*. Lean-in feminism has been influential in Colombia, and Ramos shows how, after seeing some feminist potential in these texts, she realized that they reproduce racism, sexism, and colonialism. Feminism is also difficult to sustain in the entrepreneurial world of online business start-ups, as Stephanie Newman describes in recounting her attempt to support herself with a feminist blog and an online course on how to start your own business. Jael Goldfine recounts how difficult it was to maintain her feminist ethics while working as a publicity coordinator at a music public relations firm. Interestingly, both Newman and Goldfine describe how they struggled with leaving these jobs in response to their ethical conflicts, because even as feminists, they had internalized the values of ambition and perfection. Yet leaving, ultimately, says Goldfine, enabled a return to the "feminist will" that Sara Ahmed valorizes. In the final essay in this section, Alissa Medina finds an alternative way to survive capitalism: subvert from within. Her online site, Fembot, takes on digital capitalism through various strategies that both capitalize on and undermine mainstream advertising.

In the third section, three essays focus on pedagogy. Justine Parkin and Hayley Zablotsky reflect on the challenges of integrating feminism into high school classrooms, and Addie Tsai describes her harrowing experience with a self-described white supremacist at a Texas community college. In addition to the loss of community they felt after college, Zablotsky and Tsai describe the challenges of working with an often hierarchical school administration structure.

The medical and health profession is the focus of section four, in which three women in quite different fields describe similar quandaries about how to enact feminism in what historically has been a male-dominated, white world: Rose Al Abosy in medical research, Lily Pierce in a mental health rotation at a Veterans' Administration facility, and Savannah Medley Taylor in labor and birthing. Their quite different experiences illustrate how complex and heterogeneous this profession still is: Taylor critiques the patriarchal practices in obstetrics and finds a clear alternative in her work as a doula; Pierce finds that she is able to connect with veterans through a common human vulnerability; and Al Abosy describes how the high-pressure world of scientific research frequently demeans feminist practices and modes of being.

In the fifth section, on media, four writers from different kinds of publications talk about how they wrestle with the personal/political mantra of feminism: How does one express one's politics while simultaneously engaging in a media world that still, to some degree, asks that one leave one's personal biases at home? Rachel Cromidas reflects on her move from mainstream to alternative journalism, while Reina Gattuso explores the need to organize and unionize within the competitive world of freelance journalism. Samuel Naimi analyzes the power dynamics in the world of celebrity public relations, and Sadaf Ferdowsi looks at how gendered hierarchies are maintained within social media managerial jobs.

I am grateful to the contributors for taking the time to put words to page to produce this collaborative endeavor. The vivid and heartfelt writing contained in this book testifies to the power of "theory in the flesh," and I hope readers will feel that power while reading these essays. If so, this book becomes an example of bringing together theory and practice.

Note

1. Goldberg notes, "Between 1960 and 2018, U.S. industry transformed, as the workforce shifted from one that was smaller, whiter and focused on manufacturing to one that was larger, more diverse and driven by service labor. And yet, one thing has remained the same: the gender pay gap. While it has shrunk in the past 60 years, from 41 to 20 cents on the dollar for white women and from 57 to 38 cents for black women, it has nevertheless endured" (2019).

References

Ahmed, Sara. 2017. *Living a Feminist Life*. Durham, NC: Duke University Press.

Duffy, Brooke Erin. 2017. *(Not) Getting Paid to Do What You Love: Gender, Social Media, and Aspirational Work*. New Haven, CT: Yale University Press.

Goldberg, Emma. 2019. "Why the Gender Pay Gap Persists (and What We Can Do about It)." *Washington Post*, May 14, 2019.

Hardt, Michael, and Antonio Negri. 2004. *Multitude: War and Democracy in the Age of Empire*. New York: Penguin.

Hartmann, Heidi. (1979) 1997. "The Unhappy Marriage of Marxism and Feminism: Towards a More Progressive Union." In *The Second Wave: A Reader in Feminist Theory*, edited by Linda Nicholson, 97–122. New York: Routledge.

hooks, bell. 1984. *Feminist Theory: From Margin to Center*. South. End Press: Boston.

Jaggar, Alison. 2016. "Love and Knowledge: Emotion in Feminist Epistemology." In *Just Methods: An Interdisciplinary Feminist Reader*. 378-390. New York: Routledge.

Lorde, Audre. 1984. *Sister Outsider: Essays and Speeches*. Trumansburg, NY: Crossing.

McRobbie, Angela. 2016. *Be Creative: Making a Living in the New Culture Industries*. Cambridge, UK: Polity.

Moraga, Cherríe L. and Gloria Anzaldúa, eds. 2002. *This Bridge Called Our Back: Writings by Radical Women of Color*. 3rd Edition. Berkeley: Third Women Press.

Part 1

NONPROFIT ORGANIZATIONS

AFFECTIVE EXERTIONS AT THE HUMANITARIAN FRONTLINES

Engendering Recognition of Gendered Labor and Mutuality through Feminist and Queer Theory

Kate Poor

In recent experiences working in human rights organizations, I have reoriented from the study of gender and queer philosophy to the application and analysis of theory in practice. While I have been privileged to learn from and participate in vital activism supporting folks in precarious circumstances, I have also encountered many misalignments between the theorizing and articulation of humanitarian missions and their operative execution. This essay will explore the particular manifestation of one such incongruity: the reliance on and yet concomitant deprofessionalization of gendered labor within activist and humanitarian spaces, and the incidental casualties of transferring and codifying oppressive labor practices into missions bent on social liberation.

Even if nonprofit mission statements derive from and espouse queer, feminist, anticapitalist, antiracist ideologies, their own labor policies may evidence inconsistencies that overlook, undervalue, and underpay traditionally feminine (emotional, affective, caretaking) forms of labor. Nonprofits that both depend on and dismiss feminine-coded work use labor valuations set by for-profit structures that prioritize masculinist, consumption-focused modes of production and underestimate the value of expertise and knowledge derived from the margins. I argue that activist organizations that rely on feminine-coded labor to effectuate their missions while simultaneously devaluing the work as "unskilled" and the expertise as "inherent" qualities of their female staff engender shortsighted and harm-producing infrastructures and undermine their intentions of social justice. This essay will focus on the derogation of particular intangible labors—caretaking, therapeutic advocacy, community building, and psycho-emotional healing—within contemporary direct-service settings.

The (De)valuing of Affective Labor

Michael Hardt and Antonio Negri describe the emergence of abstract production and the evolving recognizability and application of such labor's value: "In the final decades of the twentieth century, industrial labor lost its hegemony and in its spread emerged 'immaterial labor,' that is labor that creates immaterial products, such as knowledge, information, communication, a relationship, or an emotional response" (2009, 108). Within the domain of immaterial production, labor that involves the handling of emotion, caretaking, or sensitive interpersonal relating constitutes a category of work called affective labor. Affective labor requires emotional resilience, nuanced compassion, tact, empathetic gentleness, patience, and composure. Assemblages of affected experiences can contribute to the production of relationships and can constitute collective subjectivities, such as networks and communities. As I will describe later, in social service provision and emergency crisis response work, these relationships and communities created through affective labor represent vital human connectivity that fortifies and makes possible humanitarian missions.

In reminding us of the traditional subjugation of knowledge derived from emotionality and affect, Sara Ahmed underlines the historical baggage that posits affective labor as less significant than other forms of immaterial work and thus renders a common perception of the affective laborer as less useful or knowledgeable. Ahmed also emphasizes the collision of the categories of affect, emotion, and the feminine: "'Emotion' has been viewed as 'beneath' the faculties of thought and reason. To be emotional is to have one's judgement affected: it is to be reactive rather than active, dependent rather than autonomous. Feminist philosophers have shown us how the subordination of emotions also works to subordinate the feminine and the body" (2004, 3).

Vestigial hangovers from the pathologization of emotive experience—the primordial, authoritarian dismissal of feminine knowledges via diagnoses of hysteria—forge the crater of axiological skepticism of the utility of affective labor. The entanglement with pejorative valuations of emotion, caretaking, and "women's work" quells the potentiality of seeing affective perspicacity as a professional skill. Hardt and Negri further emphasize, "When affective labor becomes central to many productive tasks under the hegemony of immaterial labor it is still most often performed by women in subordinate positions. Indeed labor with a high affective component is generally feminized, given less authority, and paid less"

(2009, 111). Nonetheless, Alison Jaggar calls us to reconsider dismissals of wisdom derived from and informed by emotion: "Rather than repressing emotion in epistemology it is necessary to rethink the relation between knowledge and emotion and construct conceptual models that demonstrate the mutually constitutive rather than oppositional relation between reason and emotion. Far from precluding the possibility of reliable knowledge, emotion as well as value must be shown as necessary to such knowledge" (1989, 163). The insights hewn from commingling emotive knowledges and reason inform essential vantage points from which to interpret, understand, amend, and deliver effective humanitarian aid. In direct service provision and community-building work, particularly with populations situated in the precarious limen of housing insecurity, trauma recovery, cultural displacement, and immigration proceedings, affect is often not just a central contribution to the accomplishment of a goal but rather *the productive task* and immaterial output. Yet the tradition of associating emotion with weakness, primitivity, pathology, and the feminine, in opposition to the stoic, unbiased, rational, masculine thinker, persists as an insidious occupational hazard in many nonprofit workplaces.

Even when affective work may be the bedrock of a humanitarian mission, it remains, too often, an unacknowledged, sidelined, or undervalued element—a skill that female workers are expected to bring to the workforce naturally, without warranting professional merit. As art and technology scholar Jenny Odell elaborates, "a culture that privileges novelty and growth over the cyclical and the regenerative" (2020, 25) inhibits commensurate valorization of affective labor. She describes a 1969 manifesto written by artist Mierle Laderman Ukeles, in which Ukeles conceptualizes a death instinct, characterized by individualization and self-interest, and a life instinct, characterized by unity and maintenance. Odell writes that in contemporary work culture, the death instinct "is routinely valorized, not to mention masculinized, while the other goes unrecognized because it has no part in 'progress'" (26). The empathetic tendencies cultivated in the social dictates and performances of "feminine" socialization—that urge us to pause and consider the effects of our words and language on others; to engender meaningful reciprocal human connection; (sometimes) to be gentle or patient or merciful— may problematize "progress" toward accruing profits.

Consideration of potential human harm could impede corporate missions that stalwartly seek profits regardless of what (who) may get laid aside on the way. Jennifer Armbrust puts forward the alternate notion of a feminine economy as a system of mutuality, exchange, and growth that takes base in collaboration, interdependence, empathy, gratitude, resourcefulness, and consciousness (n.d.). Building on Audre Lorde's and Octavia Butler's articulations of feminine power defined and cultivated by supporting others and dispersing power, Armbrust asserts that a "feminine economy proposes a new set of values and a redistribution of money and power based on feminine principles." Juxtaposed to masculine power, which is defined by Butler as hierarchical, egocentric, and fearful of scarcity, the design of feminine economies, like feminine power-sharing, intends to lift everyone to an abundantly regenerative, power-diffuse common ground (Butler 1983). As Lorde writes, "The need and desire to nurture each other is . . . redemptive, and it is within that knowledge that our real power is rediscovered" (2007, 112). The emotional awareness and empathic impulse undergirding economies of "feminine" nurture make possible this vision of collectivist power dispersal, ego disintegration, and the birth and maintenance of vitally inclusive, supportive, noncapitalist spaces.

In activist and human rights settings, in which ideals of social justice often take base in the type of alternative models put forth by theorists like Armbrust, Lorde, Jaggar, and Odell, empathy, emotional awareness, and affective deftness facilitate human-centered missions. Contrary to a profit-seeking, scarcity-based model, the success of social services nonprofits hinges on effective emotional connection, community-building, power redistribution, interpersonal relationships, and established trust between clients and caregivers. Thus, affective labor constitutes an essential conduit for moving toward the mission.

Affective Caretaking at a Migrant Shelter

In my work with survivors of trauma, participation in community has proved to be essential for recovery and stabilization. Particularly for individuals whose sense of home and agency may have been assailed, the interior psychic landscape may be withdrawn and fragile. Connections forged delicately through affective relating can help trauma survivors reform subjectivity. As trauma expert Bessel van der Kolk elucidates in his volume on the corporeal externalities of trauma, *The Body Keeps the Score*, "Numerous studies of disaster response around the globe have shown that social support is the most powerful protection against becoming overwhelmed by stress and trauma. Social support is not the same as merely being in the presence of others. The critical issue is *reciprocity*: being truly heard and seen by the people around us, feeling that we are held in someone else's mind and heart. For our physiology to calm down, heal, and grow we need a visceral feeling of safety" (2015, 79). At the nonprofit that I currently work for—a Texas-based advocacy center and emergency shelter for asylum seekers and migrants of all statuses—the creation of inclusive, collective, mutually liberating community is both our goal and our means. As Alexis Pauline Gumbs and adrienne maree brown put it, "Healing comes from being kindred" (2019, 76).

The human rights abuses perpetrated at the US border—the separation of migrant families, the indefinite prison sentences that asylum seekers suffer, the militarized intimidation tactics to bar displaced people who seek refuge here—are justified in xenophobic commentary. In analysis of anti-immigrant propaganda in the United Kingdom, Ahmed deduces that "the implicit demand is for a nation that is less emotional, less open, less easily moved, one that is 'hard,' or 'tough'" (2004, 2). In my work at the migrant shelter, we push against that immovability; we work, on a broader level, toward a cultural attitude that would desire to be more open to impression and affect by another's experience—an attitude that would see the strength in mutuality as a buttress against scarcity and, on a local level, toward the manifestation of compassionate, humanist community imbued with and held up by radical hospitality, affective connections, and restorative support for marginalized newcomers.

Affective caretaking facilitates the sense of safety and welcome that we desire to offer at our shelter in hope of enabling the residents to find the security and spaciousness to begin recovery, to create connections that can provide deep, lasting support as they settle into life in the United States, and to feel trust in the workers to guide them effectively. The case workers' ability to evoke particular affectivities manufactures and maintains a safe interpersonal environment, which enables the entire project of aiding residents of the migrant shelter in their resettlement.

For many of the migrant folks who seek refuge in our shelter, the physical space of the shelter becomes the first place where they experience security and a sense of home after many months, and sometimes years, of violent displacement, unrootedness, incarceration, and separation from family. They're often paroled to our shelter directly from months of imprisonment in Immigration and Customs Enforcement (ICE) detention or from Border Patrol's *hieleras* (Garcia Lawler 2018). At our shelter, they receive a panoply of restorative and emergency response support to help them decompress, stabilize, and become independent in the United States: our staff attorneys help residents apply for work permits and orient them to the legal procedures of their case; benefits specialists enroll residents in local health coverage programs and help them apply for food stamps and other state benefits when they're eligible; English teachers offer lessons tailored toward experience level and local knowledge-sharing four nights a week; case workers enroll children in school and childcare programs, help with employment searches, and coordinate medical, therapy, and legal appointments; an on-site clinic offers health screenings and body work therapies such as acupuncture and massage; and operations staff distribute food and shelter provisions. All the residents receive three months of free shelter, during which time they benefit from additional, more intangible forms of support in community-building and relationships that shelter programming and advocates engender.

As the executive of the largest immigrant detention system in the world, the Trump administration detains the highest daily average of migrant individuals in ICE prisons in our nation's history, at approximately forty-five thousand people imprisoned per day (Kassie 2019). Many detained immigrants are eligible for parole if a qualifying citizen or legal permanent resident agrees to sponsor their release, but for those detained who have no (eligible) friends or family in the United States, migrant advocacy organizations may be the only bodies able to support their parole request and vie for their release from an otherwise indefinite prison sentence. The migrant shelter where I work is one in a sprinkling of shelters that specifically serve immigrants in the United States. We have a staff devoted to helping migrant detainees get released to our shelter to pursue their asylum cases while living freely—outside detention, they will have better access to legal representation, translation, and libraries for evidence for their case; become free from the psychological duress of incarceration and the documented human rights abuses that occur in ICE detention centers; and live in a supportive, welcoming community. Studies and statistics illustrate the overwhelmingly better odds of winning asylum when fighting a case from outside detention.

To make space for more people to get released from ICE detention and come to our shelter, three months of in-shelter hospitality remains the norm and expectation, so that our shelter can continue to offer community sponsorship to still-detained migrants, to help more detainees get paroled from detention, and to intake more folks into our services and community at the shelter. Current residents have to transition to independent housing after their three-month stay has elapsed. But three months to acclimate and stabilize, for a newcomer who may be recovering from recent trauma, non-English speaking, undocumented, impoverished, or previously homeless, may not feel like a robust period of time. Though the majority of our residents move out within three months and remain sustainably housed, initially, the prospect of having to leave the first source and place of safety and community that they may have encountered in a long while can be immensely distressing.

As an example of the precarious constellation of sensitivities that must be balanced in affective grinds, my responsibility at the shelter requires me to usher residents through the process of exiting shelter and finding new homes. Even when residents feel reluctant to move again, I work with them to identify and alleviate their anxieties about transitioning out of shelter, so that they can move toward independence with assurance in their ability to stay afloat, based on recognition of their own strengths and in confidence in the ongoing support they can access within our shelter's extended community.

I try to approach the move-out conversations gently, sensitively, and supportively, hearing and encouraging the residents to share their desires in terms of neighborhood location, price, accessibility of public transport, apartment size, roommates, and so on. Listening and engaging responsively helps me to underscore that they will be the leader in the process of finding their new home and that I will work with them to understand and realize their individual goals.

Our housing discussions also remain rooted in reality—for many migrant individuals, the high percentage of income expended on rental costs in the United States comes as a shock. Most of the shelter residents have erratic, sometimes under-the-table earnings, so our housing conversations often entail a gentle redetermination of attainable housing. I emphasize that though their first US home may not be spacious or glamorous, it will just be their first step—it can be a temporary holdover where they can save money so that one day they may be able to realize the visions of roomier American houses that they might have had. I present strategies for living economically—such as sharing rooms with friends from shelter to cut the rental costs and resource sharing via communal grocery shopping and on big purchases like cars—as both a sharing of practical advice and a method to assuage panic about the financial obligations of renting an apartment in a city known for its shrinking terrain of affordable housing options.

Of course, the conversations about moving out of shelter do not always unfold smoothly; some folks react with anger, insist on permanent residence at the shelter, accuse the shelter workers of never having cared about them if we would ask them to leave, or express despair and hopelessness. Refugees often report experiencing shame, guilt, and fear in the early stages of living in the United States—even in hospitable, blue sanctuary cities like the one in which we work, xenophobic, unwelcoming messages surround migrants and newcomers. The anger and shame elicited from hostile rhetoric can be compounded, particularly for adults, by the sense of helplessness—of having lost the dignity of being able to express oneself clearly, to move fluidly through space and exercise local cultural know-how, to continue on one's professional career path, or to earn a stable, uninterrupted income for one's family. When people respond with anger to the possibility of moving out of shelter, I recognize that their reaction is often due to an underlying fear or shame. Offering space and reassurance and trying to assist clients in identifying their triggers can help us focus on and perhaps resolve the hidden particulars of their resistance to independent living.

The notion of moving can stir up trauma for some of our residents, for whom past experiences of loss of home, forced displacement, housing insecurity, and poverty might have created profound psychological imprints. One resident once told me he could not imagine living in his own home again, after government sympathizers in his home country retaliated against his political activism by burning his house to the ground. His infant son suffocated to death in the smoke. The work of conceptualizing an imaginary future home, in which his son would never live, required this client to confront the enduring ravages of trauma and guilt that he carried.

The highest priority in trauma-informed care is ensuring the safety of the client. This mandate encompasses both physical and emotional safety. When talking about moving out of shelter, some clients might feel as if both their physical safety (shelter) and their emotional safety (care from their community or distance from triggering thoughts) are threatened. To reduce the possibility that, in presenting the impending move from shelter, I may jeopardize their sense of safety, I try to develop trusting relationships with residents early on in their time at the shelter. I find that cultivating camaraderie with individuals, through convivial, "unproductive" moments—sharing a meal, playing basketball, helping a resident understand an English-language letter, teaching or learning greetings in each other's languages, hearing stories when residents choose to share—can create a sprout of trust that enables us to work together on higher-stakes and higher-stress undertakings. Slowly evidencing commitment to their safety and well-being through affective—sometimes playful, gentle, or empathic—relating can fortify residents' feelings of reassurance and confidence in progressing together toward independent housing arrangements.

Introspective affective labor also becomes critical; as the manifest, corporeal locus of and repository for residents' angry, fearful, frustrated, or trauma-saturated responses to the notion of moving, I have to undertake a safeguarding against absorption of their ricocheting affective reactions. It's a toughening that can feel reality-splitting or estranging from my essential core; the hypersensitivity to others' emotional states that I feel as a powerful constituent of the "self" I recognize most clearly has to be tempered.

"The Queer Art of Failure"

In addition to the affective dexterity required to earn and deserve residents' trust as I guide them toward move-out, this work requires willingness to helm the circuitous navigation of the bleak array of affordable housing available to the undocumented and the asylum seekers stuck in document limbo. When asylum seekers present themselves at the US border, Border Patrol often confiscates whatever home-country identity documents they carry with them until the end of their asylum proceedings. The Department of Homeland Security does not trade their paperwork for a comparably useful and legitimate US government-issued photo ID; therefore, asylum seekers are often temporarily stranded in a government-created documentless state. Searching for affordable units for shelter residents who have no photo ID, social security number, or rental or credit history—in a saturated rental market surrounded by a mushrooming tech and finance sector that has led to skyrocketing property values, out-of-state rental competition, and the erosion of immigrant communities via gentrification and the demolition of affordable apartments—often feels like the setting for an absurdist play. Apartment complexes with low barriers to entry, and with property managers who might be willing to lease to applicants who can produce only atypical forms of identity proof, often have reputations for exploiting tenants with mandatory monthly service fees, outsize late fines, code violations, and poor-quality construction compounded by patterns of stalling on maintenance requests. And even those apartments can be hard for our residents to secure in an ever-growing city with staunch renter competition. Advocacy for the housing rights of our clients can require other configurations of affective exertion—I work to create distinct emotional milieus when addressing city and private stakeholders so that they may take seriously the mutual benefit, for them and for shelter residents, of renting their properties to migrant individuals and families and preserving the rights and dignity of their tenants.

In the stress and surprise detours of this landscape, I do not always enact my affective exertions with the finesse that such a perilously delicate project calls for. Once, a shelter resident told me he'd rather be deported back to the Eritrean war camp he escaped from than be asked to move out of the shelter. Another resolutely immovable resident never again looked me in the eye after my first attempt to discuss post-shelter housing with him.

In another instance, a resident pulled out of the fourth housing plan we had arranged for him. He gave no explanation for scrapping the effort we had poured into securing a safe, unusually affordable option for him—he told me simply that he had changed his mind. We had a tense back and forth in which I reiterated to him that he was well past the end of his allocated three months, that the shelter needed to help other folks still in detention, that he had received a wide array of support during his time in shelter and had been able to save a little money, that he'd been in a good position to care for himself at this apartment, and that we were out of time to look for more apartments. In frustration, impatience, and panic at the indefinite rerouting, I responded with a reactionary heavy-handedness that undid some of the seedling trust he had placed in my purported commitment to his well-being. In a less urgent situation, I may have slowed and recognized that his apprehension indicated weightier anxieties. He was trusting me to help him navigate those, but in that moment, I felt a panicked need to "finish," to use my time to attend to other residents, to be straightforwardly productive in an undeviating progressive sense, rather than dilly-dally, as I should have, in the curling mesh of affective relation. The absence of exerted compassion—more than his decision to step back from our work on his housing application—set us back, because the snap in that exchange teetered the conviviality, mutual comprehension, and trust between us.

It's a tottering balance; the time that I had available to care for the needs of that one resident could not stretch infinitely. I had many other clients to serve concurrently with housing assistance, and we have an urgent need to maintain the flow of residents in and out of shelter so as to continue aiding migrants paroled from detention. But my calculation of time and progress lost that led to my frustration was errant. Affective labor cannot be granularized and weighed with the mathematics that we apply to our timesheets and weekly agendas. Concern with productivity and ego—my desire to adhere to the linear, numerical guidelines of my job and move residents out punctually—corroded the relation-based, affective work I had engaged in up until that moment.

Working in housing advocacy and location for recovering, fringe, atypical aspiring tenants has further illuminated the fundamentality of openness to—maybe even finding humor in—the flexuous route. Goofiness, as manifested by stirring up playful rapport, finding humor in hard places, and seeing satire as resilience, has proved my most vital salt in retaining gumption and patience while skirting through unforeseen veers. Sages like Jack Halberstam remind us to delight in the unexpected detour, the crashed plan, and the upset of the pieces that remain and redirect us: "The queer art of failure involves . . . the embrace of the absurd, the silly, and the hopelessly goofy. Rather than resisting endings and limits, let us instead revel in and cleave to all of our own inevitable, fantastic failures" (2011, 187). The failures can redirect us to the indispensable affectivity, the ineluctably silly, the cinching safe harbors in our human connections that ferry the work. There has been no efficient, straightforward assembly line of mechanized progress in my experiences of affective labor.

It's no small joy to work in an environment that accepts and even appreciates the affective, relational abundance that sometimes derives from cyclic, roundabout efforts. Even as we aim to fulfill grant-makers' specific numbers or cellularized charts of progress, the organizational values at the shelter privilege rapport, community, and emotivity. My boss frequently cries at our staff meetings; community-building with and offering refuge to displaced people is work emphatically sinewed by emotion. A day at a migrant shelter in the era of vigilante Trumpian xenophobia might entail a million depleting violations: a client is picked up by ICE, jerked away from his family, and imprisoned; a resident loses her asylum case and faces deportation; a community member learns that her husband perished in the spillages of civil war violence back home; another resident confronts wage theft by a local employer; and another's youngest son is kidnapped by gang members in the last country they crossed en route to the United States. Often, our affective labor necessitates a performance of emotional composure when working with the fractured, healing psyches of our clients, but when staff are not engaged in direct service provision, we share earnest support for our emotional experiences. It's a rare occupational privilege that I cherish.

Counterbalancing (and coexisting, sometimes inexplicably and absurdly with) the experiences of horror, rage, and trauma at the shelter is a delight in the eccentricity, curiosity, and social justice passion of our eclectic community. Providing shelter and hospitality for othered, marginalized people is based in subverting the material oppression and immaterial affect in xenophobic rhetoric, hostile immigration policy, and dehumanizing incarceration. Conviction in the transcendence of bringing together our individual oddities and our variegated cultural customs blurs divisive borderlines and replaces "us" and "them" binaries with ambiguity. I'm reminded of the jubilance in the curiosity and togetherness in the hodgepodge community of our shelter most days—when we creatively string together disjointed syntax with the only words we recognize in each other's languages and we're met with or we offer patience and chuckling; when two residents, from different planes of existence in age, homeland, language, sexuality, and experiences of displacement, teach each other popular dances from home; when a French-speaking resident shares a poem he wrote with his Urdu-speaking friend who says, "Que bueno, amigo," having no French words with which to understand or respond himself; when we linger in a tiny, grungy room in the back of a sweltering homeless shelter in the midst of Texas summer to surprise our newest resident (an eighteen-year-old who arrived directly from youth detention one day prior) with *tres leches* cake and raucous, enthusiastic renditions of "Happy Birthday" in seven languages. This parade of playfulness in pursuit of recovery and of the capacity for rejoicing that comes with conviviality is a stride toward Donna Haraway's call "for pleasure in the confusion of boundaries and for responsibility in their construction" (2019, 7).

This work of ragtag community composition touches Haraway's description of urgent (which she describes as both "serious" and "lively") troublemaking to counteract the devastating forces of displacement that characterize the contemporary moment: "Staying with the trouble requires making oddkin; that is, we require each other in unexpected collaborations and combinations, in hot compost piles. We become-with each other or not at all" (2016, 4). For a postmodern queer theory student, this work of furthering the wacky, off-kilter spread of affective care in a compassionate activist community is existentially and viscerally engrossing. When I think of the privileges of the existential freedom of my work, I think of poet Ross Gay when he writes, "How threatening to the order our bodies are in nonproductive, nonconsumptive delight" (2019, 231). There is such pleasure in working outside the reign of capitalist constrictions of production, in a radical field that instead constructs itself on the nonconsumptive subversive delight of affective labor and community-building.

Commodifying the Soul

As Rebecca Solnit writes of finding meaning through activism, "When [our ideals] are realized there's joy and joy is itself an insurrectionary force" (2016, xviii). But acknowledging the privilege of earning wages through joy-giving and soul-feeding work requires analysis of who can and who cannot easily access jobs that may be existentially rewarding but low paying. Even though affective labor may constitute the crux, the backbone, and the main engine of an organizational mission, roles with high affective and caretaking responsibilities are nonetheless devalued (i.e., undercompensated) as a result of the disparagement and deprofessionalization of labor traditionally seen as "women's work." Humanitarian and social work labor forces are—as a consequence of the low wages—disproportionately white. Immense discrepancies in the economic power of white households versus households of color in the United States, coupled with the devalorization of affective or caretaking work, often enable white workers to access low-wage but existentially or intellectually stimulating jobs more effortlessly than would-be job applicants of color or applicants from less economically privileged backgrounds for whom such undercompensation may present too heavy a burden.

The racial disparity in social work is an alarming disservice not only to aspiring workers who are shut out of personally meaningful opportunities but also to the participants in social service programs who may be best served by native speakers of their mother tongues and service providers more familiar with their cultural backgrounds. As a white, native-born American citizen who has never undergone forced displacement or homelessness, I know that I cannot provide certain services or counsel to my clients as expertly or as gracefully as my peers with lived experience. A disproportionately white or economically privileged staff hinders vital knowledge-sharing from people with lived experience of racism or economic hardship. By offering low-paying opportunities that are often more attainable for white or already well-off, non-wage-dependent individuals, nonprofits perpetuate race and class barriers. This reification of exclusivity of opportunity for mostly white or middle-class people goes against the missions of nonprofits that purport to fight against racial or economic oppression and reduces the profundity of the quality of care for clients.

Aggravating the problematics of underpaying social service workers, this work often requires laborers to undertake high occupational risks. In his study of "the soul at work," Franco Berardi asserts that Post-Fordist labor models, by tying our souls and identities to the products of our labor, have grated and flattened the buoyancy of our spiritual, vital core: "The soul, once wandering and unpredictable, must now follow functional paths in order to become compatible with the system of operative exchanges structuring the productive ensemble. The soul hardens and loses its tenderness and malleability. . . . The immaterial factory asks instead to place our very souls at its disposal: intelligence, sensibility, creativity, language" (2017, 192).

Berardi describes the "immaterial" workplace—labor involving the mind and spirit—as a site for subsumption of the soul as a capital-producing apparatus. The detethering of affective labor from its fleshy form as a medium for human togetherness and the reformulation of affective relation-making as a skill can cause an estrangement that affective laborers sometimes experience.

When affective labor takes place in humanitarian missions, where the assembly path may be more loop-to-loop than traditionally efficient operations, the work does not call to objectify the soul for profit-making ends, but rather to commodify the soul for objectives driven by social justice values. So though the purpose and process of optimizing the soul's productivity in activist and for-profit organizations may differ, the individual laborers similarly gamble, in stitching their souls into their work—estrangement from one's sense of vitality and relation to the world is, in both for-profit and activist instances, at stake.

Thus, although fulfilling work provides existential mooring to those who can sustain low wages, which can feel reassuring in a culture that aligns self-identity so closely with labor, even the most ecstatic uplift derived from labor can still risk alienation. Moreover, no amount of existential sustenance can replace the basic need for living wages and safe work conditions.

Erasing the input exerted and consequently diminishing the value of labor is particularly harmful to workers in organizations that engage in risky affective labors like emotional triage, crisis intervention, and direct work with traumatized populations. The risks that workers undertake by proffering emotional connections and care are manifold. Vicarious or secondhand trauma, particularly in understaffed organizations that rely on flexibly defined boundaries, and in which caseloads are overstretched, training is limited, and supervision and support are nominal, can have devastating effects on helping professionals. The TEND Academy, an organization that conducts research and creates resources for organizations undertaking such work, offers a list of some of the ways secondary traumatization can impress on and restrict the body of affective laborers: "exhaustion, insomnia, headaches, increased susceptibility to illness, sore back and neck, irritable bowel, GI distress, rashes, breakouts, grinding teeth at night, heart palpitations, [and] hypochondria" are common side effects (n.d.). It also articulates some of the ways overexposure to and absorption of others' trauma can diminish quality of life through behavioral and emotional changes, such as

> increased use of alcohol and drugs, anger and irritability at home and/or at work, avoiding social events, impaired ability to make decisions, feeling helpless when hearing a difficult client story, difficulty with sex and intimacy due to trauma exposure at work, compromised care for clients, engaging in frequent negative gossip/venting at work, impaired appetite or binge eating, emotional exhaustion, negative self-image, depression, increased anxiety, difficulty sleeping, feelings of hopelessness, guilt, reduced ability to feel sympathy and empathy towards clients or family/friends, resentment of demands being put on you at work and/or at home, dread of working with certain clients/patients/certain case files, hypersensitivity to emotionally charged stimuli, insensitivity to emotional material/numbing, difficulty separating personal and professional lives, failure to nurture non-work related aspects of life, suicidal thoughts.

Compounding the hazards to mind and body in affective labor, I observe that leadership's concern for staff safety—physical and emotional—is often sidelined rather than seen as a necessary pillar of the ultimate mission of the organization. Humanitarian organizations often rely on young staff who are willing to work for low wages and often have little experience taking precautions against secondary trauma or recognizing when their flexibility regarding workplace conditions leads them to be taken advantage of. Young (particularly female) workers may feel less capable of asking for adjustment to conditions or saying no to a workplace demand, as a result of conditioning against expressing an individual (self-oriented) need or feeling the need to prove themselves as competent and capable as young and new workers.

For example, affective laborers in frontline humanitarian work often find themselves beholden to erratic schedules, which may entail work at any or all hours of the day and night and rare or scattered days off. The unpredictability and the around-the-clock expectation complicate the feasibility of separation and restoration from emotionally challenging work. The body and mind thus have diminished capacity to recuperate.

Relatedly, workers engaged in affective brokerage and linkages with traumatized clients may feel consumed by emotional discharge that tends to slop outside the physical parameters of the worksite. Pieces of our attention and deep strains of affective awareness are often oriented toward the unfinished struggles of the individuals we intertwine with at work. Leaving a physical space does not automatically precipitate an easy delinking of affectivity. Thus, workers undertake the risk of a factionalized psychosphere, in which the possibility of being subsumed by life-or-death crises—that are not currently present in the flesh—threatens presence of being when not at work.

The unintended or unconscious attentiveness to work matters outside work hours is not compensated. Unpaid time spent agonizing in the shower, processing chaos that rests in the subconscious through nightmares and stress dreams, waking up to panicked messages from clients, or emotionally steeling oneself for a delicate intervention on the commute to work besieges many of my coworkers who engage in frontline affective labor.

Affective labor also connotes an element of risk associated with the erotic. Femme folks, when forging emotional caretaker relationships with displaced, dehumanized individuals who may not have been emotionally held, listened to, surrounded by caring community, or erotically tapped in a long time, open themselves up to the potentiality of misinterpretation of caretaker intent and the accompanying psychic and visceral risks. We can hold compassion for the confusion of different place-based cues pertaining to gender, sex, and flirtation, as well as for the dislocating trauma of incarceration, solitary confinement, and displacement that can lead one of our residents to a wayward search for erotic reconstitution. But organizational leadership too often fails to hold parallel awareness of or accountability for the increased risks and consequences that their female staff may endure—such as sexual harassment, physical violations, and assault—when engaging in affective relationality.

I have seen many leaders at humanitarian organizations dismiss risks and hazards that their employees suffer in order to expend full attention and resources on care for clients (even though, of course, clients cannot be efficaciously cared for when their caretakers are overstressed or burned out). When working in conditions constructed from biopolitical hierarchies that do not prioritize their well-being, affective laborers confront a slew of corporeal risks.

For example, we offered several years of shelter to a middle-aged man who survived a stroke that left him largely nonverbal and with a minor motor disability. He had also been charged with a sexual violence felony before living at the shelter, and unlike most residents, who move out after three months, he stayed longer, because the combination of his disability, immigration status, and criminal record left him with few options for other care facilities. Most of the time, he was a quiet but curmudgeonly resident that other residents and volunteers liked to dote on and take care of. But when agitated, he frequently flew into rages, brandishing his fist and thwacking other residents and volunteers with his cane. He was once arrested for violent assault on the shelter property. He also sexually violated multiple female staff members who were running the shelter alone on the overnight shift. After many violent transgressions, it became clear to many of us on staff that other residents, volunteers, and staff members should not be put at risk for this one man's care, particularly when he demonstrated no desire to rehabilitate his behavior. The offenses he committed had been brought up to our boss on numerous occasions, in email, in meetings, and in private, but she consistently diminished the harm he committed ("He has been really good for several weeks!" "You'd be grumpy too if you were in his position"), accused us of "gossiping" when discussing how to protect our community from his violations, and dismissed calls for him to be relocated to other homeless shelters. She deployed guilt appeals that put undue responsibility for his survival on victims of his assaults: "If he goes out there, he won't survive. You would really ask him to leave, knowing he'll be killed?" To be asked to de-escalate violent tantrums, to calm other residents who have been perturbed by his anger, to call the ambulance for other residents who may have been physically harmed in his rage, to settle the turbulent psyche of an aggressor, to reassure volunteers or visitors who may have witnessed the scene, and to engage in any affective or caretaking labor at all for a man who has sexually violated you while alone in the shelter, particularly during the night hours, is an unjust ask. After two years of collective protest against the protection of this resident at the risk of the rest of the community, he was moved to a different transitional housing program. Though my boss eventually grew exhausted with our complaints and gave in to the consensus decision, she made clear that she did not agree with our protest.

Other biohazards include entry-level staff engaging in blood-related medical care for residents with communicable, terminal diseases and driving residents to the public tuberculosis clinic after they've received a positive exam result. Staff have been pricked by bloodied needles used by hepatitis C–positive residents and contracted tuberculosis at the shelter. Particularly for staff in low-wage jobs and in states like Texas where workers' compensation is not guaranteed, conditions that unnecessarily and cavalierly expose staff's bodies to biohazards evidence a misguided bifurcation in prioritization of care for human life—a stratification that presupposes vulnerability entirely on the side of the client and negates the possibility that the service provider may need protective conditions or be vulnerable.

This one-sided notion of vulnerability flattens the possibility of complicated experience, thereby reducing, essentializing, and dehumanizing both staff and shelter residents. When laborers at the shelter think about the ways in which we're compassionate to the injustice the client has experienced, injustice that we perhaps feel implicated in as American citizens and thus hyperresponsible for undoing, we can be susceptible to allowing the importance and urgency of the clients' care totalize and halt the possibility of weighing the risks in tasks asked of workers. Leadership suppresses the reality of the hazards for staff because they desire to make things right for the client who has suffered such injustice; thus, if done in the noble pursuit of aiding the "truly needy," leaders may see jeopardizing workers' safety as permissible or as not truly risky, as workers' vulnerability is not recognized in this framework.

Instead of creating safer work environments, many frontline organizations run through tired cycles: frustrated, burned-out staff leave after their calls for better conditions go unheeded, and new staff come in without knowledge of or personal grievance with the legacy of problematic conditions. They handle the high risk, intense labor, and low wages for as long as they can—a period suspended by leadership's affirmation of the nobility of their precarious work—until they, too, burn out and are replaced by new, disposable employees.

The glory that sometimes is ascribed to undertaking big risks further problematizes the binary of human need. Rather than create conditions to preempt and reduce risk and compensate employees so as to allow them to take restorative care of themselves, frontline nonprofit and activist groups too often romanticize the selflessness of the archetypal martyr and the risks he or she undergoes in service of a noble justice mission. It's a bizarre ossification of the white savior binary that reads as gaslighting; a staff member's perseverance through an unnecessary challenge or risk becomes recast as a positive indication of strength, unflappability, and commitment to the cause.

Though the work of bringing about a large-scale professional valorization of affective labor has begun—many organizations do offer professional training and development for frontline workers, hire workers with advanced degrees in relevant training or robust experience in direct-service work, and compensate affective laborers at the front lines at a livable, commensurate rate—many other humanitarian organizations find excuses to instead maintain a turnstile of young, disposable laborers.

The Effects of "Founderitis"

One of the challenges in implementing structural changes in nonprofits that would beget care and justice for all community members—clients and staff alike—is the hold on power and the stratification of priorities by leadership. "Founderitis" is the debilitating organizational condition in which leadership, generally founders or directors entrenched in lifting or transforming an organization to its current incarnation, hold inordinate control. Particularly in nonprofits, where projects promise no revenue streams, founders and directors fight tooth and nail to keep their visions afloat. The dissolution of borders between the individual identity of the founder and identity of the organization is too common—founders become their projects, and projects become the founders. Though founders and leaders may be well used to fighting the status quo and rejecting the establishment as it pertains to the suppression of their client population, when their own institution comes under scrutiny, too many are quick to disprove criticism, and sometimes, as a consequence, they throttle creativity that could lead to positive change.

Scarcity politics also unfortunately undergird much of nonprofit dynamics and can compel leaders to hierarchize injustices. Leaders and grant writers, as countercultural and radical as their work and philosophies may be, are grubbing for money under the same capitalist boot as their for-profit counterparts. When the question of pay raises comes up, leaders underline their shoestring budget, which, they remind us, has to stretch to meet so many people's needs. Though understanding of the finite resources nonprofits have at their disposal, I am always interested in why the core facilitators of human-centered projects—the humans carrying out the labor—are not prioritized and why the organization's own struggling employees do not fall under the category of people with needs.

Several years ago, when working for a human rights organization focused on eradicating and protecting against the exploitation of gendered labor—ironically, as it goes—I participated in some informal organizing with fellow staff. We were earning an unlivable, barely minimum wage; we all had second or third jobs to support ourselves. In a meeting with our boss, she suggested that we had succumbed to the temptation of greed and had allowed our desires to overshadow the true needs of the vulnerable survivors of labor exploitation whom we worked with.

She responded to our call for higher wages with a confounding conflation of femininity and frivolous consumptive desire: "If you want to be able to go the mall and get your nails done, this is not the right kind of job for you." My sputtering reaction was to remind her that we were asking for a living wage so as to be able to make rent without working sixty-hour weeks. My colleague later pointed to a more essential question: Why should she morally malign a coworker for enjoying some aesthetic, indulgent, playful recuperation after spending many hours engaged in emotionally sapping labor? Why should feminine joy be mutually exclusive with important social justice labor? In the iconography of the self-sacrificial martyr, there's no room for self-softness, self-doting, or self-need, only for self-sacrifice.

The leaders' refusal to admit how they reproduced, within their own organizational structure, parallel versions of the very conditions we were meant to be working against evidenced an insular, neocolonial (subject vs. savior) conception of who deserves labor justice. The hypocrisy of a labor rights organization that purported to advocate for gender justice but undercut the value of the affective labor that sustained its mission and underpaid its own female workers colored my day-to-day work experience with shoots of anger.

In another collective bargaining gathering at a different human rights organization, a colleague reminded those of us gathered not to let the director leverage her individual hurt and portrayal of emotion to shame or silence our legitimate calls for better pay and conditions. Knowing that we were sensitive and empathetic to others' pain as affective laborers, my coworker urged us to be mindful of our susceptibility to being quieted through emotional appeals. It was a vital message—I recall her words often in preparing for tough conversations with senior staff whose egos, defined by self-identification as social do-gooders, easily feel assailed when staff express grievances. Her warning exposes the many dimensions of emotional acuity required to bring about justice for undervalued laborers in human rights organizations.

In those collective organizing conversations, we prepared against the fatalist positivity of leadership at that organization. Perhaps a by-product of decades of crisis intervention, leaders glossed over and suppressed every workplace issue raised with a call to look at the silver lining, a humorist bent, or a validation of having handled a dangerous or challenging moment well. They pushed back against logical analyses with deludedly optimistic spins until we would find ourselves disoriented in a farrago of mismatching realities ("We *like* turnover because it brings in new energy! People *don't want* higher wages because 'roughing it' is important in self-discovery! This is unskilled work; we don't need trainings! I think everyone's doing great—let's not talk about this kind of stuff so we can keep morale up!"). I find this unnerving "positivity gaslighting" (a term coined by a coworker in an organizing session, also known as "brightsiding") to be a commonplace tactic that protective founders and leaders use to deflect and deny the reality of kinks and corollary damage in the operations of their missions.

I love adrienne maree brown's theory of generating abundance—"By tapping into the potential goodness in each of us we can generate justice and liberation, growing a healing abundance where we have been socialized to believe only scarcity exists" (2019, 3)—and I believe it offers a useful counter to the rationale nonprofit leaders put forth to explain the suppression of worker wages. If frontline workers, who engage in risky and exhausting affective and emotional labor, were paid well enough to live, able to pay their bills without stress, enabled to pursue restorative activities and recuperation outside work rather than go to their second or third job or flop on their couch because they can't muster the energy or afford to go out, then they would have more abundant resources in their psychic and visceral repositories to pull from when at work. If affective laborers were better able, with financial resources and trainings, to take care of themselves— inside and outside the workplace—they might be able to fend off burnout, continue to provide specialized services, and stay on in frontline roles, meaning that organizations would not ritualistically flush away institutional knowledge and clients would receive more expert care. Investing in structural care for staff, so that they can provide the best order of services, is also justice for the clients we serve—staff would be better emotionally regulated and energized and would have more experience and knowledge to apply in complex crises. The abundance that could be realized through caring for all humans involved, not just the clients, may generate sustained outputs and draw in more material (financial) opportunities.

Krista Tippett, founder and host of the *On Being* podcast, in conversation with writer-activist Darnell Moore, summarizes Moore's contention that when we engage in tough, critical conversations with people we disagree with, we evidence a caring—we honor our companions enough to take on emotional work together and to become vulnerable to their reactions: "In fact, to be honest is an act of love" (2019). Rather than viewing constructive criticism and calls for better conditions as an attack or personal affront, I wish that founders and directors would see evidence of their staff's deep love for the founders' projects. Offering critical visions of how an organization could evolve is a risk for staff to undertake—they risk agitating or angering their boss and losing credibility and trust, and missing out on promotions and raises. Opening to those forms of vulnerability attests to a profound commitment to the mission and an active hope for the longevity of the project. It's the opposite of personal avarice over collective mission; it's the exposition of a desire—to extend and enhance the project—that outweighs the peril undertaken in speaking up. It's a demonstration of the staff's commitment to take on surplus affective and material work in order to help the organization evolve constructively.

The Contingency of Vulnerability

There's growing recognition of feminist and queer thought regarding the contingency of vulnerability on togetherness and reciprocity and how those forces of interdependency can effectuate the dispersion of power. In articulating her wish to see "more trembling, more unknowing" from leaders, Maggie Nelson speaks to the emergent trendiness of vulnerability (2019, 68). I have hope in the possibility that, through the mainstreaming of radical theory in social media, meme pages, magazines, and public watchdogs, nonprofit leadership can come to introspect on the postcolonial need to disintegrate, as best one can, ego and self-image from their work and dissolve saviorist dynamics that dehumanize and disparage both clients and staff. I have hope that the spread of knowledges from the margins will push nonprofits to see how both their laborers and their clients become collateral damage in the churn-and-burn models of frontline workplaces; to recognize that people of color need to be offered conditions, welcome, and opportunity to lead organizations that work with populations of color; and to acknowledge that traditionally feminine forms of labor enact, facilitate, and comprise vital mainstays of human-focused service work. With the mainstreaming of radical theory, there's nervousness about dilution and malappropriation, but there's also the optimistic potentiality that more people will become enthralled by the bright, crucial questions about human connection and condition that radical race, queer, and feminist philosophers explore. It inspires hope that livable wages and safe conditions will be seen not as bonuses but as necessary provisions to enable sustained social justice work.

Many online labor justice, antiracist, and feminist communities serve as accountability boards. In addition to sharing job postings, they draw public attention to organizations whose publicly asserted values do not match the treatment of employees who work for them. Their influence has motivated organizations to become more transparent with pay, exposed the problematics of panel organizers that complacently offer platforms to all-white speakers, supported strikes and union creation, and called out repeat offender organizations with multiple reports of taking advantage of female and LGBTQ workers and workers of color. These virtual spaces have also engendered conversations and knowledge spreading on how to handle and subvert racial bias, sexual harassment, erratic work schedules, lack of paid leave, and other forms of oppression that are perpetuated, though often unacknowledged, in nonprofit and activist spaces, where ostensible commitment to social justice too often expunges scrutiny and exonerates harm production. These communities also buoy union and collective bargaining efforts, offer comic relief and morale lifting, and unite labor activists.

I'm trying to sort through my desire to embody as much fire-mouthed commitment to justice as a more freshly impassioned version of myself. In a conversation with a friend and fellow activist half a decade ago, we tittered with anxious wonder, speculating about why folks grow moderate with age. As I contend with the necessity of finding balance in pushing back when I can and settling when I am overfilled, I worry that I am lurching toward that foreseen threshold of out-of-touchness in which "progressive" older folks fall prey to the pitying young leftist's concession of "Well, at least she's trying." Accepting less than the radical ideal is a heartbreak, particularly when we find ourselves foreclosing on fundamental principles of justice in order to keep other pieces of our projects or our souls going, in order to rest at night, in order to stave off emotional and mental breakdowns. I'm trying now to implement and rest in perimeters that steady my pace so as to enable me to continue, for the long haul, in exhausting but meaningful affective healing and social justice work.

In my (unhurried!) disentanglement from the social theory classroom and integration into the working field of social change, I'm looking for balance in both tempering and preserving the fire, of pushing to make my workplace more liberating and accepting that regardless of how socially minded and radical an organization's mission may be, moving the transformative ideologies of feminist, queer, and antiracist theory into the grind of the twenty-first-century workplace presents everyday compatibility issues. As I continue to prod my workplace toward neater fusions of theory in practice, I'm trying to find peace when progress is slower than I would want it to be, to hold myself accountable when I could have pushed harder, and to find grace for when I fought for organizational change that didn't come about. I return to the providence of queer and feminist theorists to find restoration; to rethread hardened or fragmented pieces of myself with sensitivity, curiosity, grit, and wonder; to embrace the unexpected saplings that can grow from wreckages; to remember the deliverance in humor; and to become awash again in all the reasons why one can hang on to hope. In the face of resistance, the hard, rambunctious, meaningful troublemaking may give birth to slightly more mutually freeing, trembling, affect-conscious awakenings tomorrow.

Note

This essay is dedicated to Maddie, Cecelia, Miriam, Rose, Elena, and Collyn. In many dimensions of the incongruous and the absurd, your support, humor, and interdependent care were life-saving. Thank you.

References

Ahmed, Sara. 2004. *The Cultural Politics of Emotion*. New York: Routledge Taylor and Francis.

Armbrust, Jennifer. n.d. "Proposals for the Feminine Economy." Sister. Accessed September 30, 2019. https://sister.is/proposals-for-the-feminine-economy.

Berardi, Franco "Bifo." 2017. *The Soul at Work: From Alienation to Autonomy*. New Delhi: Aakar Books.

brown, adrienne maree. 2019. *Pleasure Activism*. Edinburgh: AK Press.

Butler, Octavia E. 1983. *Wild Seed*. London: Sidgwick and Jackson.

Garcia Lawler, Opheli. 2018. "The Iceboxes at the Border." The Cut, December 26, 2018. https://www.thecut.com/2018/12/what-are-las-hieleras-iceboxes-used-by-cbp-at-the-border.html.

Gay, Ross. 2019. *The Book of Delights*. Chapel Hill, NC: Algonquin Books of Chapel Hill.

Gumbs, Alexis Pauline, and adrienne maree brown. 2019. "The Sweetness of Salt," 26–31. In *Pleasure Activism*, by adrienne maree brown. Edinburgh: AK Press.

Halberstam, Jack. 2011. *The Queer Art of Failure*. Durham, NC: Duke University Press.

Hardt, Michael, and Antonio Negri. 2009. *Multitude: War and Democracy in the Age of Empire*. New York: Penguin.

Haraway, Donna J. 2016. *Staying with the Trouble: Making Kin in the Chthulucene*. Durham, NC: Duke University Press.

——. 2019. *Manifestly Haraway*. Minneapolis: University of Minnesota Press.

Jaggar, Alison M. 1989. "Love and Knowledge: Emotion in Feminist Epistemology." *Inquiry* 32 (2): 163–73. https://doi.org/10.1080/00201748908602185.

Kassie, Emily. 2019. "How Trump Inherited His Expanding Detention System." Marshall Project, February 12, 2019. https://www.themarshallproject.org/2019/02/12/how-trump-inherited-his-expanding-detention-system.

Lorde, Audre. 2007. "Sister Outsider." In *Sister Outsider*, 110–113. New York: Penguin.

Nelson, Maggie. 2016. *The Argonauts*. London: Melville House.

Odell, Jenny. 2020. *How to Do Nothing: Resisting the Attention Economy*. London: Melville House.

Solnit, Rebecca. 2016. *Hope in the Dark: Untold Histories, Wild Possibilities*. Edinburgh: Canongate Books.

TEND. n.d. TEND homepage. Accessed October 1, 2019. https://www.tendacademy.ca.

Tippett, Krista. 2019. "Darnell Moore—Self-Reflection and Social Evolution." On Being Project, August 8, 2019. https://onbeing.org/programs/darnell-moore-self-reflection-and-social-evolution.

Van der Kolk, Bessel. 2015. *The Body Keeps the Score: Brain, Mind, and Body in the Healing of Trauma*. New York: Penguin Books.

SUBJUGATED KNOWLEDGE

Listening to LGBTQ Homeless Youth

Sassafras Lowrey

I decided to major in women's studies having no idea what it was. It was 2002, and I was seventeen, homeless, and queer. I held the Portland State University course catalog on my lap as my bus bounced down the street, and as I flipped through the course offerings, I saw something called "queer studies" as part of something called "women's studies." I circled it. This might not be the ideal way to pick an undergraduate major, but for me it set into motion a profound educational experience in which for the first time I felt valued and gained a language to talk about and understand my experiences with gender, sexuality, trauma, and survival.

In those years, feminist and queer theory became a way to name my experiences—not just as an individual but as part of a larger community and culture. I learned not just to put language to oppression but also how to use that language as a building block for organization and mobilization. For example, as an independent study course, I organized a gender-neutral bathroom campaign on the campus, not only (successfully) lobbying the university to include gender-neutral bathrooms in the designs of new buildings but also creating physical maps that were distributed across campus for trans, genderqueer, and nonbinary students to learn where safe(r) bathrooms were located (before my work, the university did not actually have a complete count of where gender-neutral bathrooms on campus were). At the end of that semester, I graduated with a bachelor's degree in women's studies, committed to turning that organizing work into a career.

When I decided to major in women's studies, I got a lot of questions about what I would do with the degree. It didn't have a direct translation into a job or even a career path. While some people found that nerve-racking, I found it free-ing. Feminism gave me a lens for understanding my experience as a nontradi-tional, (formerly) homeless, queer, genderqueer student with PTSD. Feminism had empowered me to believe that I could build any kind of life I wanted, and the intersectional skills I gained in the classroom provided me with a lens for un-derstanding marginalization and professionally channeling it into my creative work as well as into the nonprofit careers I would go on to pursue. Eventually, however, I found that the nonprofit world where I found work was not what I had envisioned for one important reason. It did not value one of the primary characteristics of how I defined feminism: actively listening to and incorporating the voices of the people it purported to empower.

"Subjugated Knowledge"

My first job after college was at a national LGBTQ organization working on me-dia advocacy and analysis. I soon transitioned out of that role and into LGBTQ nonprofit management. My nonprofit career culminated in my employment as director of an LGBTQ homeless youth drop-in program, where I worked for nearly eight years managing a team of staff that included social workers, direct service providers, and street outreach workers as well as interns and volunteers. At the same time, I juggled direct-service responsibilities with youth and man-aged large private and government contracts.

When I was hired to create this program in one of the oldest and largest LGBTQ youth organizations in the United States, I thought about that first experience of walking into the queer theory classroom at Portland State, and of reading queer and feminist theory texts. I had felt exhilarated by seeing marginalized bodies like mine reflected on the pages, and I wanted to re-create that sense for the homeless youth in my program. I wanted them to see their own identities as they walked in the door of the shelter, to encounter staff members who were people of color, queer, or margin-alized in other ways. For me this seemed like a logical move, but to my coworkers, it was confusing and astonishing. They believed in a hierarchical workplace where staff were markedly different from the people we helped.

I define my leadership style as centering my feminist principles and ideas. Key to this style is recognizing how our lived experiences and identities influence who we are everywhere in life, including in the workplace. As a hiring manager, espe-cially as a white queer person who was formerly homeless but was also in a posi-tion of power at an organization that served primarily youth of color, I tried to hire applicants who were LGBTQ people of color and also formerly homeless—meaning they had been personally affected by the same issues facing our clients.

This would give youth the opportunity to work with adults who looked like them and who came from similar communities, neighborhoods, and backgrounds. I also created a peer outreach worker position and filled it with a recently homeless LGBTQ person who did outreach, connecting with youth on the streets and letting them know about services and supports that they could access.

For me, being a queer feminist professional affected every aspect of the job, from who I hired to how I dressed and presented myself in the workplace. This meant not hiding my queer tattoos and not conforming to hetero- or homonormative ideas of "workplace-appropriate" attire. It also meant that I talked openly with youth members about issues ranging from politics to sex, listening carefully to their words and recognizing their insights about their own lives. In doing so, I was recognizing their "subjugated knowledge," a concept used by Patricia Hill Collins in her book *Black Feminist Thought* to describe the knowledge African American women possess about their own lives but that is not recognized as worthy knowledge by dominant forces. As Hill Collins says, "Starting from the assumption that African-American women have created independent, oppositional yet subjugated knowledges concerning our own subordination, contemporary U.S. Black women intellectuals are engaged in the struggle to reconceptualize all dimensions of the dialectic of oppression and activism as it applies to African-American women" (2000, 13). Grounding "theory" in the particular experiences of African American women produces knowledge that will likely not be recognized as valid by dominant groups, says Hill Collins, because the language and methods used to express this knowledge are not considered valid, or scholarly, or sophisticated. As she explains, "Subordinate groups have long had to use alternative ways to create independent self-definitions and self-valuations and to rearticulate them through our own specialists" (253). Hill Collins positions herself as one of these "specialists," negotiating the move back and forth between the realm of academic theory and the everyday life experiences of Black women in the United States. In so doing, she aids in the process of making subjugated knowledge more of a political force, which is so important because "dominant groups aim to replace subjugated knowledge with their own specialized thought because they realize that gaining control over this dimension of subordinate groups' lives simplifies control" (286).

As a person in a position of power within the agency, I sought to occupy this mediating role while making clear that I was allied with the youth. I also called out and challenged the status quo. The oft-cited rationale "Because that's the way that we've always done it" wasn't good enough for me if the way business had always been done resulted in policies and procedures that failed the most marginalized youth—typically our long-term street homeless youth, youth struggling with substance use or mental health challenges, youth of color, and transgender youth. Feminism was my foundation and reinforced my fundamental belief that the most vulnerable people need to be uplifted and seen as the experts of their own lives, and my women's studies education gave me the language, strength, and resolve to continue to push against oppressive structures within the organization.

One of the challenges I found in my work was that even in a queer organization, it was cisgender gay men whose voices and perspectives were systemically prioritized on leadership teams. This was true even when these men had displayed abusive and inappropriate conduct in the workplace, including yelling at and threatening me and other women and gender-nonconforming colleagues. While this was personally frightening and professionally disheartening, my feminist education prepared me well to continually push back against those agency norms, to utilize my resources (in human relations), and to continue to uplift the voices of the most marginalized youth and staff to make shifts in programmatic strategy and approach, to design innovative programs, and to insist that the voices of youth be brought into program designs and decisions.

I learned one thing very well: feminists aren't always popular in the workplace. My values and approach to the work caused a lot of conflict with my peers in management who were uncomfortable with having to talk to people whom they perceived as difficult or challenging (read: homeless or formerly homeless). Many of my peers in management positions were attached to the idea that as adults they knew better than youth what those young people should do with their lives.

The belief in adult-led decision-making was particularly visible regarding decisions homeless youth made about where they lived or stayed—a central component of their sense of self, or what Hill Collins would call their "self-definitions." My approach was to center harm reduction and trauma-informed care perspectives, both feminist philosophies insofar as they center the idea that people (in this case homeless LGBTQ youth) are the experts on their lives and that our job as adult providers is to listen to them and recognize that they are best equipped to both understand the systems where they receive services and make decisions about what services they will receive. As an adult advocate, my job is to help youth get what they want and need, not to tell them what they should prioritize.

For example, consider a situation in which a youth told me that she felt safer living on the streets, sleeping in the subway or in a park, because she had experienced physical or sexual assaults in the adult shelters (a common experience). She could not obtain a youth shelter bed because she had turned twenty-one and aged out (youth shelter beds are only available to those under the age of twenty-one; however, drop-in programming for homeless youth goes up to age twenty-five). At times there was a waiting list (it's not uncommon in New York City for two hundred youth to be on a waiting list for a youth shelter bed). In this situation, my job was to ask that young person what I could do to support her, listen, and meet those needs as best I could. This might mean providing a space in the drop-in center where she could take a nap before going out onto the streets, or giving extra to-go meals, blankets, socks, and toiletries that she could bring with her onto the streets that night.

Overwhelmingly, my colleagues wanted to approach the relationship with youth from positions of power, in the interest of "simplifying control," as Hill Collins describes it. They struggled to believe that youth could make decisions about their lives—even though the majority of the youth we had worked with had been on their own on and off the streets for some time. These staff would insist on telling youth that they would be safer in shelter and that they couldn't or shouldn't go back to the streets. These staff who had never experienced home-lessness themselves would at times even go so far as to label youth as having be-havior problems, which could result in loss of access to the drop-in center or other consequences if staff felt that youth weren't appropriately respectful of their (adult) perspective and guidance.

My colleagues' top-down approach to youth work was not only ineffective, it also eroded trust between youth and my team, which was predominantly made up of formerly homeless queer staff who had been brought on specifically to work with this population. It was exhausting and disheartening. I tried to use my posi-tion of privilege to shelter the youth and my staff from the structural misogyny and patriarchal values that informed direct interactions with youth, as well as the larger issues of what was deemed appropriate behavior for clients.

Unfortunately, my attempts to make the organization youth centered failed. Just shy of eight years, I left my director position to pursue my passion of writing full time (I had been effectively working two jobs for many years, writing and pub-lishing on nights and weekends around the demands of my day job). It was a strategic career decision to transition to being a full-time author and also a re-sponse to my own burnout resulting from the agency's failure to address work-place physical and psychological violence (I was assaulted by a client), which was of course at odds with my feminist approach to the work. Despite my leadership position, I felt I had run out of options to create a more proactive response to protect myself, staff, and youth, as the agency showed resistance to incorporating a more feminist approach. Because of the inherent structural inequality of the organization that those in leadership were unwilling to do anything more than pay lip service to, I reached the conclusion that the youth whom the agency was theoretically designed to serve were never going to be given the type of decision-making and leadership role in the running of the agency that they deserved. I had run out of options for trying to pressure the organization to take youth expertise and leadership into account when making programmatic decisions. Their knowledge, it seems, was destined to remain subjugated within the structures of this nonprofit.

Ultimately, it was my feminism that helped me gain the strength to leave not only my job but also my career in LGBTQ nonprofit management. Feminism helped me to reframe the leaving not as giving up but rather as embracing my passions to expand my career and go full time as a freelance writer, author, and writing instructor.

Alongside community organizing, a core component of my undergraduate academic studies was centered on the act of creativity and healing for marginalized communities. In that regard, this career shift feels like a full-circle embracing of what I fell in love with as an undergraduate student. Working in nonprofits was (at times) rewarding, and there were concrete ways my work could benefit communities that I was invested in; however, I felt routinely as though I was unable to achieve my full potential in the work. This career shift has enabled me to reframe and recommit myself to work that I feel uses my biggest strength—reaching people through writing and more specifically creating content by and for marginalized queer people in which we are able to see our lives, bodies, desires, communities, and families reflected on the page. To reach others, to inspire, uplift, or offer representation to the communities I call home is a profoundly feminist act.

Reference

Hill Collins, Patricia. 2000. *Black Feminist Thought: Knowledge, Consciousness, and the Politics of Empowerment.* 2nd ed. London: Routledge.

THE PATRIARCHAL ROOTS
OF PHILANTHROPY

Lauren Danzig

After I graduated from the University of Chicago's undergraduate program, known for its core curriculum, I entered my graduate program and eventually the professional sphere heavily influenced by capitalist criticism and feminist theory. I took on life after college as an abiding skeptic, grounded in strong beliefs about the moral deficiencies of capitalism and its inextricable relationship to patriarchy. My worldview was strongly informed not only by my education but also by my position as a cisgender white woman from a hyperliberal, suburban, upper-middle-class community in the Pacific Northwest.

Leaving college, I wished to be able to join a feminist socialist society like the one I read about in my gender studies classes—the Chicago Women's Liberation Union, influential in the 1970s in the very neighborhood where I went to school. The Hyde Park Chapter of the union laid out its philosophy in an essay called "Socialist Feminism: A Strategy for the Women's Movement": free, humane, competent medical care; people's control over their own bodies; attractive, comfortable housing; a varied, nutritious, abundant diet; social respect for the work people do; free, quality public education; and more. In this work, the authors state, "We share the socialist vision of a humanist world made possible through a redistribution of wealth and an end to the distinction between the ruling class and those who are ruled" (Hyde Park Chapter, Chicago Women's Liberation Union 1972, 3). In such a society, capitalist patriarchy would disappear, and most forms of philanthropy would be unnecessary because every individual's most basic needs would be met.

In many ways, the campus community at the University of Chicago mirrored these principles of feminist socialism. As an undergraduate, I enjoyed unlimited access to competent medical care, room and board, quality education, and more; these necessities were very intentionally built into student life. My most essential needs were met, paid for by scholarships and loans that I was privileged to access. Very few of these necessities are provided under the systems and structures characteristic of American capitalist patriarchy. When I graduated, I needed to make a living and figure out how to support myself without any of this assistance. At the same time, I hated the idea of working in corporate America.

I believed I could circumvent direct participation in (and, therefore, implied support of) the political economy of capitalist patriarchy by working in the field of social services, so after graduating, I enrolled at the Columbia University School of Social Work to study advanced clinical practice. Having lived in two major American cities, Chicago and New York, I had seen exactly how capitalist patriarchy alienates, vilifies, and impedes class mobility of the poor, and I wanted to fight back by connecting people to public resources. If the rich were never going to pay their fair share of taxes, at least I could take part in facilitating access to the few public benefits and resources that did exist.

After a year as a clinical student, the emotional labor of direct practice felt insurmountable. I had difficulty creating separation between my personal life and my work. Though the clients I worked with brought exceptional resilience, expertise, and resourcefulness to their situations, I felt defeated by the enormity of the challenges that stood in their way. One client whom I remember well was elderly and homeless, living with schizophrenia, diabetes, and other comorbidities. He wandered out of the shelter he was living in and never returned; I have no idea what happened to him and still wonder whether he is alive. While completing a field placement at an elementary school, I had a first-grade client who often showed up to case management in dirty clothes with bruises on his arms, eyes glossed over with exhaustion. I remember that the day he lost his winter coat, in order to teach him a lesson, his guardian refused to buy him a new one despite the harsh New York City winter weather. At six years old, he would walk to school alone at sunrise, arms stiff at his sides in unwieldy layers of cotton and wool.

During this time, my mind was constantly occupied with concerns about how my clients were faring, where they were, whether they were hungry or in pain or lonely, and what else I could possibly do to support them as a social work student. I found it overwhelmingly difficult to not use my personal time and resources to support clients and struggled with whether and how to make the best use of my various forms of privilege within the context of direct practice. I labored, for example, over the professional ethics of whether to buy that first-grader a new winter coat. This overinvolvement with casework was paralyzing, and I was dismayed by the feeling that the advocacy I was doing for individual clients was ineffective and temporary. I felt I would be better suited to address social issues on a broader scale and decided to switch from the advanced clinical practice track to an administrative curriculum.

As a white woman, being repeatedly shut down by racist and oppressive public systems for the first time was an important experience. Engaging in the emotional labor of client-facing social work and experiencing firsthand the harmful and complex barriers that prevent people from achieving safety and stability was crucial to my understanding of systemic oppression, which I had previously engaged with mostly in academic settings. Sitting with the emotional discomfort and vicarious trauma of client-facing work led to a crucial period of self-reflection that I was very privileged to be able to unpack in clinical supervision, during class, and in my own therapy. And making the choice to opt out of this kind of discomfort and switch to a macro-level area of social work practice was a privilege that I anticipate will have ripple effects throughout my career.

Soon after changing academic tracks, I realized that nonprofit management is mostly about financial management and raising money; of course, nonprofit organizations can only run programs with adequate funding and administrative infrastructure. Though I struggled with the reality that governments fail to tax the rich sufficiently to create the social safety nets necessary for a fair society, I entered the field of philanthropy with the perspective that fund-raising could be an alternative means of wealth redistribution.

After working in the field for several years, it is now clear to me that private-sector philanthropy flourishes under capitalist patriarchy. Gender and class hierarchies are unambiguously present in this work. Just read through practically any nonprofit's annual report or event program, and you will almost certainly see the word *patrons* on the back cover with a list of major donors, with *patr-* being the Latin root word for *father*.

Recent studies on high-net-worth major donors and presented in a report called *Women and Giving* found that although single women in the study gave more money to charity than single men (Women's Philanthropy Institute 2019), the men in the study were more strategic about giving than the women and tended to have higher net worth (Fidelity Charitable 2017). According to the report, when it comes to high-net-worth major donors, women may be more confident about which causes to support, while men may be more confident about which of their financial assets to donate, such as stock or liquid assets, and when to donate in order to maximize benefits, including tax deductions. Within the boundaries of my own anecdotal experiences as a fundraiser, I believe men who donate are also more likely than women donors to subconsciously act on peripheral variables, such as the gender dynamics present in philanthropic transactions, when making decisions about which organizations to support.

In the field of philanthropy, the term *major giving* describes the type of donation that can seriously transform the capacity or impact of a charitable program or project. For example, when a donor purchases a building for a university or hospital, their gift would fall under the category of major giving because it adds a significant level of capacity for the organization to expand its programs and services. In the major giving specialty, fundraisers are assigned a portfolio of high-net-worth donors and prospects and are tasked with cultivating those relationships with the organization, leading to major gifts. The culture of major giving is more accommodating of meetings in personal settings like dinners and cocktail hours, and these relationships have the potential to become quite involved over time, depending on how much attention and communication the donor prefers to receive. The power imbalance characteristic of this type of relationship, paired with the fact that most fundraisers are women,[1] as well as with the common practice of cultivating these relationships in more personal settings, introduces multiple layers of gendered interpersonal dynamics to navigate.

Several colleagues over the years have expressed marked awareness of gender dynamics in the woman fundraiser–man donor dyad, particularly in the specialty of major giving. Indeed, some women fundraisers may intentionally maneuver around these dynamics to their advantage, capitalizing on the gendered dynamics of philanthropy. This strategy recalls Judith Butler's well-known notion of the social construction of the gendered binary:

> If gender is instituted through acts which are internally discontinuous, then the appearance of substance is precisely that, a constructed identity, a performative accomplishment which the mundane social audience, including the actors themselves, come to believe and to perform in the mode of belief. If the ground of gender identity is the stylized repetition of acts through time, and not a seemingly seamless identity, then the possibilities of gender transformation are to be found in the arbitrary relation between such acts, in the possibility of a different sort of repeating, in the breaking or subversive repetition of that style. (1988, 520)

Undoubtedly, some actors in philanthropy do not realize they are performing a set of acts that maintain the illusion of a seamless identity. However, others most certainly do realize their performance. In fact, by consciously playing up a "stylized repetition of acts" that mimes the understanding held by the "mundane social audience" of the dominant conventions of femininity, women fundraisers may exercise a subversive performance of gender in order to strategically leverage existing oppressive gender conventions that portray women as helpless and thus obtain the donation. In theory, this type of strategy would motivate men donors to write a donation check out of benevolence to the beholden woman fundraiser, or "damsel in distress," rather than out of support for her cause, though the two are not mutually exclusive and may actually have a compounding effect.

Within the context of the capitalist patriarchy, however, some donors are much more motivated by peer recognition than by more gendered factors like those just described. For example, a donor motivated by elements of the capitalist patriarchy rather than by the charitable cause itself may perform charity by making and announcing a public donation or perhaps by bidding on a high-value auction item at a charity gala in order to deliberately quantify and demonstrate their wealth among peers in a socially acceptable way. By doing so, these donors also seize the opportunity to substantiate their apparent altruism among their social network.

This type of philanthropy sustains the capitalist patriarchy that necessitates it because philanthropic recognition gives the donor additional social and political capital among a highly curated wealthy audience. Additionally, charitable contributions in the United States are tax deductible, which decreases tax revenue that could otherwise be funding a social safety net and comprehensive public resources, resulting in the inequality and power-hoarding that is characteristic of capitalist patriarchy.

In addition, other forms of fund-raising, such as grant writing, play into the gendered dynamics of perceived ability to save people or solve gendered social issues like reproductive justice and gender-based violence. Often, grant proposal forms will include a section soliciting a client success story, in which the grant writer is tasked with explaining in tidy linear terms exactly how the services provided by the nonprofit organization helped the often feminine client escape a terrible fate. Further, grant writers must often propose measurable success metrics in grant proposals, such as number of women housed, meals served, or hours of counseling provided, in ways that reflect white-male-dominated constructs of legitimacy and success. This focus on measurability, outcome metrics, and linear client success stories also keeps the focus on individual lives and salvations, rather than challenging a capitalist system that perpetuates these gendered issues.

These are just some of the manifestations of gender politics and patriarchy in the field of philanthropy. My academic grounding in gender theory has at once made it easier for me to identify and decode the power structures at play in my work, while also making it more difficult for me to ignore particularly obvious demonstrations of sexism and classism in the field.

This paints somewhat of a gloomy picture of the world of philanthropy—at least within the context of American capitalist patriarchy. Certainly, my academic background in gender and sexuality studies has been helpful in identifying abuses of power and authority, money worship, sexism, heteronormativity, and the ubiquity and inherent inequity of capitalist patriarchy. I would much prefer to be aware of these dynamics and have a philosophical grounding in how to think about them than not be able to recognize and think critically about them at all.

I am also very hopeful that the field of philanthropy will continue in its current trend of becoming more inclusive and community centered, led by the people and groups it seeks to support. With the encouragement of thought leaders in the field, an increasing number of private foundations have begun to adopt practices like participatory grant making, through which funders engage the communities they support in the grant-making process. Modeled after years of leadership and practice in communities that have typically been left out of organized philanthropy (Witte 2012; Barclay 2012), these more grassroots practices are beginning to be incorporated into what is considered to be mainstream philanthropy (Eikenberry 2005). Meanwhile, other funders, including major individual donors, are increasingly giving unrestricted donations that enable the recipient organization to decide how best to steward the funds, rather than dictating exactly how the money must be spent. With increased use of progressive practices like these, the field of philanthropy becomes more democratic and equitable over time.

The Hyde Park Chapter of the Chicago Women's Liberation Union authors write, "Our own particular relationship to ideology has two special functions. First, it provides ideas which guide us, defining the framework and reason for our actions. Second, it defines our view of the world concretely, thus providing a system of analysis through which women can understand socialist feminism as a world view" (1972, 7). The union authors' view of ideology is resonant and describes precisely the way that I view my grounding in feminist academic theory. Whether this grounding is practical or productive is not the question; what matters most is that it adds a rich dimension to my career and underscores my vigilance in my practice of feminist philanthropy.

Note

1. According to the Census Bureau American Community Survey Public Use Microdata Sample One-Year Estimate, nearly 70 percent of fund-raising professionals are women.

References

Barclay, Akira J. 2012. "The Value of Giving Circles in the Evolution of Community Philanthropy." 2012 Emerging Leaders International Fellows Program. Graduate Center, City University of New York.

Butler, Judith. 1988. "Performative Acts and Gender Constitution: An Essay in Phenomenology and Feminist Theory." *Theatre Journal* 40 (4): 519–31.

Eikenberry, Angela M. 2005. "Giving Circles and the Democratization of Philanthropy." PhD diss., University of Nebraska Graduate College.

Fidelity Charitable. 2017. *Women and Giving: The Impact of Generation and Gender on Philanthropy.* Boston: Fidelity Charitable. https://www.fidelitycharitable.org/content /dam/fc-public/docs/insights/women-and-giving.pdf.

Hyde Park Chapter, Chicago Women's Liberation Union. 1972. "Socialist Feminism: A Strategy for the Women's Movement." https://dukelibraries.contentdm.oclc.org /digital/collection/p15957coll6/id/617.

Witte, Deborah. 2012. "Women's Leadership in Philanthropy: An Analysis of Six Giving Circles." PhD diss., Antioch University.

Women's Philanthropy Institute. 2019. *Womengive 2019: Gender and Giving across Communities of Color.* Indianapolis: Indiana University–Purdue University Indianapolis. https://philanthropy.iupui.edu/institutes/womens-philanthropy-institute/research /women-give19.html.

Part 2
THE BUSINESS WORLD

"WOMAN, YOU ARE THE ONE DOING IT WRONG"

A Decolonial Conceptualization of Colombian Working-Class Femininity

Laura Ramos-Jaimes

After completing my graduate studies in gender and policy in 2015 in London, I returned to my home in Colombia, prepared to encounter a chauvinist workplace culture in Bogotá. However, I arrived at a research center where I joined a feminist research team. We were diverse women whose progressive statements were well received in the institution. We published a book on critical lessons from South America about women's economic empowerment, and we executed a regional research project on education and technology from a gender and diversity perspective.

I began trying to translate feminist theory into practice in the workplace and decided to familiarize myself with those US authors whose focus was giving pragmatic solutions to overcoming sexism in the business world. I read *Lean In: Women, Work, and the Will to Lead* (Sandberg 2013); *Playing Big: Find Your Voice, Your Mission, Your Message* (Mohr 2014); and *Women Don't Ask: Negotiation and the Gender Divide* (Babcock and Laschever 2003). These best-selling authors acknowledge that patriarchy and sexism are structural problems for women in the work world, but they focus on why individual women are afraid of confronting these obstacles. They argue that we have internalized sexism and negative stereotypes about ourselves. According to these authors, women are not taking advantage of the opportunities available in the labor market because we lack the will to lead, fail to find our voices, and do not successfully learn how to negotiate.

As I gave workshops to young and middle-aged women who aspired to succeed in the business world, I used Sandberg, Mohr, and Babcock and Laschever as my main sources of inspiration. I worked on turning their statements, theses, and arguments into practical guides for working women in Colombia. This approach worked for a while—or at least, I thought it was working. I found resonance in their messages, as did some participants in my workshops. However, I also found myself growing emotionally and physically tired and feeling disconnected and disengaged from Colombian women's issues. I realized that in using this corporate feminist discourse, I had actually contributed to the reproduction of a workplace misogyny that was underpinned by a colonial victim-blaming discourse.

After many workshops and presentations, I reached a conclusion: these authors implicitly address the kind of woman who resembles them and find solutions only for her. They posit a woman whose only obstacle to a successful career is her gender, disregarding her class, ethnicity or race, sexuality, language, nationality, disability, culture, and religion. This woman is also portrayed as mainly reproductive and, thus, the recipient of monetary and economic resources produced by her productive counterpart—the male breadwinner. She learned her femininity via nonviolent gender socialization—at school, through the messages of mass media, and through gendered toys at home. Because obstacles to advancement are the patriarchal structures that punish them for being feminine, solutions to overcoming sexism in the workplace assume that solidarity with other women is based solely on their gender identity.

The problem is that each of these assumptions coincides with white, middle-class—and upper-middle-class—heterosexual femininity (Windsor 2015), a femininity that does not correspond to Colombian conditions. By positing such a femininity, the authors I analyze participate in a colonial discourse that cannot account for discrimination against Colombian women in the workplace (or for other women in the United States, for that matter). This literature does not have the theoretical grounds to integrate our colonial legacy, which is gendered, racist, classist, and overtly violent. I address this literature under the rubric of colonial corporate feminism.

Instead of problematizing this solipsistic approach, I decided to problematize the implementation of this literature in places in the Global South like Colombia from a decolonial perspective. I represent a Colombian femininity as one that is built on the materiality of almost falling under the poverty line, defaulting, and running out of money to pay for school. It is about recognizing myself as a woman who comes neither from a family trapped in a poverty spiral where social mobility is statistically unlikely, nor from a privileged family with full-time homemakers who have time to pick up their kids from school or even go to parents' meetings. I depict my professional and personal journeys to explore how these books resonated with me in the first place. Then, by analyzing the main arguments of this literature, I identify how I contributed to the reproduction of misogyny by neglecting the Colombian gendered colonial trauma.

I delve into Colombian coloniality by defining three aspects that concern Colombian women: gendered coloniality, gendered socialization through violence, and the denial of such violence.

The Colombian Context

Colombia merits attention because of its apparent paradoxes. Our most basic paradox is that we are the most stable democracy and economy in South America and the Caribbean with, at the same time, a fifty-year-old armed conflict against the oldest guerrilla force in the world, the FARC-EP.[1] With no history of lethal coups, military regimes, or the perpetuation of populist leaders in power, Colombia also has the most stable macroeconomic indicators of the region.[2] Nonetheless, we bear the burden of millions who have been violently displaced from their homes,[3] thousands who have disappeared,[4] and a significant economic cushion in the illegal markets. In terms of gender, paradoxes are present as well. Women have reached gender parity in education, have one of the highest levels of labor participation in the region, and evidence more social mobility than men do (Araujo Vallejo 2014). However, women are more likely to be unemployed (14%) than men are (8.7%) (Departamento Administrativo Nacional de Estadística 2019), and despite having more years of education, women earn 81 percent of men's salaries with the same levels of education (Osorio 2015). Also, on average, women work two hours and ten minutes more than men per day (Departamento Administrativo Nacional de Estadística 2018).

Colombian paradoxes start to make sense once our colonial history is included in the analysis. Coloniality survives colonialism, and Colombia is no exception (Quijano 2000). Our country was gestated through the violent encounter of Europeans, Africans, and Indigenous people. Driven by the belief in a racialized hierarchy (Mezilas 2015), Europeans plundered the Americas, slaughtered Indigenous people, and enslaved Black Africans. This violent past remains in our collective memory. It constitutes our colonial traumatic legacy, for such memory is material. It survives through acute inequality,[5] methodical violence against poor populations incited and sponsored by the Colombian state (e.g., massacres),[6] the virtual absence of Black people in elite universities, and the absence of Indigenous people in white-collar jobs. Our patriarchal system cannot be explained without taking into account our colonial history, and neither can this colonial history be understood without an analysis of patriarchy (Cumes 2012). These conditions continue to shape the experiences of Colombian women today—and these experiences are not consistent with those that Sandberg, Mohr, and Babcock and Laschever standardize.

Reading Sandberg, Mohr, and Babcock and Laschever

The overall message from this literature is that, as women, we have internalized oppression to such a point that we act as our own oppressors. The main mechanism is fear, which prevents us from reaching our full potential. This literature summons women to stop reproducing what the patriarchy does in terms of segregation, doubts about our skills, and internalized biases against ourselves. What resonated the most with me from these books was that they included many of the strategies that I had been using in my own life and gave me additional advice.

The three books all recognize that feminism has paved the way for younger generations but also that there is still a long way to go because, they say, women are scared. According to *Lean In*, the solution lies in each individual woman's decision to overcome fear and find solutions to reach top positions in organizations. *Lean In* states a clear theory of change: once women reach the top, gender equality will trickle down. Getting to the top is about leaning in, "being ambitious in any pursuit" (Sandberg 2013, 10). According to Sandberg, ambition is thwarted by "fear of failure," fear of going against the norm, and the internalization of negative stereotypes (24). Thus, not reaching the top of organizations and corporations is due to what is inside of us. Sexism gets under our skin, we internalize it, and then we reproduce it. It is our duty to question and change ourselves before thinking about external conditions.

After reading *Lean In*, I felt reassured about some decisions I had made to advance in my career. For example, I was eighteen years old when I had my first job interview. I applied to be an English teacher in a vocational institution in Bogotá. During the interview, I felt so certain about my teaching skills that I confidently "leaned in" toward my interviewer's desk. I placed both my elbows on the desk and enthusiastically talked about the idea of being a teacher. I got the job and worked there for a year. This gave me the experience I needed to be hired as an English teacher at my own university, which is a renowned institution in Colombia. For a while, I talked about that interview as a slightly funny, embarrassing moment yet ultimately a positive event in which I occupied more space than my interviewer and disregarded the hierarchy separating us. However, after reading Sandberg, I stopped feeling self-conscious and thought that perhaps it was because I confidently leaned in and bargained about the condition that he hired me despite my lack of experience.

Playing Big (Mohr 2014) complements *Lean In*'s career-driven approach. Although Mohr has a less corporate approach, it aligns with Sandberg's main idea and rationalization: playing bigger "is having the vision of a more authentic, fully expressed, free-from-fear you and growing more and more into her, being *pulled* by this resonant vision rather than *pushing* to achieve markers of success" (10). Yet it is a challenge because the "inequality of men and women has also left internal effects on us" (xxv). Mohr goes deeper into this psyche. First, she talks about an "inner critic" as the obstacle left by the person who took care of us, treating us as weak, helpless girls; this person laid the groundwork for fear in our decision-making process during adulthood. Then, Mohr presents the "inner mentor," the future, wise woman we could become if we overcome our fears in the present. When we let the mentor talk, she assuages our critic and guides our path.

The inner critic's anxiety is due to us caring too much about what other people think (Mohr 2014). We have learned to diminish the strength of our messages and our abilities so we are not judged as rude, masculine, and grating. To do so, we use expressions like "just," "sorry, but," "Does that make sense?," "kind of," and "almost" and substitute a statement with a question. As a low-status group, women cannot be warm and competent at the same time. This is a white man's privilege. Mohr's invitation, however, is to rise above the fear of being judged as arrogant by focusing on truth, service (as our skills could be of help to somebody who is looking for someone with our experience), and visibility, thus learning to talk in assertive and concrete ways about ourselves.

Thanks to Mohr, I stopped feeling responsible for other people's feelings regarding my achievements. In the Colombian context, studying at the Universidad Nacional de Colombia is a great achievement. When I mentioned the name of my university, most men said things like, "Then it is not very hard to study there." Thus I played a game. If I was not in the mood, I just avoided talking about it at all. If I was in the mood, I continued the conversation with sarcasm, joking about how some people projected their shortcomings onto my life story. Those jokes were not well received. Reading *Playing Big* taught me that I should neither lie by omission nor thwart and sabotage my own story with sarcasm. Talking about my achievements was not being arrogant; instead I was telling the truth and being visible.

Finally, *Women Don't Ask* (Babcock and Laschever 2003) is about women avoiding negotiating because of our internalized fears about making demands. The authors mainly use data to show that the gender wage gap is largely explained by working women's reluctance to negotiate. This reluctance relates to the lower levels of dissatisfaction in the workplace that women feel compared with what men feel. When a person feels dissatisfied, she will want to change her conditions and status. However, women tend be satisfied with less compensation than men do, so we are less likely to take action to change our salary conditions.

Satisfaction correlates with expectations. Because throughout childhood we learn that we will obtain less than men, we undervalue our work compared with the value men give to theirs. Babcock and Laschever (2003) argue that women working for love instead of money is one of the problematic traits in women's subjectivity. This pattern "cuts across economic, class, and racial lines" (44) and is present beginning in childhood because of gendered treatment, such as toys and gifts: "One of the things that men are conditioned to think they should get is money. Becky, 50, journalist, recalls that when she was a child her brother was given gifts of stocks, but she was given dresses" (68). Thus, "grateful to be paid at all, many women accept what they are offered without negotiating" (68).

This reading affirmed my childhood, since I experienced many of the conditions that it points to as beneficial to build a confident character in girls. My parents gave my brother and me gifts with similar prices and gender-neutral colors—his bike was green and mine was orange. Once, my father gave us the same amount of stocks for our birthdays. After handing us some weird pieces of paper with holographic labels and signatures, he said, "Each of you has to take care of your own money. These are your future savings."

Thus, when I facilitated workshops based on these books, I was convinced their advice was correct. And I still believe that these workshops somehow helped both participants and facilitators. For example, they taught us to identify when we had behaved chauvinistically toward our female coworkers. The problem began when I assumed that I was performing the "correct" femininity, which Sandberg, Mohr, and Babcock and Laschever used as the reference for their understanding of women. Despite presumably being physically weak, sensitive, and nurturing, I believed I was turning that femininity to my advantage. I thought I was only teaching a strategy to grapple with sexism in the workplace, but I realize now that I started feeling superior to the other women, as they did not perform the same kind of white, upper-class, heterosexual (and correct) femininity. Although I cannot elaborate here on the basics of psychoanalysis, I think it is safe to assert that superiority is an expression of the inferiority complex. I evidenced it by applying a femininity disconnected from the materiality of being a working-class woman in Colombia. I was neglecting my gendered colonial trauma.

Gendered Colonial Trauma

Our colonial wound is also a gendered colonial trauma. *Trauma* refers to the effects on a person's psyche of an extreme experience in which the person authentically thinks that his or her life is endangered (Ortega Martínez 2003). It is possible to talk about collective trauma when the extreme experience is a common situation that brought individuals together in shared social suffering (Mezilas 2015). This social distress is a way for individuals to avoid loneliness and to collectively process trauma.

In particular, the colonial trauma corresponds to the collective responses and efforts of the colonized to discredit and condemn colonialism (Mezilas 2015). The main rebellion against the imposed European ways of doing and thinking was to preserve the colonized cosmogonies through memory (Mezilas 2015). The aim is to rescue and value ancestral memories and in that process to resignify signs and symbols as symbolic weapons against hegemonic forces that overtly denied the human condition in the colonized for more than two centuries.

The denial of Indigenous people's and Black Africans' humanity by European thinkers was the cognitive violence that legitimized the physical violence against the colonized (Santos 2014). Blatant violence was the colonial technology; it was the means to instill "fear, inferiority, dread, genuflection, despair, and obsequiousness" in millions of human beings (Cesaire 1955). In this sense, colonialism generated traumatic responses from the colonized as they tried to overcome and compensate for systematically imposed inferiority.

As colonized people rescued their memory in the midst of colonial violence, enslavement, and dispossession, they engaged in a *criollización* process. This process involves multiple cultures constantly crossing the imaginaries possessed by each population at the moment of the colonial encounter (Mezilas 2015). Now that the region is the target of neocolonial phenomena, *criollización* still develops, in uneven yet tangible fashion. In short, *criollización* allows us to understand that we are the unpredictable sum of intersecting cultures in a meeting zone, currently shaped by free labor and neoliberal conditions (Glissant 2006).

Both colonial trauma and *criollización* produce gendered responses. The embodiments of femininity and masculinity were defined, oppressed, and exploited differently by colonial violence. In contemporary Colombia, our gendered heritage is shown through the use of gender-differentiated stereotypes about Indigenous and Black Colombians to rationalize their current disadvantages. Stereotypes about Black men as lazy and Indigenous women as meek are still commonplace. The gendered aspect of our colonial trauma thus has particularities that interact with class: Who are those women who work? Who are those men who do not work? Are they Black, Indigenous, rural people?

Because of this history—a history that is still playing itself out in the present—any neglect of these conditions reproduces colonial racism and sexism. Thus, assuming—as I did—that Anglo-Saxon authors who disregard social, economic, and racial hierarchies are capable of prescribing the undoing of gender oppression is to be complicit in a violent discourse and practice. These practices deny our *criollización* and collective wound as expressed in the configuration of a working-class femininity.

Working-Class Femininity in Colombia

In the corporate feminism discourse, the authors acknowledge that people are socialized following gendered traditional roles; there is thus the potential for addressing social and historical contexts. However, their assumptions about gender roles elide difference and specificity and thus do not capture the kind of sexism that we experience in Colombia.

First, these authors assert that gendered socialization is based on women internalizing that we are "recipients" of economic resources, as opposed to the masculine "providers." Yet in Colombia, women are socialized to work and provide for their families. Colombian (colonial) productive systems have depended on the productive (and, certainly, reproductive) labor of poor, Black, Indigenous, and rural women. Although women get paid less than men, women get paid; informality, instability, underpaid jobs, and underemployment are the usual for Colombians, both women and men. In this context, women do not face the dilemma of the white middle-class woman that corporate feminist discourse describes—a dilemma that puts forward the privilege of choosing between a career and full-time domestic activities. It is a privilege because that dilemma is typical of a woman whose household could thrive with a single breadwinner's income. Given the historical labor conditions in Colombia, income that solely comes from male labor has not been enough to sustain a household.

Indeed, the construction of femininity in Colombia revolves around motherhood, yet it is a providing motherhood. This point coincides with the argument of the analyzed authors, who assert that women are socialized to provide care in the domestic sphere; however, a Colombian mother must *guarantee* economic resources. Certainly, being a working woman in Colombia has its various degrees of sexist sanction; for example, if women in heterosexual relationships earn more than their partners, or spend more time outside than inside the household, they are met with disapproval.

I grew up in a working-class setting. Stay-at-home mothers were considered privileged or exceptional. If women in my family had not worked, their families would not have had the option of social mobility or even survival. I grew up with the ingrained idea that both parents worked for remuneration, although they followed a sexual division of labor. My father's mother sold women's shoes and purses, while my mother's mother was a dressmaker who rented out rooms in her house. My great-grandmothers worked to get their own income as well. My father's grandmother was a maid and cook, and my mother's grandmother was a prison guard.

By contrast, the gendered assumptions of colonial corporate feminism only recognize one femininity—the one that chooses between being productive and being reproductive. Assuming this choice in Colombia functions as an oppressive mechanism, as it becomes a prescription about what a woman is. During my workshops, women acknowledged their disadvantages, and for many of them, it was a radical revelation. However, once I explained how we contribute to those disadvantages through our behavior, many expressed their sentiments that the feminine traits I described were foreign to the roles they assumed in their contexts. They did not feel described by the qualities of a woman dedicated to receiving instead of providing, not negotiating for a raise or expressing her opinion in the workplace, or being passive. Some of them even recalled the violent experiences they overcame because they were the breadwinners of their families, with or without a heterosexual partner. They did encounter a sexist environment, but they did not identify with the individual traits we posed as the problem. At the end, sometimes workshops became an exercise in trying to convince them that this research was "the truth." Still, many of the participants were reluctant to accept this analysis.

Second, this corporate feminist discourse assumes that the internalization of gender roles happens solely through nonviolent socialization, such as education and gendered toys and gifts. *Women Don't Ask* is the only one of the three books that acknowledges that there are situations in which women's bargaining and purchasing power and higher positions also generate violent backlashes: "At a construction site in New York . . . the men took a woman's boots and hacked them to bits. Another woman was injured by a male coworker; he hit her on the head with a two-by-four." However, even though their "interviews produced numerous stories of 'punishment,'" Babcock and Laschever (2003, 97) do not follow up on this violence.

Colombia is widely known for its high levels of interpersonal violence.[7] A substantial component of our socialization process is to internalize fear and inferiority through violent means, which is part of our colonial legacy. This legacy is also present in our gendered socialization. We learn to be the right kind of women and men not only through education, discourse, and intergenerational expectations but also through overt violence used to punish nonnormative gender performance.

For example, the Afro aesthetics of my hair defined my socialization process. My hair was either a political statement or an obstacle to progress, depending on the political views of adults around me. My father's family comes from a Black region. Though my brother and I are light-skinned mestizos, my appearance is closer to our Black background. I never straightened my hair. As a child, I could not bear that painful process, so my parents did not adhere to the discourse that said that my hair needed to be controlled. During the time I facilitated the workshops, three men attacked me with stones thrown from a convertible car. I was leaving a hair salon in the upper-middle-class area of Bogotá wearing a natural Afro hairstyle in all its amplitude. It was nighttime and lights were scarce. When I stepped onto the sidewalk, stones rained on me while these men yelled that this was not a neighborhood for Blacks and questioned what I was doing in *that* hair salon—a very famous one in Bogotá. Shaking, I braided my hair and continued on my way back home. I embody one version of the Black heritage in the *criollización* process. I have constructed my identity as a light-skinned mestiza with thick, big, Afro hair in a dialectic and tense movement between rejection and acceptance, denial and affirmation (Gomes 2011). Thus, patriarchal violence is not merely about giving girls dresses and boys stocks for Christmas. Racist and elitist sexism physically attacks women when they disrupt the norm.

This personal experience illustrates that premising feminism on the experiences of white women from the United States does not provide any way to address the fact that stones literally fell on me because of my female Black aesthetics. To work for social change in Colombia requires one to recognize the threat of daily, systematic violence. Otherwise, our silence is a denial that leads to a victim-blaming discourse, as used to happen during the workshops I facilitated. Such a discourse states that the victim is partially or completely responsible for the violence that somebody else enacts on him or her (Miller, Markman, and Handley 2007). It frames violence as an event generated by a deficiency of the victim (Garland et al. 2017). The victim is different from the people who do not experience such violence, for the latter's "correct" behavior allows them to dodge the violence. A consequence of this discourse is that perpetrators are exonerated by society and themselves. Thus, the perpetrator's responsibility decreases as the victim's responsibility increases. My discourse in the workshop did not take into account participants' socioeconomic background; I treated everyone in the audience as equally needing to overcome her tendency to settle for less.

To tell women that, because of our internalized fear, it is more likely for us to both experience sexism and fail in the work world is a way of sending a victim-blaming message: if you experience sexism, you will be held accountable for complicity in it. What I have since realized is that walking down the street with Afro hair should not generate a racist and sexist attack, just as a woman accepting a given salary does not mean she is responsible for the wage gap. Telling women that this violence is their responsibility because of the internalization of traditional gender roles and fear to face norms is to deny the systematic violence that controls the performance of our nonwhite, working-class (and "incorrect") femininity.

Finally, *Lean In*, *Playing Big*, and *Women Don't Ask* assume that there is a trickle-down effect in terms of reducing sexism, which follows the advancement of women in the work world. The trickle-down effect states that economic growth will benefit society at large because those who accumulate wealth—thanks to the lack of regulation of the markets on distribution—will generate employment and better conditions for the rest of society. It is a natural effect that rests on the good intentions of those who accumulate wealth. This theory has been far from confirmed in the economic realm, yet the authors analyzed here take it outside the economic sphere and use it to explain how an individual woman's success enhances the conditions of the women who follow in her footsteps.

When I returned to Colombia after graduate school to work, the head of the administrative area of the research center was a light-skinned, upper-middle-class Colombian woman. She regularly treated her staff badly: yelling, mistreatment, and silence were standard responses to direct questions. During more than two years, I never witnessed her behaving in such a way with men, only with women. Perhaps it was because all the administrative staff were women, and she oversaw them directly. Also, her workload was stressful and not many people valued the clerical work she did for the center. However, the fact that this woman was in a top position in one of the most important institutions in Colombia was no guarantee of dignified treatment toward women. Assuming that the trickle-down effect functions in terms of gender equality is to disregard the reality that women also reproduce sexism. In bell hooks's words, patriarchy has no gender (2010); furthermore, she says, "We are all participants in perpetuating sexism until we change our minds and hearts, until we let go of sexist thought and action and replace it with feminist thought and action" (2000, 87).

Conclusion

The corporate discourse in which I participated was bound to backfire at some point. Amid organizing conferences and workshops, I dyed the lower part of my thick black hair a bright blue color. A woman reacted to it by telling me, "It is unacceptable that you, the face of a company, a representative of the most important research center in Colombia, have done that. In addition to being a woman, you added another obstacle. You look unprofessional and no one will take you seriously." At that moment, I saw what I was doing. I realized that I was contributing to the reproduction of stratification among women by creating divisions among women—those who behave correctly and those who bring sexism on themselves. I was disconnected from my own context, which was the hardship that women in my family and hometown overcame and the strength they exhibited in facing structural sexism that placed them in a disadvantageous position in the labor market. I felt the emptiness of rejecting my own story.

Working-class femininity in Colombia is the result of a gendered colonial trauma that characterizes our process of *criollización*. We are the unpredictable result of an unequal, inefficient, and colonial economic system that forces marginalized populations to have a source of income on their own or starve. This system is colonial because it follows a racialized hierarchy of bodies, where there are limits to your freedom to determine where to be, how you talk, and in what venues you participate. Our sexism is based on economic inequality, racism, classism, colonialism, and systematic violence. Being an active member of Colombian society who seeks to change those conditions of oppression requires that we give our own story the place it deserves. Otherwise, we will recycle stereotypes and historical constructions—such as white, urban, US, middle-class femininity, which touts a colonial corporate feminism. A feminism that requires the exploitation and exclusion of marginalized women as well as thwarting our chances of finding solutions to overcome patriarchal practices that are particular to our Colombian context is not really feminism at all.

Notes

1. FARC-EP stands for Fuerzas Armadas Revolucionarias de Colombia—Ejército del Pueblo (Revolutionary Armed Forces of Colombia—People's Army). They were founded in 1964, but the official starting year of the contemporary Colombian internal armed conflict is 1948, with the assassination of the presidential candidate Jorge Eliécer Gaitán.

2. Colombia began 2017 as the most resilient Latin American economy, before the decrease of commodities prices (OCDE 2017).

3. In 2017, then-president Juan Manuel Santos recognized that 8.3 million people had been displaced by the internal armed conflict.

4. In 2018, the Centro Nacional de Memoria Histórica (National Center of Historical Memory) announced that eighty-two thousand people had disappeared in Colombia in the context of the internal armed conflict.

5. Colombia has one of the highest Gini coefficients in the world at 49.7.

6. The Inter-American Commission on Human Rights found that the Colombian state was responsible and guilty for the La Rochela massacre (in which twelve people were publicly executed by paramilitaries in 1989), the Mapiripán massacre (in which the paramilitaries used an airport of the state to land in the municipality and tortured and killed forty-nine people during five days in 1997), and the Pueblo Bello massacre (in which thirty-seven people disappeared and six were killed by paramilitaries in 1990) (Carvajal Martínez 2015).

7. Colombia has been on the list of the world's most violent countries for several years, a status it shares with the United States. However, with the signing of the peace agreement between the government and the FARC-EP guerrillas in 2016, homicide and other violence rates have dropped dramatically.

References

Araujo Vallejo, V. 2014. "Movilidad social en Colombia: Un análisis de la evolución de la movilidad educativa por género." Thesis, Universidad del Valle.

Babcock, L., and S. Laschever. 2003. *Women Don't Ask: Negotiation and the Gender Divide.* Princeton, NJ: Princeton University Press.

Carvajal Martínez, J. E. 2015. "Los fallos de la Corte Interamericana de Derechos Humanos: Colombia y la mirada de la justicia internacional." *Prolegómenos* 18 (35): 103–20. https://doi.org/10.18359/dere.813.

Cesaire, A. 1955. *Discurso sobre o colonialismo.* Paris: Présence Africaine.

Cumes, A. E. 2012. "Mujeres indígenas, patriarcado y colonialismo: Un desafío a la segregación comprensiva de las formas de dominio." *Anuario Hojas de Warmi* 17. http://institucional.us.es/revistas/warmi/17/7.pdf.

Departamento Administrativo Nacional de Estadística. 2018. *Encuesta Nacional de Uso del Tiempo (ENUT): 2016–2017.* Boletín técnico. https://www.dane.gov.co/files/investigaciones/boletines/ENUT/Bol_ENUT_2016_2017.pdf.

——. 2019. *Mercado laboral por sexo: Trimestre móvil febrero–abril 2019.* Boletín técnico. https://www.dane.gov.co/files/investigaciones/boletines/ech/ech_genero/bol_eje_sexo_feb19_abr19.pdf.

Garland, T. S., C. Policastro, T. N. Richards, and K. S. Miller. 2017. "Blaming the Victim: University Student Attitudes toward Bullying." *Journal of Aggression, Maltreatment and Trauma* 26 (1): 69–87. https://doi.org/10.1080/10926771.2016.1194940.

Glissant, É. 2006. *Tratado del Todo Mundo.* Barcelona: El Cobre.

Gomes, N. L. 2011. "O movimiento negro: Ausências, emergências e a produção dos saberes." *Política & Sociedade* 10 (18): 133–54. https://doi.org/10.5007/2175-7984.2011v10n18p133.

hooks, bell. 2000. *Feminism Is for Everybody: Passionate Politics.* Cambridge, MA: South End.

——. 2010. *Teaching Critical Thinking: Practical Wisdom.* Hoboken, NJ: Taylor and Francis.

Mezilas, G. 2015. *El trauma colonial entre la memoria y el discurso: Pensar (desde) el Caribe.* Pompano Beach, FL: Educa Vision.

Miller, A. K., K. D. Markman, and I. M. Handley. 2007. "Self-Blame among Sexual Assault Victims Prospectively Predicts Revictimization: A Perceived Sociolegal Context Model of Risk." *Basic and Applied Social Psychology* 29 (2): 129–36. https://doi.org/10.1080/01973530701331585.

Mohr, T. 2014. *Playing Big: Find Your Voice, Your Mission, Your Message.* New York: Penguin Group.

OCDE. 2017. *Estudios económicos de la OCDE: Colombia.* http://www.oecd.org/eco/surveys/Colombia-2017-OECD-economic-survey-overview-spanish.pdf.

Ortega Martínez, F. A. 2003. "Crisis social y trauma: Perspectivas desde la historiografía cultural colonial." *Anuario Colombiano de Historia Social y de La Cultural* 30:45–96. https://doi.org/10.15446/achsc.

Osorio, V. 2015. *De cuidados y descuidos: La Economía del cuidado en Colombia y perspectivas de política pública.* Medellín, Colombia: Escuela Nacional Sindical. http://biblioteca.clacso.edu.ar/Colombia/ens/20170803044636/pdf_905.pdf.

Quijano, A. 2000. "Colonialidad del poder, eurocentrismo y América Latina." In *La colonialidad del saber: Eurocentrismo y ciencias sociales—Perspectivas Latinoamericanas,* edited by E. Lander, 246. Buenos Aires: Consejo Latinoamericano de Ciencias Sociales. http://bibliotecavirtual.clacso.org.ar/ar/libros/lander/quijano.rtf.

Sandberg, S. 2013. *Lean In: Women, Work, and the Will to Lead.* New York: Alfred A. Knopf.

Santos, B. de S. 2014. *Epistemologies of the South: Justice against Epistemicide*. New York: Routledge.

Windsor, E. J. 2015. "Femininities." In *International Encyclopedia of the Social & Behavioral Sciences*, 2nd ed., edited by J. D. Wright, 893–97. Amsterdam: Elsevier. https://doi.org/https://doi.org/10.1016/B978-0-08-097086-8.35015-2.

HOW TO MARKET ANTICAPITALIST FEMINISM

The Making of an Online Socialist Agenda

Alissa Medina

As an aspiring writer in my early teen years, I reluctantly devoured women's magazines. *Seventeen* magazine was my bible. Every month I religiously ran to the mailbox to retrieve the newest issue, pop open the glossy cover, and view the contents. In spite of my excitement, staring into the faces of the celebrities posing on the cover didn't feel very empowering. As I turned the pages, I would compare myself to the women on them. I was enthralled with the toxicity of it all: I wanted to take all of this advice and be deemed perfect according to their standards, all while secretly knowing I never would be.

Since these magazines are shaped by heteropatriarchal capitalism, it's not surprising that they bring women advice on fixing their imperfections so that buying what's inside will be validating to one's femininity. The male gaze prevalent in these pages reinforces the idea that women are the ones who need constant improvement through the purchasing of products, furthering the notion of sexism in capitalism that we need to be physically perfect to be desirable to men.

By the age of sixteen, I could take it no longer. In 2009, I started my own blog, *Reasons to Be Beautiful*, with the mission of creating a collective voice that represented individuals dismantling societal notions of beauty and femininity. Precisely because I belong to the demographic to which these magazines cater—heterosexual white women—I wanted to critique their assumptions about heteronormativity as a marketing device. Investing my time and energy in *Reasons to Be Beautiful* made me feel as if I was actively working to subvert everything I was seeing on TV and in magazines. I could exercise some agency by resisting their idea of the "ideal woman," forgoing the need to constantly feel feminine by purchasing products.

By joining an anime fandom site called GaiaOnline and issuing a call for like-minded writers, I found my future editorial partner, Stephanie Watson. In 2014, the community blog was revised and *Fembot* magazine was officially established as a result of an outburst of radical creativity led by young, predominantly women-identifying writers. *Fembot* officially started to gain traction in 2019 within the online feminist community, and we now reach more than one million people a day through social media. Finally, after ten years, Stephanie and I have seen the fruition of our unpaid labor within the confines of a society riddled with toxic masculinity, racist rhetoric, and heteronormativity. As *Fembot* took shape, we also expanded our critique to include magazines that may consider themselves feminist because of their articles on strong women and so on, but that simultaneously run nonfeminist ads and marketing campaigns. Many of these magazines are monetized by beauty and fashion industries that capitalize on women's insecurities.

The name Fembot was chosen to subvert the derogatory nickname given to feminists by online men's rights activists. The crowdsourced online Urban Dictionary defines the word *fembot* as "a woman who is an uber-feminist. As in, such a feminist she's a robot." The name, a satisfying response to the current political climate that inspired this misogynistic definition, provokes daily chats, weekly meetings, and the constant questioning of how to define feminism.

Soon *Fembot* embodied an anticapitalist, antipatriarchal, and anti–white supremacist mindset marketed to women and nonbinary individuals. I had been taught as a women's studies major at the University of California, Riverside, that inclusive feminism for positive change should follow the intersectional feminist model. From Professors Jane Ward and Chikako Takeshita, I learned that gender is just one critical lens for analyzing oppression, and that we also need to integrate the voices of antiracist, LGBTQ, and global women's rights activists. There was a fairly seamless transition from academia to *Fembot* in terms of applying intersectionality and inviting contributions from people who have experiences with discrimination. Our mission statement says,

> Fembot Magazine is a fully independent online magazine concerned with the need for diverse voices in intersectional feminism and social justice. By inviting marginalized folk to share their feelings with the world, our mission is to create a diverse and safe online community of writers and creators. We aim to share with you a platform that ignites conversations and allows for diverse perspectives. Popular websites for women are generally run by white men in power. We want to take back our space on the internet by giving you a site that promises no click-bait, no gimmicks, just real perspectives.

My decision to challenge capitalism from within capitalism—something I never really needed to contemplate as a student—sparked a desire to see change personified in a magazine. I worked diligently to put that theory into practice when creating *Fembot*.

In the remainder of this essay, I explore the mechanics of *Fembot*: How can we, as anticapitalist feminists, disrupt capitalist practices, especially when we are constantly fighting the rise in online heteropatriarchal rhetoric, which is largely neo-Nazi, pro-life, and antifeminist, while simultaneously combatting the rise in capitalist feminism? How can *Fembot* and the marketing behind it mobilize individuals without caving into capitalist tendencies?

Fembot frequently critiques the capitalist feminism of competitors like Bustle, *Vogue*, *Marie Claire*, and Hello Giggles. I define capitalist feminism as a phenomenon of pro-women marketing schemes that are portrayed as feminist. Capitalist feminism is the rampant misuse of feminism masked as inclusion for profit. It produces a narrow concept of the category of "woman" and a narrow understanding of femininity that relies on individual empowerment, self-confidence, and self-esteem. By calling on women to take up more disciplinary practices of femininity (time, pain, money), such publications reinscribe women's worth (which is defined by our self-esteem and self-worth) to be centered in appearance. Online magazines for women are also exclusively cis-heteronormative. There's a strong relationship to patriarchy and capitalism embedded in their business models, which in turn problematizes the agenda and success of present-day, fourth-wave feminism.

Capitalist feminism's proponents argue that it does realign and question patriarchy's relationship to capitalism by sharing narratives of empowerment for women. These narratives have been used to gain a niche market: the changing perspectives of the new generation labeled as the Zs and millennials. For my definitions, I am drawing on theorist Zillah R. Eisenstein's *Capitalist Patriarchy and the Case for Socialist Feminism*, where she says that capitalist patriarchy works to "emphasize the mutually reinforcing dialectical relationship between capitalist class structure and hierarchical sexual structuring" (1979, 7). Capitalist feminism takes it a step further when people in power use it as a means to masterfully represent the oppression of women and market products accordingly so that they receive monetary gain from the sexual division of labor and society.

Bryan Goldberg, tech entrepreneur and founder of the women's website Bustle, captured capitalist feminism at its zenith. As he wrote in 2013, "I've raised $6.5 million to build and grow my new company: Bustle.com. We have an opportunity to completely transform women's publishing. . . . A lot of very wealthy advertisers care about reaching young women. If we can become the largest website in the Female 18–34 category, then we can become a billion dollar company." What Goldberg didn't mention was Bustle's focus on white, cis-heteronormative, popular topics catering to a marketable demographic, no matter the pro-woman stance the website has. For example, articles on preventative Botox urge young women to start treating their wrinkles now—at a very high price. Other articles give relationship advice assuming heteronormativity and sex advice assuming hetero desire. By using what the new generation is interested in—celebrities, media, self-care, and empowerment—they create an atmosphere of synthetic feminist ideals for venture capitalists to prey on by advertising to young women in the form of banner ads alongside these articles. Take, for instance, the dominating Boost Mobile ad next to images of Toni Morrison in "Toni Morrison Saw a Path to Being Comfortably & Authentically Black" (Monique 2019). Meanwhile, contributing writers, many of them struggling to make ends meet, are paid sub-minimum wages: the compensation for one article submitted to Bustle is four cents a word, according to WhoPaysWriters.com ("Bustle," n.d.).

Fembot is an anticapitalist subversion of competitors like Bustle. We acknowledge that while there is no outside to capitalism, there is room from within to critique it and to reflect on our own complicity. *Fembot* produces over fifteen articles a month, most of which call out the marketing motives of big companies, but we approach our critique with a recognition of our own complicity—another trademark of subversion. Take, for instance, an excerpt from an article by Beatriz Kaye written in April 2019, "I'm Anti-capitalist, but I'm Obsessed with McDonalds": "Eventually, I put that McNugget down long enough to think about how my neighborhood is receiving my money. The only place I frequented more than McDonald's is a quintessential Brooklyn mainstay: my bodega. . . . How does the proximity of my money to a business-person's pocket affect the amount of respect I think they deserve? Capitalism and its demise are lofty ideals that are widely passed around on the internet, but how are we applying these concepts into real life?" This personal essay explores a feminist's desire for fast food and other capitalist products. The writer reflects on her complicity when confronted with purchasing from empires like McDonalds that dehumanize their workers under the guise of an affordable meal. Kaye questions the effects of her obsession and realizes that the small-business owner at the bodega down the street should warrant a deeper loyalty. The narrative also incorporates moveable digital images, known as GIFs, which are dispersed throughout the article to make it relatable and entertaining to the reader, thus drawing on the same mechanics that sites like Bustle and Hello Giggles use and showing that for-profit tactics can be rearticulated.

Other articles on *Fembot* expose the marketing intent of companies, television shows, movies, and novels in pop culture. Intersectional feminist writers use our platform for critical analysis of culture to reveal the tactics of websites and businesses. For instance, Vixen Temple, a New Zealand feminist writer by day and stripper by night, critiques how e-commerce sites like DollsKill harmfully exploit stripper culture as a fashion statement in her article "DollsKill Uses Sex Workers as Props but Doesn't Care about Our Rights" (2019). Bethany Killen critiques the lack of consent in HBO's teen show *Euphoria*, which sexualizes teenagers as entertainment, in "'Euphoria' Doesn't Understand the Concept of Sexual Consent" (2019). And I have shed light in my own investigative piece on how Planned Parenthood's collaboration with Miley Cyrus and Marc Jacobs stole creative concepts from a popular feminist baker on Instagram named the Sweet Feminist (2018). These articles, and many others like them, work to hold readers accountable for their choices and actions regarding feminism in theory and practice.

In another subversive strategy, *Fembot* uses digital marketing tactics in the form of memes and Twitter replies. Because we cycle news stories with opinions daily, we often have to deflect trolls away from our comments section. For instance, our warning underneath all Facebook posts reads, "FEMBOTS. We know the comments section can be triggering—that's why we take an active approach as editors to provide a safe space for you. We want to encourage you to join our FB groups where we post the same posts but the comments section is more regulated and embraced by like-minded feminists. We NEED to have conversations about what's important to our activism. JOIN US."

The virality of the internet produces a cesspool of content, spam, and Trump-era propaganda. By encouraging followers to escape and seek refuge with other intersectional feminists in our online group, we are able to grow our mailing list and encourage readers to submit questions on feminism and participate in community building. With topics ranging from "How Do We Address Classism within Feminist Circles?" to "How Do You Explain Pansexuality to Someone Who Thinks It's the Same Thing as Bi?" our readers are encouraged to participate in a feminist discourse with the editors. *Fembot* integrates readers' questions in order to enter into an inclusive dialogue with other online feminists found throughout Instagram, Facebook, and Reddit. By injecting an anticapitalist attitude into Facebook comments, Twitter replies, and Instagram posts, the website sparks an initiative beyond female empowerment and explores how intersectional feminism can create community within the space of the internet. The trolls that swarm the comments provide an algorithm boost that allows for posts to be visible in social media feeds. By deflecting them and bringing attention to their malicious behavior, *Fembot* is transparent in how it must tolerate—and challenge—hatred in return for activism to be visible.

Furthermore, *Fembot* recognizes that not all businesses are evil. We are currently working to collaborate with business partners that share the same values and goals of intersectional feminism. For example, we welcome businesses that are unable for financial or other reasons to promote themselves on mainstream advertising platforms, including sex-positive companies, birth control providers, CBD and homeopathic wellness brands, and other companies marginalized in a heteropatriarchal society. By openly welcoming feminist small businesses as partners, *Fembot* hopes to grow and develop to a point where it is possible to pay writers a living wage by the end of 2020. The online sphere is the ideal space for feminists like the staff and readers of *Fembot* to challenge societal norms and combat capitalist feminism, one meme, tweet, and article at a time.

References

"Bustle." n.d. Who Pays Writers? Accessed August 15, 2019. http://whopayswriters.com/#/publication/bustle.

Eisenstein, Zillah R. 1979. *Capitalist Patriarchy and the Case for Socialist Feminism.* Monthly Review Press. https://fembot-mag.com/about-fembot/. Mission statement. January 18, 2021.

Goldberg, Bryan. 2013. "I've Raised $6.5 Million to Build and Grow My New Company: Bustle.com." Pando, August 13, 2013. https://pando.com/2013/08/13/ive-raised-6-5-million-to-build-and-grow-my-new-company-bustle-com.

Kaye, Beatriz. 2019. "I'm Anti-capitalist, but I'm Obsessed with McDonalds." *Fembot*, April 30, 2019. https://fembotmag.com/2019/04/30/anti-capitalist-mcdonalds.

Killen, Bethany. 2019. "'Euphoria' Doesn't Understand the Concept of Sexual Consent." *Fembot*, July 23, 2019. https://fembotmag.com/2019/07/23/euphoria-doesnt-understand-the-concept-of-sexual-consent.

Medina, Alissa. 2018. "Shame on You Miley Cyrus, Marc Jacobs, and Planned Parenthood for Stealing from Our Fav Feminist Baker." https://fembot-mag.com/2019/06/04/shame-miley-cyrus-marc-jacobs-planned-parenthood-stealing-fav-feminist-baker/.

Monique, Joelle. 2019. "Toni Morrison Saw a Path to Being Comfortably & Authentically Black." Bustle, August 7, 2019. https://www.bustle.com/p/how-toni-morrison-created-space-for-black-women-changed-the-way-i-love-myself-18554447.

Temple, Vixen. 2019. "DollsKill Uses Sex Workers as Props but Doesn't Care about Our Rights." *Fembot*, August 1, 2019. https://fembotmag.com/2019/07/31/dollskill-uses-sex-workers-as-props-but-doesnt-care-about-our-rights.

THE PERILS OF PERFECTION FEMINISM

Stephanie Newman

I have a roster of go-to anecdotes about the stereotypical sexism I faced when starting a business in my twenties. There was that time a man I met for coffee suggested I go into sex work to help finance my business. Shortly afterward, a client told me the stock photo of a woman on my PowerPoint presentation wasn't attractive enough; he wanted me to replace it.

This is the world in which entrepreneurial women function. It's so explicitly sexist as to evoke audible groans, even laughter. We feminists know things like this happen. I know these stories aren't a reflection on me but rather a product of a misogynistic environment. They represent the types of obstacles I had imagined encountering.

It is much harder to make sense of how I bumped up against walls I didn't know existed. While running my business, I felt I was constantly making tradeoffs between my feminist values and the desire to build a profitable company. Most days, I questioned my fitness as a feminist business owner. Ultimately, when my business failed two years after it launched, I didn't know where to hang the blame: on my own shortcomings or on a system of oppression so subtle it eluded my recognition.

My business, an online media platform, was called Writing on Glass, the name a reference to both the glass ceiling and the power of the written word. Its mission, at first, was to make feminist theory more accessible. I wanted to show how the ideas of feminist scholars like bell hooks, Audre Lorde, and Simone de Beauvoir could help improve women's lives in Trump's America. "I believe that some of the best wisdom is hidden inside books written by trailblazing women long before the internet," I wrote in the fall of 2016, for the first iteration of the website—published the morning after the presidential election. I still remember drafting the copy in a café on Manhattan's Lower East Side, surrounded by other twentysomethings watching Hillary Clinton's concession speech on their Mac-Books. With my latte and pumpkin yogurt, I felt both hyperaware of my ridiculous privilege and humiliated by my naïveté about how this election would turn out. I was alight with the possibility of doing something, as other white people in my socioeconomic bracket liked to say.

From the start, Writing on Glass seemed like the meeting point of my passion for feminism and my desire to start my own business. I had been unhappy in my career since graduating college and had left my management consulting job months earlier to freelance as a strategist and writer. Starting my own media business had been a dream I was always too scared to pursue. Declaring my feminism on the internet had once felt scary; by 2016, it just felt necessary. Black Lives Matter had swept the nation after policemen murdered Trayvon Martin and Michael Brown. A new wave of social justice–minded media was emerging, with online publications like the Establishment and Everyday Feminism analyzing feminist issues. If I had the privilege to speak up for women's rights and amplify others' voices in this political moment, why wouldn't I?

And so it began. Within weeks, I had over one hundred email addresses on my newsletter list and was collecting essays from contributors. It was fun, thrilling even. I treasured these pieces and felt honored that these writers entrusted their work to me. I received positive reinforcement from peers congratulating me on "taking action," though in reality I had done little more than publish a webpage. Still, it felt inherently feminist to pursue this opportunity. What if I could be part of a new class of feminist entrepreneurs whose companies would actually promote social change? What if I could encourage other women to start their own businesses, businesses that didn't treat workers unfairly or wreak environmental havoc?

I can still see the glittering fantasy: cultivating a strong community of writers, publishing new articles three times a week, holding events to discuss important feminist cultural issues, releasing an illustrated encyclopedia of feminist scholars, starting a subscription book service that sent out new feminist releases each month. The possibilities seemed endless. The promise of a feminist business—this anticorporate, humanistic version of "having it all"—was so tantalizing to me that I deluded myself into thinking the journey would be as easy as following my passion and encouraging others to do the same. I believed I could start a company that would cherish the human experience and also support me financially.

I think you know it didn't end up that way. The path of my business was less like a yellow-brick road and more like a poorly constructed obstacle course, where the "obstacles" weren't clearly labeled and the finish line continually receded into the distance.

In October 2017, eleven months after I launched Writing on Glass (and one day after the *New York Times* broke the story on Harvey Weinstein's sexual predation), I attended a talk by Chimamanda Ngozi Adichie. On stage, Adichie said something that has stayed with me since. She told the audience that the pursuit of perfection struck her as immature, referring to the "extremist idea of purity" within feminism. "It's so easy to fall afoul of the ridiculously high standards set there," she remarked (*New Yorker* 2017).[1] She was right. When I started my business, I was immature. I was twenty-five. I wanted to do everything right, or at least in a way that aligned with my personal beliefs.

In the early days of Writing on Glass, I tried very hard to avoid "corporate feminism," the frequently maligned practice of co-opting feminist messaging to sell products and services to women without benefiting women's rights. As Andi Zeisler, cofounder of Bitch Media, writes in her 2016 book *We Were Feminists Once*, "Reinscribing feminism as something you . . . consume, rather than something you do, accomplishes nothing—not for you as an individual, and not for how women as a whole are viewed, valued, and validated in this culture" (80).

Exemplifying the paradox that is corporate feminism are companies that produce "I'm a Feminist" T-shirts made out of environmentally detrimental materials, created only in sizes deemed socially normative and sewn in a factory by underpaid women who work ungodly hours. Compare that with a company that could unhypocritically call itself feminist in nature, perhaps a fashion brand that makes size-inclusive clothing, prioritizes fair pay, and ethically sources its fabrics.

It is much harder to build the latter kind of company. As Zeisler notes, "The companies that make feminist body lotion, feminist energy drinks, and feminist t-shirts are not interested in putting themselves out of business by actually changing the status quo" (2016, 256). I did want to change the status quo, and I knew that meant building a company on a foundation of social awareness. Starting with a clean slate was, I thought, the beauty of building a business as a socially conscious person. Rather than inherit the legacy problems of stodgy, old companies— male-only executives, biased hiring practices—I could build an organization that was inclusive from day one. In my head was one of Audre Lorde's most famous quotes, "For the master's tools will never dismantle the master's house." I would not be using the tools of the patriarchy to build my business. No fundraising from venture capitalists, who only give 3 percent of their funding to women anyway. No "hiring" unpaid interns to save on costs. If I was going to talk the talk, I was certainly going to walk the walk.

Unfortunately, walking the walk often meant stumbling. As I mentioned, I wanted to ensure that Writing on Glass took an intersectional approach to feminism. I was no stranger to Kimberle Crenshaw's concept of intersectionality. In her 1991 essay "Mapping the Margins," Crenshaw writes, "Because of their intersectional identity as both women and people of color within discourses that are shaped to respond to one or the other, the interests and experiences of women of color are frequently marginalized within both" (1244). The term *intersectionality* had already blazed through the internet, reaching a wide and nonacademic audience twenty-five years after Crenshaw first coined it in 1989 as a way to describe the overlapping systems of racist and sexist oppression to which women of color are subjected. By 2016, the word had already started to backfire, with Twitter users rolling their virtual eyes at all the white women using the term in their social media bios as a signal of their allyship. Claiming a knowledge of intersectionality was, at first, a sign of awareness of the nature of systemic oppression; soon it became a signifier of co-optation, something privileged people said to try to sound in-the-know.

I suppose my first blunder was to become one of these women. In November 2016, I sent my first Writing on Glass newsletter to a media contact I admired, a woman of color whose own email newsletter focused on issues of race and gender and taught me a lot about my blind spots. Yet my blind spots persisted. The content I sent her and called "inclusive" featured Gloria Steinem and Elizabeth Warren. In an email back, she pointed out to me that my approach didn't seem inclusive at all. It was a generous response, one that she certainly didn't owe me, and one I'm not sure I would have sent in her shoes—if, for instance, I got an email newsletter from a man claiming to have started a feminist site that featured, well, mostly men. I apologized, told her how embarrassed I was, and committed to doing better in the future. But I also felt a kernel of discomfort start to expand. If I could make a gaffe this innocently and this quickly, would I end up hurting people, making others feel excluded or unseen?

I couldn't stomach the idea of letting that happen. Instead, I started working harder to avoid mistakes and adhere to my feminist philosophies. Take the question of labor. The entrepreneurs I knew in media were hiring unpaid interns to save on costs. This had long struck me as unethical—how could a company not pay an individual for his or her labor?—and I had seen the repercussions of this business model play out in real time. Several of my friends had wanted to become journalists. Because they couldn't afford to accept unpaid internships at major New York–based media organizations, they were systemically shut out of the industry. I watched as twenty-one-year-olds with trust funds acquired the necessary experience as interns to help them get editorial jobs after graduation; the rest of my friends had to figure out how to actually get paid. I had long considered this practice one of the sins of the media industry, and while I knew I was far less powerful than a large media corporation, I still didn't want to fall into the same trap.

Aside from hiring a few hourly contractors (about all I could afford), I tried to do everything myself. My stake-in-the-ground approach to feminist business meant that I spent my time in ways other business owners might consider wasteful. For instance, I often combed through stock photos, an industry term for photographs licensed for commercial reuse, to ensure that the images of women on my site represented true diversity. The subjects of my interviews often provided me with their own photographs to feature, but the majority of my articles were not interviews, and I knew as well as the next blogger that professional-quality images were essential to increasing my site traffic. Searching out diverse stock photos was a taxing process that often left me feeling guilty, like I was mishandling my time. Internet business gurus said that founders should be doing strategic things, not administrative tasks. But it was important to me to pay attention to these details, as I thought a good feminist founder should. So while I was running statistics on my stock photos, other entrepreneurs in my community were fund-raising and building out their company road maps. Is it any wonder that my business didn't skyrocket?

Then there was the question of my business model. While I devoted mornings to building out Writing on Glass, I spent afternoons doing the consulting work that actually paid me. I parlayed my management consulting experience into a service helping mostly white, wealthy men write business plans for their new ventures. I took the money they paid me and funneled it into Writing on Glass. On good days, I felt a bit like a feminist version of Robin Hood, taking money from the leaders of the patriarchy and then devoting it to undermining the patriarchy itself. On bad days, I felt delusional. I could easily see myself as a wannabe entrepreneur whose business model was so convoluted it was hard to even articulate.

I knew I had to start making money from Writing on Glass. Because digital advertising paid very little (and seemed like a "master's tool," so to speak), I decided that my flagship product would be an online course that I could sell to my readers. This was scalable, and it was focused on creativity and education, two ideals that continued to anchor my business. Over several months in early 2018, I built a four-week online course called Feminist Incubator. I described the course as a way to "build your freelancing income and jumpstart your creative dream— the feminist way." There were a handful of other women doing similar work, which signaled to me that the market existed. Jennifer Armbrust of Sister had a successful online course called Feminist Business School, which helped entrepreneurs create businesses using feminist principles. Kelly Diels, a feminist marketing consultant, started a company to resist the "female lifestyle empowerment brand," instead selling a feminist copywriting certification program on writing "effective copy through the lens of justice" (n.d.). Conferences like ZebraCon took the idea of the unicorn business (a startup valued at $1 billion or more, most likely funded by venture capitalists) and turned it on its head, encouraging feminists to build socially conscious and sustainable businesses that they loved.

Each of these enterprises challenged the concept of corporate feminism. There was nothing "corporate" about them. I don't know the numbers behind them, but from the outside, they appeared to be thriving. They allowed their founders to be themselves, making an impact while also earning a profit. How does one build a feminist business like these women did? I yearned for answers. My intention for Feminist Incubator was to turn this phenomenon into a blueprint that other entrepreneurial women could follow.

And so I got to work. I interviewed nearly every self-proclaimed feminist entrepreneur I could find on the internet, publishing their insights in the interviews section of Writing on Glass. Soon, my company's mission evolved from making feminist theory more accessible to helping other women build businesses. I found that while very few people were interested in paying to learn about feminist theory, many—or at least more—were interested in paying to learn about business. Every day for months, I worked on the course. I created the curriculum, collaborated with coaches who taught me how the online course ecosystem worked, researched the software and tools I needed to use. I wrote a new business plan specifically for Feminist Incubator, specifying my target audience, pricing, and marketing plan. I launched a new website specifically for the course. Every module I filmed myself, and every slide deck I presented was hand-created. My videos led students through business basics, from strategy and vision to sales and marketing to operations and financial modeling. Each lesson had a feminist angle, whether that be negotiating for fair pay, prioritizing collaboration over competition, or recognizing unconscious bias.

I was extremely proud of what I created. I was also very, very tired. After announcing that Feminist Incubator had opened for enrollment, I shut myself into my bedroom and slept. I awoke to a phone notification telling me that the first student had purchased my course for $249. A few hours later, another enrollee. I spent the afternoon in a state of euphoria.

But after six enrollments, the new students stopped coming, and I ended up earning $1,500 from a course I spent hundreds of hours creating. At my hourly consulting rate, I could have spent twelve hours working with a consulting client and earned the same amount. I didn't love that fact, but the people who needed my products—young, socially conscious creatives, often women of color—didn't have much disposable income. I was providing these women and nonbinary folks with an affordable course to help them start their own businesses. If that meant making some financial sacrifice on my part, I figured I could handle it.

Where did that leave me? Serving a lot of people for very little money, watching my income levels sink, and continuing to turn to male clients to pay me well for the exact consulting work I had quit my day job to escape (the kind where clients complain about "unattractive women" in their PowerPoint photos). This was nothing like what I had envisioned when I set out to build a socially conscious company. On top of the stress of building a business—the financial instability, the constant self-nagging to work 24/7—I carried the additional, self-imposed burden of doing it all in a way that was beyond criticism. This didn't make me a martyr. It just made me exhausted.

In late 2018, my business imploded. This was not the result of my disappointing course sales or even my feminist exhaustion. Instead, it was the result of a male client who broke a consulting contract and refused to pay thousands of dollars he owed me for months of work. Without that income, I couldn't afford to pay my bills, let alone self-finance Writing on Glass and Feminist Incubator, and I became temporarily reliant on my fiancé's income. Despite my best efforts at being a feminist business owner, I had ended up financially dependent on men—first my male clients, then my husband-to-be. I hated that fact. Even more than that, I hated the knowledge that this made me lucky. Other women in my shoes could have been in dire financial straits. I had drained my savings account and compromised my mental health, but I was fortunate to at least have a safety net.

After I left Writing on Glass behind, it took months for me to see the picture with clearer eyes. I understood that I had been holding myself to impossible standards. I also recognized the extent of the adversity I faced, which went far beyond rude comments from men over coffee. I had never taken time to really consider the various threats against my well-being. None of the dozens of business books I read featured a blueprint for answering customer support emails while losing your reproductive rights, or watching white supremacists chant about killing people of your religion while you prepare your blog posts for the week. Yet this is what I tried to do. So did many folks with even more on the line: people of color, people identifying as LGBTQ+, the disabled, undocumented immigrants. My respect for their struggles and their work grew every day, along with the knowledge that my privilege had made every step of my own journey more manageable—even the steps that felt steepest.

After all this, I'm still not sure how one remains passionate about feminist solutions without losing oneself inside the problems. I do know it has more to do with resilience than with perfection. I tell myself it is okay that I didn't figure out how to be a labor hero while supporting myself financially. And it is also okay to acknowledge that I was working within a system that was not designed for my participation, let alone my success.

Note

1. Adichie gave this talk on October 6, 2017, at the New Yorker Festival in Manhattan.

References

Crenshaw, Kimberle. 1991. "Mapping the Margins: Intersectionality, Identity Politics, and Violence against Women of Color." *Stanford Law Review* 43, no. 6 (July): 1241–99.

Diels, Kelly. n.d. Homepage. Accessed December 15, 2020. https://www.kellydiels.com.

New Yorker. 2017. "Chimamanda Ngozi Adichie on Liberal Cannibalism." YouTube video, 8:45. Posted October 9, 2017. https://www.youtube.com/watch?v=fo3OZWPOa3g.

Zeisler, Andi. 2016. *We Were Feminists Once: From Riot Grrrl to CoverGirl, the Buying and Selling of a Political Movement*. New York: Public Affairs.

CIRCUITOUS PATHS FROM UNIVERSITY TO WORK, AND FINDING FEMINIST WILLFULNESS ALONG THE WAY

Jael Goldfine

When I graduated from college, I was a flawed but vigorous and joyful feminist. I felt full of feminism and its side effects: energy, community, hope, and confidence, as well as the liberating kinds of doubt and discomfort. Becoming a feminist was, as Sara Ahmed describes it in *Living a Feminist Life*, "sensational" (2016, 21).

During my senior year in 2017, studying feminist, gender, and sexuality studies at Cornell University, I completed a rigorous, praised honors thesis. I felt that I'd made a small but important discovery about feminism while living out the war cry of the "personal is political." I wrote about an underground music scene that was unleashing young women's unruly, unprofitable affects, such as insecurity, sadness, anger, and shame. I argued our feelings-in-revolt were wrenches, or at least pebbles, in the gears of neoliberalism, given how, as Ahmed quotes Marilyn Frye, "oppression involves the requirement that you show signs of being happy with the situation" (2016, 54). I dreamed that we were changing the world at basement shows, organizing a happiness strike through earbuds and playlists and tweets.

Writing that thesis shaped my understanding that feminism could be inconspicuous, pleasurable, and everyday. I enjoyed that idea while at college. It was a happy place to be a feminist. Teachers and companions were all around me. I lived in a house full of feminists. We lived interdependently, shared emotional and physical labor, and reveled in our collective intellectual dynamism. I had daily discussions with a cohort of women also engaged with feminist theory. We talked about trauma and theory and television and grassroots politics and queerness. We discovered what it meant to take care of one another: that it was an option to value community and each other over, or at least as much as, individual success—surely, a blow to the neoliberal university. I fell in love with a feminist, and we structured our relationship to compensate for the power differential between us. We tried to keep in mind that we were just a bunch of extraordinarily privileged students talking over eggs and coffee. It was difficult. Our care and our conversations felt powerful and significant.

As any gender studies student paying attention would, I felt nearly as conflicted about all of this as I was in love with it. I dwelled on the prospect that my own comfort and inclusion at the university, especially within its nominally alternative spaces, came at the expense of others'. With classmates and friends, in seminars and at home, I fretted over the gap between theory and praxis, as well as the masturbatory futility of my fretting. I was peripheral to the student organizing scene, more likely to skip class to comfort a crying girl than attend a letter-drop or rally. I rationalized that although I might not be participating in what Ahmed calls the "loud acts of refusal and rebellion" that the word *feminism* brings to mind, I was dedicated to quieter, personal ones—expelling misogyny from my life, investing in female friendships, breaking down my perceptions of acceptable femininity, and questioning concretized histories of sexism—without thinking much about whom these acts benefited.

As a student, I contemplated race, gender, and power constantly. I emailed professors who lacked sexually and racially inclusive data. I argued in class and with my liberal parents about the Obama administration's expansion of immigrant detention and the flawed notion of the "enlightened moderate." I struggled and sat with criticism from a people-of-color student group over the organizing methods of a feminist group I was in. I applied Judith Butler and bell hooks to *Moby Dick*. I wrote columns for the school newspaper on topics like *The Walking Dead*, George Condo's paintings, and the Grammys through the lens of race and gender. I reviewed women's music and parsed my own misadventures with pop culture. I kept arguing with my parents.

Leaving school, I felt empowered and excited to wage the daily battle with the world and myself that feminism entailed—to live as a part of the "struggle for a more bearable world" (Ahmed 2016, 1). It seemed self-evident that I would carry the feminist values, questions, and struggles with me.

A year out of college, however, found me painfully, deeply alienated from feminism. The workplace and world that I discovered outside school seemed irreconcilable with my beliefs: too hostile, too broken, too capitalist, too wrong. The care and conversations, the playlists and tweets, that once sustained me felt puny in my back pocket as I faced down the hypercapitalist working world, like bringing a knife to gunfight. I felt as impotent, cynical, and alone as gender studies had once made me feel strong, hopeful, and connected.

This book is about how gender studies and feminist theory shape students' lives in the workforce. When I sat down to consider the question, my initial thought was that they hadn't, and this was the problem. However, it's truer to say that feminist theory didn't shape my working life in predictable or immediately obvious ways. I thought that I gave up on feminism because the world was too inhospitable. But my gender studies education is what let me ultimately reject this complacent, uncritical life and imagine alternative ways of navigating the workforce. Feminism rose up in me as shame, alerting me that I'd formed unsustainable bonds, in pursuit of unsustainable ends. Feminism let me break them and intentionally choose different ends. I lost feminism, but still, feminism was how I located myself.

I don't wish to use this essay to confess to being a bad feminist or student of gender studies. I also don't intend it as a criticism of the excellent program I studied in. Rather, I want to draw attention to the insidious pressures of neoliberal capitalism, which feminist students, like everyone else, face as they're recruited into the workforce. I want to ask what these pressures look like, and how they operate particularly in the lives of millennial women. I want to ask what kinds of contradictions or vulnerabilities might be naturally produced within feminism formed in a classroom, which leave us prone to such pressures after we leave school. I want to ask what returning to feminist commitments can look like, and what internal and external reorganizations of one's life that process may entail.

In the end, I'm glad that I got lost. In locating myself, I've had to confront exactly what feminism did and didn't mean to me. In this process of reflection, it became clear to me that the circumstances of my feminist becoming resulted in my feminist undoing. As Ahmed says, "In pursuing a path partway, in turning back, I learned about that path" (2016, 48).

For me, returning to feminism meant leaving a bad job. It's important to address the privilege inherent in this choice. When I left my job, I shared a cheap apartment with my partner, which meant I could live off what I'd saved and my wages as a barista while I worked as an unpaid intern. As a college-educated, middle-class white woman with supportive parents and no debt, I had many different levels of security in making this choice. A less privileged person could not choose to quit their job because they were unhappy or politically alienated; most work is unhappy and politically alienating. The fact that there are so few ways to earn a living doing happy, fulfilling work is its own issue, one that is exacerbated by the lack of an American social security net, universal health care, and mass union membership, which makes it a privilege to leave a job where one is unhappy or treated poorly. In retrospect, it wasn't actually my bad job that made feminism impossible. As many authors in this book can likely testify, a bad job isn't an impossible place to practice feminism (it might be a very important place to do so).

Leaving my job was not an act of feminist rebellion, or even an inherently feminist decision. But it was something that was very difficult for me to do, because of neoliberal capitalist myths and logics about the nature of work and careers that I'd become attached to. Those beliefs were what made feminism feel impossible. Those beliefs were what I had to quit.

After college, armed with my gender studies degree, I threw myself into the workforce more or less at random and got a job making $35,000 a year as a publicity coordinator at a music public relations firm in Brooklyn. The work itself was corrosive. My job was to coerce journalists into writing about bands who hired the company I worked for. It was depressing to sell music—often, bad music—and witness up close the flow of cash, connections, and capital that powers the music industry. Each day of manipulating, groveling, flattering, lying about, and exaggerating the "devastating" quality of my clients' lyrics or the "propulsive" nature of their guitar playing felt like participating in a scam I didn't know was going on. I wanted to confess everything to the writers on the other end of the phone. Emailing hundreds of journalists and getting no replies was no less demoralizing than seeing a mediocre band get a magazine feature because they had a lot of Instagram followers.

Publicity is a bastion of regressive entertainment industry norms that glamorizes checking your email 24/7 and screaming on the phone. My boss, a chic, bubbly twenty-five-year-old, was volatile, punitive, and fond of humiliating me, sometimes publicly. The stakes of the company's work were treated as dire, although a music publicist's greatest professional achievement will be booking a band on *Saturday Night Live*. Missing a news item as I sifted through Twitter to find mentions of our clients was a mistake beyond the pale. I tried to appease my boss by being perfect, leaving the office late at night, coming in on weekends to complete the bloated workload, taking every slack-lashing with a smiling face, and apologizing for mistakes I didn't make. I developed a Pavlovian response to my office intercom and anxiety rituals around checking my email.

My descent into workaholic misery disturbed and disgusted me even as I couldn't stop it. I thought about my job twenty-four hours a day. I relied solely on my partner for support, isolating myself from friends, with whom I dreaded answering the question, "How are you doing?" Each morning when I stood on the train platform, I fantasized about getting on the train in the opposite direction, taking it to the end of the line, the airport, anywhere.

To work so hard at something I hated so much created a dizzying dissonance that seemed to go beyond the classic office job grievance of work being "meaninglessness" or "soul-sucking." I hadn't anticipated that publicity would be meaningful or soul-pleasing. But I'd never imagined the type of self-alienated despair that comes from trying to succeed at a game in which you've somehow staked your self-worth, despite disagreeing with both the object and the rules.

I internalized the badness of my situation as failure. "Maybe you are disappointed with yourself, or with a world, because you are not as happy as you expected to be. . . . (Why am I not made happy by this? What is wrong with me?)," Ahmed writes, capturing my self-flagellation (2016, 57). My failure to thrive in my first adult job made me feel like I was a lazy, spoiled child, though I'd held service-sector jobs since I was a teenager and was working sixty-hour weeks. *What did you think it would be like? What would you do if you left? Work harder.* When I examined my situation more honestly, I burned with shame. *What are you doing here?*

Ahmed warns, "Turning off feminism might be necessary to survive the world that we are in, which is not a feminist world. . . . Sometimes it might even seem that it is as or even more tiring to notice sexism and racism than to experience sexism and racism: after all, it is this noticing that makes things real" (2016, 31). I went into a political fetal position, observing but not acting. There was much to notice around me. There were so many ways I could have put a good-faith effort into living and struggling for feminism, even in a bad situation—things I could have spoken up about, ways I could have been what Ahmed calls "willful" (66). I'd moved into a gentrifying neighborhood, where my presence was actively harmful to my working-class neighbors and neighbors of color. In the office, clients were pitched to ghettoized press lists based on gender, race, and sexuality. We were expected to lie or manufacture results before conference calls. My superiors talked frequently about unhealthy dieting and made derogatory comments about the appearances of our female clients. We were required to attend an all-staff workshop from a "crisis PR agency" that taught us how to "protect" clients should they be accused of sexual misconduct.

But I became numb to local and immediate injustice—in my office, in my neighborhood, in my life, in my relationships. I only engaged with politics through melodramatic nihilism. *Capitalism is killing us all!* When I imagined the future, instead of trying to articulate and respond to what I found disturbing about my workplace or capitalism, I fantasized, nonsensically, finding the softest corner of it to hide out in, working with children maybe, or moving off the grid. I dreamed of never again working for pay, or being forced to help anyone make money.

Feminism involves embracing conflict. Ahmed writes, "A feminist killjoy lives and works in a contact zone" (2016, 190). But I felt the slightest vibrations might shatter me. My gender studies education had much to say about mental illness, toxic relationships, abuses of power, complicity in violent systems, and, of course, labor and capitalism. But I felt both too emotionally weak to wield the tools of feminism that had changed my life in college and, politically, too pessimistic. Unlike at college, in this new world, the consequences of willfulness and of feminism (punishment from bosses, unemployment, creating tension in the workplace) were unfamiliar and frighteningly serious. Feminist victories seemed so implausible as to hardly be worth it.

"At times, it can be tempting to think: it would be easier to screen things out," Ahmed writes. "Personally I don't think that is an easy option. And I don't think that it is always an option: because having let the world in, screening it out would also require giving up on the subject you have become. I think this is a promise: once you have become a person who notices sexism and racism, it is hard to unbecome that person" (2016, 32). I tried to give up on myself. I tried to screen out the world and subdue my feminist consciousness in exchange for a clearly demarcated, comfortable path through the postgraduate years and the rewards capitalism offers for following it. It took me about a year to realize that the costs of doing so were higher than the costs of living with feminism.

When I reflect on my transition out of college and first year in the workforce, I'm shocked and confused to recognize so little willfulness in this story. *How did that happen? How did I go from happy, empowered feminist to that fearful, paralyzed figure?* At first, the answer seems like bad luck: that the job I got out of college happened to be the one it was. Yet it seems likely I would have had the same reckoning anywhere, albeit less impeded by depression and anxiety, because the real issue that led to my personal crisis was that I'd unconsciously staked my self-worth on a narrative about professional success and a normative career path. This narrative was guiding my choices—not financial practicality and certainly not feminism. How did I get lost in these murky waters, when my gender studies background ostensibly should've served as a buoy?

In retrospect, my decisions were the result of the logics and norms that surrounded me like water at a prestigious university: logics of complicity, logics of inevitability, logics about happiness and goodness, logics about paths, logics about which types of paths brought happiness and goodness. Ahmed writes a lot about paths: "A path gives life a certain shape, a direction, a sequence" (2016, 45). She writes a lot about direction. She explains that "power works as a mode of directionality, a way of orienting bodies in particular ways, so they are facing a certain way, heading toward a future that is given a face" (43). She writes about crowds of bodies and how they move: "When there are so many, you have a crowd, a thickening, a density. You are carried by that flow: it might even save you energy" (45). Ahmed uses these terms to talk about the directional forces of patriarchy, heteronormativity, and whiteness, but they can aptly be applied to the forces of neoliberal capitalism and classism.

It is strange to think of myself as adrift (implying powerlessness) within systems that bestow me with significant power. I am far more the beneficiary of neoliberal capitalism than I am the victim of it. The cognitive dissonance of writing this essay brings to mind Rebecca Liu's essay in the feminist film journal *Another Gaze*, "The Making of a Millennial Woman." Criticizing the universal "we" used to praise contemporary feminist media about millennial women like the protagonists of the TV show *Fleabag* or Sally Rooney's novel *Normal People*, Liu writes, "The many socioeconomic divisions that mark our generation are flattened beneath the vague language of collective burnout and mutual suffering that comes with living under the boot of capital . . . not so much as a unifying call to arms but a convenient erasure of difference. It allows the most powerful among us to divest themselves of the idea that the world is something that they can actually build, not just endure" (2019). Her critique is crucial—the faulty millennial female "we" that Liu charges with over-universalization is indeed rampant, at least in media and online discourse. When it's used to praise the kinds of art she discusses, it exaggerates the significance of private, individual feminist struggles and triumphs and undermines the need to address public, collective issues of injustice. I am vulnerable to using it. It shaped some of the self-theorizing that I found so empowering in college, and if I am not careful, it might be lurking behind this essay.

It is key to the concept of intersectionality that the acknowledgment of someone's vulnerability doesn't prevent them from recognizing their power in other contexts. I believe it's useful and even necessary to recognize how capitalism harms people at every level. Subjects of neoliberal capitalism of every class are subjected to its violence: its precarious labor conditions, the alienation of compulsory selfishness, the cruelty of the profit motive. Focusing collective liberation efforts on the unequal nature and scale of capitalism's harm is crucial. But recognizing that all of us lead less fulfilling lives under the mandates of capitalism may be what makes those in privileged positions feel more accountable.

Although normative paths, identities, and modes of direction are exactly what my gender studies education taught me to challenge, after graduation I became obsessed with getting a job. Not in a particular industry or in pursuit of a particular passion. Not out of financial necessity: my parents expected me to support myself after school but were happy to have me live with them while I figured things out. I simply craved the validation of being hired and paid. I didn't question where my urgency came from. I don't remember feeling curious or skeptical about these desires. I didn't seriously consider the forces shaping my relationship to work, or what my feminist commitments meant when it came to my career.

I don't suggest that a gender studies education should lead students into ideo-logically pure work. There is no pure work, and this book specifically documents the challenges and possibilities of cultivating feminism in un-feminist workplaces. I also don't suggest that the best or most useful application of a gender studies education is in the political sphere. There are many ways to do politics outside the government, advocacy work, or organizing. However, the relationship between work and feminism is important to consider, and my lack of intentionality meant that I ended up following rules I didn't agree with. Ahmed writes, "The hardest work can be recognizing how one's own life is shaped by norms in ways that we didn't realize, in ways that cannot simply be transcended" (2016, 43).

Capitalism organizes us through fairy tales and ghost stories. Ahmed claims that, minor updates notwithstanding, "the happy stories for girls remain based on fairy-tale formulas: life, marriage, and reproduction, or death (of one kind or another) and misery" (2016, 49). As a student of gender studies, I'd debunked all kinds of fairy tales about marriage and reproduction. However, other stories about how to acquire a good life lay dormant in my subconscious, untouched by femi-nist knowledge. They rose to the surface as I began to make decisions about my life as an adult. I'd unconsciously become devoted to a certain "image of a good life," as Ahmed writes, that had been "screened in front of me" (50). The fairy tale I'd internalized was banal: prestigious, intellectual, white-collar job right out of college, a retirement account, health insurance, the correct answer to the ques-tion, "What are you up to these days?" But it was powerful. Perhaps even more powerful was the ghost story I'd internalized about a basement-dwelling, jobless college grad, symbolizing the end of American abundance and prosperity. I'd learned that millennials would be the first generation to not out-earn their par-ents; instead, we'd be lucky just to hold on to the social position they were born into. I read articles about parents being burdened by their children's debt and un-employment into old age. I had been told that, even as a graduate from a presti-gious college, my access to a good life was becoming increasingly precarious.

My fears were somewhat exaggerated given my class privilege and the fact that I graduated into a prosperous economy solidly recovered from the 2008 financial crisis. But of course they weren't really about falling into poverty or being ruined by student loans. My anxiety was about validation, inclusion, and comfort. I was afraid of the invisibility and awkwardness of failing to start on the path of the good American life. These fears were at least as potent as, if not more so than, any actual desire I had for that path.

I did desire the comforts of the middle class, including secure income as well as the privileges bestowed through rituals of inclusion. But underneath my class anxi-ety as a millennial, I'd later discover evidence of a more archaic kind of American classism—a belief in the moral goodness of employment. I bought into the myth that employment was a sign of social and psychic health, while alternatives signaled dysfunction and deviance. I never would have said that I believed good people had jobs and bad people didn't. I knew America's economy was designed for some people's prosperity and others' poverty, and that people's ability and opportunities to work are defined by their ability, class, and race, among other factors. But I was incredibly uncomfortable with the idea of myself as a person without a job. What excuse did I have? Of course, not all types of work are celebrated like the job I expected to secure (white-collar, salaried, intellectually stimulating), and many employed people are still shamed for "failing" to "rise" from low-wage or service work. However, there is a baseline American fantasy work ethic, evident in the way politicians talk about "hardworking people," that I'd internalized.

Sister to this trope was the seemingly inherent virtue of ambition. *Ambitious* is a compliment in our society, a convenient lubricant of capitalism. For me, there was always a gendered tint to "ambition." The modern happy story for women, somewhere in between birth and marriage, now includes an ambitious, fulfilling, impressive career. Beyond that, it was suggested to me that happy lives, in general, were lived out by ambitious, career-driven women. As a gender studies student, I'd critiqued the misogyny of corporate feminism and rejected the idolization of the power-suited girl-boss. Even if I understood the girl-boss was a foot soldier for the patriarchy, it still felt unacceptable and problematic to be an unambitious, apathetic, or idle woman, as if to do so would reaffirm sexist conceptions about women's status or capabilities. While there are acceptable or attractive ways to be an unambitious man (the charming slacker), there was something specifically undesirable and repulsive, morally and aesthetically, about an unambitious woman. Filtered through my own political lens: if she objects to pursuing capitalism, she has no excuse not to be working indefatigably for the revolution. So even while deeply ambivalent, I performed ambition, hoping it might become real.

My hapless entry into the workforce is certainly evidence of how insidious the self-perpetuating logic of American neoliberal capitalism is; of how impossible it is to extract yourself from a crowd you don't realize you're in; of how beguiling and seductive the stories about a good life are, and how frightening the prospect of losing out on that life can be. However, as a student of gender studies, I was ostensibly better prepared to be willful in the face of these kinds of orienting forces, which every student faces. Yet capitalism's fairy tales and ghost stories remained in my consciousness, sealed off from my apparatus of feminist critical analysis. I forgot what I knew.

Neoliberal capitalism's paths, crowds, and directions are one piece of the answer to the question of how I found myself compelled to turn feminism off. But the answer also has much to do with how I'd built that feminist apparatus to begin with: its fragility, its scope, and the extraneous commitments that become entangled in it.

Every feminist has a different story. Everyone has a different experience at college. Many feminists will never go to college, and most will never study gender studies. But among those who do, I suspect that there are many who find feminism like I did. People who are drawn to study feminism are likely to be those who've experienced alienation. When you find feminism, it makes you feel less alienated, less like an alien. It's easy to become attached to feeling unalienated and at home. I know this was true for me: I became a feminist over a period of my life during which I became settled, happy, and at home. As a result, my feminism became settled and happy. Feminism became a home.

So from the beginning, my feminist knowledge was contradictory. I knew the inherent unsettledness of feminism. Being a feminist means being willing to live feeling unsettled, like an alien, out of place, and not at home. Feminism means living, as Ahmed says, perpetually in crisis, because we keep asking the question of how to live (2016, 196). Gender studies had taught me that feminism was never static, always challenging itself, challenging settledness.

I remember feeling so invigorated when I came to see this perpetual conflict and motion at the heart of gender studies. I remember a conversation from a seminar about one of the discipline's pedagogical debates. We read a scholar who asked whether gender studies departments (given how they risk ghettoizing knowledge, or may be based on outdated constructs altogether) should be dissolved and their faculty distributed throughout the university to bring feminist perspectives to each department. The conversation didn't end up settled (it never is), but the class reached the consensus that gender studies departments weren't houses where distributable knowledge was stored but rather machines for collective willful questioning, capable of self-inquiry—machines that couldn't function if stripped for parts.

Nonetheless, within the parameters of the university, feminism settled into a fixed shape and moved into a certain home. Feminism became a particular set of critical exercises, questions, conversations, activities, and affects. Feminism became raised hands in class, emails to professors, and arguments with parents and men. It became meals and chores and conversations over eggs. It became listening to and caring for women and receiving care in return. It became my relationship. It became song lyrics and my favorite bands. It became personal essays about my dad and articles about TV shows. It became organizing lectures and reevaluating the inclusivity of the application for our house and attending certain meetings and not others. It was questioning power at a university, asking how we could use our power toward feminist ends, and fighting our complicity in its un-feminist purposes.

All of these phenomena are valid and useful exercises of feminism. But I suspect they replaced feminism as a question that must be asked over and over again and became feminism itself. This is natural, in a way. It was the result of how I reoriented myself against the norms and flows of power that had given shape to my life, from childhood through college. My twists and turns freed up new space in the world, easing the cramped estrangement I'd carried all my life. It was tellingly easy, as someone with racial and class privilege, to find a comfortable new position. There were painful and humbling moments, such as when I grappled with the scarred history of feminism and the extent to which I was a beneficiary of this system. But I reached a level of comfort with how to negotiate and redress these discomforts that still let feminism harden into a comfortable shape. The pleasurable shape my life took on overshadowed the apparatus that allowed me to mold it that way. Naturally, this set of orientations and habits proved inadequate as my world changed shape. I was unprepared to hold on to my feminist commitments after college. They crumbled.

Happiness is another question. Ahmed is one of the most adamant feminist critics of happiness. In her book *The Promise of Happiness* (2010), she explores how happiness is often constructed as an end point, the goal, in pursuit of which we make certain choices and not others. In *Living a Feminist Life*, she says, "Happiness: what we end up doing to avoid the consequence of being sad. Happiness is a way of being directed towards those things that would or should make you happy" (2016, 49). In our society, certain things are said to bring happiness (marriage, employment, children), while others are warned to bring sadness (being single, queer, or unemployed, not having children). She proposes, drawing on Audre Lorde's *Cancer Journals*, "[Lorde] shows how making our own happiness our first responsibility can be how we turn away from injustice" (239).

I became happy while I became a feminist and, in part, due to becoming a feminist. As feminism became my cause, sneakily, so did happiness. I became addicted to my own happiness, to the detriment of both my feminism and my happiness. My pursuit of happiness helps explain why I was so unwillful in my choices after college. I was seduced by the happiness promised by the American story of a good middle-class life, which, I believed, depended on beginning a linear, traditional career immediately after college. I saw a career, ambition, and a job as happy social goods, irrespective of my feminist commitments. Ironically, even when I was miserable at my job, I was terrified to leave because I believed that having a job meant happiness.

Ahmed doesn't suggest that practicing feminism requires being unhappy. But she does say that it requires "stay[ing] unhappy with this world" (2016, 254). My world at college had become so happy that I stopped being unhappy with the world. I confused feminism's joys with joy as a feminist end. I stopped struggling with the world. Having given up this struggle already, it was not so counterintuitive to thoughtlessly join my classmates pursuing the same happy, social goods. It was easy to follow the crowd down the normal, clearly marked path after school, rather than struggle with the world or struggle with what my feminist commitments meant in it.

One of Ahmed's killjoy principles calls for a new understanding of happiness, one that returns the concept to its root word, *hap*, which means chance. She argues that a neoliberal notion of happiness removes hap, making happiness something you work for rather than something that happens to you. This is dangerous, she says: "The narrow scripts of happiness are precisely about the violence of the elimination of the hap. . . . When we stumble, when we are in line, we might feel ourselves as the obstacle to our own happiness. . . . Can we let ourselves be in the way? Can we be willing to be what seems to be our undoing?" (2016, 265). She proposes we take on a different notion of happiness, which is "as fragile as the bodies we love and cherish. We value happiness because it is fragile: it comes and goes, as we do. I am willing to let happiness go; to allow anger, rage, or disappointment to be how I am affected by the world" (266).

I find it shameful to acknowledge my selfishness and ignorance. However, I suspect that for those who find feminism in college, and for whom college is a happy place, this messy conflation of happiness, home, and feminism, which makes it difficult to keep hold of feminism after school, is common. I think that it's important to honestly acknowledge how and why it is difficult to hold onto feminism in the world. If we don't, it's easy to start believing the ugly story they tell. They say we become feminists at universities not because those of us who are privileged discover devastating violence and injustice for the first time there—or those who are less privileged learn how the violence and injustice in their own lives is systemic—but because universities are where people "experiment." Our minds are filled with fantasies of transforming society into something fair and just. These fantasies are as wonderful and empty as plastic toys. We become angry and vindictive and oversensitive like children. We stomp our feet and wave our arms and make unreasonable demands. They say that after a few years "in the real world," we'll find ourselves jaded and reformed, living happy normative lives. We'll see for ourselves that the world is more complicated than we ever imagined. We'll be convinced that the world we theorized in college is impossible and only minor tweaks can be made. We're supposed to mock our younger, more radical selves. As the myth goes, "Feminism is a phase."

I began to believe this story, and it was heartbreaking. As painful and shameful as it is to acknowledge my failures as a feminist, succumbing to this story is much more excruciating and humiliating. As much as it can cost to be a feminist in the world, accepting this story is much more costly. Accepting it is to resign oneself to a lifetime of pain and shame.

Being humbled in feminism can teach us about our attachments and commitments. We can use feminist shame as a resource. What does it look like to turn feminism back on? Can we return as more resilient, more critical, more willful feminists than before?

I left my job as a publicist after visiting a feminist friend across the country. When I walked into her apartment, she asked me, "How are you?" I began to cry. She said, "You don't have to feel this way. You can quit."

It's not immediately clear how this part of the story relates to Ahmed's text, or my analysis of it. In some ways, it seems to run completely counter. I left my job because it was diminishing me and because I decided I couldn't be a part of a system that commodified art and that commodified me in such diminishing ways. Although I am now criticizing how I made happiness my cause as a college feminist, ultimately, I left my job because I was unhappy. I left it, to some extent, in pursuit of happiness. What my friend told me was, "You don't have to *feel* this way." I had abandoned my commitments and followed the crowd to this job because I had been told that it and the life it signified would make me happy. If I left simply in order to try out another strategy for happiness, what would I have really learned?

This is an unsettling question. I'm grateful to be unsettled by it. I don't think happiness was my only end in quitting. For one thing, it didn't make me happy. Actually, I was miserable. I spent the summer after I left my job waking up when my partner would leave for work, paralyzed with anxiety that I had nowhere to go. I applied to work at restaurants and cafés and started an unpaid internship at a magazine two days a week. As I walked around in the middle of the weekday and took the subway with children and elderly people, I felt viscerally out of place in the roaring human traffic of New York City. I felt illegitimate at parties, where I had no answer to "What do you do?" I found myself face-to-face with all my classist anxieties and neoliberal conditioning. I was the boogie man, the millennial in the basement (who, classically, can also be found holding an unpaid internship or a Brooklyn coffee shop job). The path I had been on was unbearable, but it was well lit and crowded. The one I was on now was lonely and dark. I turned away from the story I'd been told led to happiness and goodness (employment, the ambitious career woman) and turned to face one about unhappiness and badness (unemployment, the millennial in the basement). I had to discover for myself that so many other stories are possible.

There's nothing disruptive or illegible to our society about a white, college-educated twenty-three-year-old quitting her first job out of college. Being briefly unemployed does not constitute being "outside the system." I don't mean to exaggerate the significance or radicalism of the act of quitting a job. But the story I'm trying to tell about feminism ultimately isn't about rejecting work or capitalism. It's about breaking capitalist paradigms in order to craft feminism deliberately in adult life and becoming aware of the incomplete, fragile, and contradictory parts of feminist knowledge. In quitting my job, I broke through something; I did something I didn't think I was allowed to do. I learned to become skeptical of happiness as an object to orient life around.

I had the option to discover these truths and untruths by exercising agency over my employment. This was privilege: leaving a job is rarely an option, whether for personal or political reasons, and not having to work at all is much rarer. But it's also not the only way I could've learned these things. Quitting was breakage. It was a snap. Ahmed says, "Willfulness comes up to explain a breakage, to stop a chain reaction" (2016, 167). When I quit my job, I recognized willfulness in my story. I ended a chain reaction. This break was harder than choosing to study gender or cultivating feminist friendships or living in a cooperative or arguing with my parents. A "feminist snap," she says, is "about how we collectively acquire tendencies that can allow us to break ties that are damaging, as well as invest in new possibilities" (162). This snap can look like many things—a thought, a conversation, an internal readjustment.

My snap didn't lead to happiness. I sat with my unhappiness while I asked the questions I had failed to ask when I left school: *Do I need to be a person who does feminist work? What does feminist work look like? What does work that doesn't diminish me or others look like?*

I have a new job now. I work as a writer for a magazine. I have an answer for people who ask what I do, though I no longer relish it like a prize. There is much to notice in the way of sexism and racism where I work and in the work I'm expected to do. There are many ways that neoliberal capitalism structures the terms of my work and diminishes me and my coworkers, as well as the subjects of our stories. Though I'm now taking notice of and turning toward injustice, instead of away from it, I recognize how I am still moving in a certain direction, associated with a particular future. Ahmed writes, "To be shattered can be to experience the costs of our own fragility: to break, to reach a breaking point" (2016, 163). My feminism was hard and brittle, and I experienced the costs of that fragility. The first time I experienced a snap, feminism exploded for me in a sensational rush of connections. It didn't come after a shattering. As I rebuild a feminist consciousness suited to navigating capitalism as an adult, I have been slower and more careful in what I am committing myself to.

I am committing to willfulness. To unsettledness and discomfort. To refusing happiness as a cause and to staying unhappy with the world even when I am happy. To a notion of happiness that is fragile, in order to allow for the anger, sadness, and disappointment of living in an unhappy world. Many of these ideas are a part of Ahmed's "killjoy manifesto." It would be convenient to end this story by invoking the militant killjoy, hard at work at her feminist assignments. But this is not a neat story, and I don't want to tidy it. Ahmed says, "We have been taught to tidy our texts, not to reveal the struggle we have in getting somewhere" (2016, 13). I want to live with the killjoy manifesto in full. But I am still grappling with its commitments and consequences. I feel strong in some. Others are difficult. As Ahmed says, "The task is to stay with the difficulty, to keep exploring and exposing the difficulty" (163).

References

Ahmed, Sara. 2016. *Living a Feminist Life*. Durham, NC: Duke University Press.

Liu, Rebecca. 2019. "The Making of a Millennial Woman." *Another Gaze*, June 12, 2019. https://www.anothergaze.com/making-millennial-woman-feminist-capitalist-fleabag-girls-sally-rooney-lena-dunham-unlikeable-female-character-relatable.

Part 3
PEDAGOGY

LETTER TO A WHITE SUPREMACIST

Addie Tsai

Author's Note

This essay recounts an experience I had while teaching a student who identified as a white supremacist in an Introduction to Creative Writing course in an English department in a community college in Texas. Within the classroom, I was able to teach radical texts that interrogated race, sexuality, gender, and class, but this pedagogical attention to social justice did not protect me from students for whom these texts seemed to only serve as provocation for their own fidelity to homophobia and racism.

The student's communications over social media were threatening to me, as a queer, nonbinary, Asian person. And these threats were exacerbated by a lack of attention from my institution, where I have worked in a permanent, full-time capacity for the past decade. Although I teach in the most diverse city in the country and support a largely minoritized student population, I still teach in the state of Texas, which as a whole supports very conservative policies. Most relevant for this story is the fact that the community college at which this experience took place recognizes Campus Carry, Texas Senate Bill 11, which has permitted handgun license holders to carry concealed handguns on all campuses of this institution and into many of its buildings. This policy went into effect on August 1, 2017, and my encounter with the white supremacist occurred during the fall semester of that same year.

Although I do not feel that my job security as a full-time professor (with a renewable, yearly contract) is in jeopardy, the institution did away with tenure across the entire institution many years ago, which could have provided a certain kind of support from the administration that I felt was lacking when I spoke to the dean of students regarding the concerning behavior and communication from this particular student. I was also aware that this institution has a history of inaction due to fear of lawsuits, so it is possible that could have also informed how the administration failed to adequately respond.

Given the number of school shootings that have been happening across the United States, combined with my own awareness of how little a professor truly knows about the stability of any one student, particularly in this political climate, I felt extremely vulnerable to the unknown scenarios that could have taken place. This feeling was exacerbated when one administrator basically dismissed a possible threat to my life and safety, a reaction that confirmed my sense of how unprotected so many of us feel at a time when tempers run high and gun control remains a growing concern, particularly in the field of education, where school shootings and acts of terrorism are on the rise.

> Dear White Supremacist Student Whose Name I No Longer
> Remember,

I know that this is a letter I will never send.

I consider myself a generous person, no longer to a fault (I have my therapist to thank for that), and I am making an intentional choice not to hold your name in the recesses of my memory. Each time I try to recall your name, the forces that I've spent the last four decades building to protect my body will help me no longer remember your name on the roll sheet next to the checkbox that I marked "absent" on the computer, the variation of your name that popped up on my phone to indicate you'd sent me a message, and then another, and then another, or the same name on the same roll sheet next to the checkbox that I clicked to permanently remove you from the course.

As Cathy Caruth says, "The historical power of the trauma is not just that the experience is repeated after its forgetting, but that it is only in and through its inherent forgetting that it is first experienced at all" (1995, 8). I do recall, however, that your name was unremarkable. It was the first and last name of a white American student that I'd read a hundred times before, and so when you did not show up for the first day of class, I didn't pause to think much about it.

But that all changed when you walked into the room.

Before I knew what details to retrospectively take note of and to reframe in a new light, your body immediately instilled in me a familiar fear, but not one I had often encountered in the classroom, and not for many years.

There was the time that I played an episode of *Mad Men* for an introductory composition class ten years ago, the one where the junior ad man harasses the new secretary as the department's "fresh meat," and a young, white, cis man enrolled in the class waited until every other student had left the room to approach me.

He was tall and thin, wearing a white T-shirt, gray trousers, sneakers, and a smile that made me feel like a broken-off piece of a dollar bill sticking out of the gutter.

He asked if I had a boyfriend. If I was married. If I was engaged.

I said yes, yes, yes, anything for him to leave me alone.

It didn't work. He retorted that I was only telling him that so that he would leave. Which is to say that he knew his advances were unwanted. And he didn't care.

Later on, I would go back in time and scrutinize each moment of the class in which I showed this episode and discussed sexual objectification and harassment with the students only to be sexually harassed immediately following the lesson.

I questioned what I wore. I questioned the attention I attracted to my body when I leaned my bottom against one of the tables that was not occupied. Did I wear a skirt that day? Were my legs exposed? Could you see the indentations of the lace on the bra that I wore? Did I look too long at one student or another, or this student in particular?

After I scrutinized my behavior in the classroom, it didn't take long for me to pick apart the fact that instead of saying that this student's question about whether I was single was inappropriate, I answered the question as though it were an acceptable one to ask of a professor. I have never told anyone this, nor have I confessed the shame I feel that I have withheld this information.

Once I'd told the student that I was engaged, married, with partner, yes, all of those things, and once he'd refused to believe that answer as true, I tried a new tactic.

I'll see you next class! I exclaimed, staring at the door, hoping longingly for another class of students to enter the room, but finding no easy way out.

His eyes bore through me like a strip search.

He left the room. I remained until the little hairs, standing straight as soldiers, fell back against my thighs. I remained until my hands stopped knocking against the underside of the desk at the front of the room, where I had gripped them in my lap until the dark beige of them had turned white as the walls that confined me, isolated in my terror of the what-ifs.

At some point, somehow, I went on with my day, and I wrote the chair of my department an email about what the student had asked me. Unusually, I received an immediate reply: Come see me in my office ASAP. I was so used to being marginalized, to being asked to tolerate the small and large abuses, that it didn't even occur to me that this was a protective measure, a measure to keep me safe.

My pulse quickened, my breath grew shallow at the base of my throat. I assumed what I always assume when an authority figure needs to see me at once. She is furious with me. She will fire me. She will yell at me.

This is just a slightly deviated version from years of growing up in a house with a dominant and violent Chinese father, years of growing up in a house where a man who loved me also required me to accept the small and large abuses. I was taught, again and again, to expect that Baba would be furious with me, that Baba would yell at me, that Baba very well might hit me.

The heat I imagined striking off my department chair's glare, taut limbs, like a ball of fire pushed out of the body in its targeted attack toward me, was the same heat that rose to a shriek that pierced my ear drums, the same white fury that bruised my naked bottom when I wet my pants, when I forgot my jacket at day care, when I temporarily jammed the glowing gold combination lock on my father's briefcase.

I'm sorry, Baba, I said inside my head. The coils were magic and I'd hoped if I wore your blazer and striped tie of brown diagonals, and could gain entrance to what lay behind those numbers, that maybe I wouldn't be afraid of everything either.

But that's not what happened.

My department chair marched me up the stairs and around the corner and down the hall to sit at a round wooden table across from an administrator whose position I no longer recall. My chair explained that I had been harassed, and that the student needed to be placed in another instructor's class immediately.

The man lifted his brown hand and twisted his mustache. My chair placed her black hand on the table in front of him. A reckoning.

The administrator: *Well, if it happens again—*

And before he could finish, my chair: *If it happens again, Addie could be dead. I won't risk it.*

Before that moment, I hadn't known yet what it would mean to have someone's rage enacted in a professional space in order to keep me safe. That is largely because the only bodies that were expected to keep me safe were ones whom I also felt endangered by. My father did everything he could to feed us, clothe us, bathe us, and provide for us with what he was and what he could offer—a Chinese immigrant single father of three children. But he was also the man who terrified me. I would detail the fears he provoked within me in a journal that came with a lock and key, which I hid between the mattress and the box spring every night before I went to sleep.

I might end up in an emergency room one day.

One day he might go too far, and I won't wake up.

I will die in this room, because I will be too afraid that he will kill me if I try to leave it.

But here was this woman, in the body of a person my father hoped I would fear, who enabled me to live without fear instead. Who insisted on my safety. A gesture I imagine she would barely remember today, so many years later, but who left an indelible mark on me, one that insisted on my vitality and on my body being honored.

The semester you appeared in my classroom was no ordinary semester. This was the post-Harvey semester, a semester in which excuses were the norm, a semester in which I would excuse any student for any reason because we were all connected to one another through the tragedy of a city that almost drowned. Some homes filled with water. Some homes became the sacrificial lambs—offered up in order to save the lot.

I had been lucky. Our little bungalow was just high enough to miss it, tucked into one of the many miraculous pockets of safety that weren't expected. The water curled up the curb each night, and then crept back to where it began. The only thing I lost was my belief that my city wouldn't drown, and a pink cruiser I had hoped to learn to ride one day.

It was for this reason that when you wrote me to tell me that you had a work injury and you hadn't been cleared to attend class, I accepted it without question. After that first email, I forgot about you. I assumed you'd end up like most students who write the first day of the semester to give a story of why you couldn't attend. That maybe you would drop the class after a while, or never show up again at all.

A month in, suddenly, there you were. An apparition. A wasp hiding in plain sight. I was tending to a student and didn't hear the door open or the hinges squeak as the door made its way closed again. I was not ready for how you would appear to me, how I had been taught to receive a body and likeness like yours. Perhaps I will never be ready.

You were around five feet ten, white. You had the kind of build that looked as if you might have been muscular once, lifting weights at the local gym long into the night. Your belly strained against your T-shirt, your arms swelled. The swelling was the first sign of trouble. Your eye had clearly been cut, and it twitched as you asked me to explain what you'd missed. What most disturbed me, however, were the markings on your face and your left hand. A 5150[1] in black ink above the wounded eye, a Reichsadler[2] on the left hand. The Nazi symbol under the eagle quivered as your hand shook while you spoke.

I took a long, studied look at you, and I felt a new kind of fear. It was not the fear provoked by my father, or the student who sexually harassed me, or the disappointed authority figure. This was a new fear, and one I chastised myself for, one based, initially, off what I imagined your life was like outside that classroom.

I assumed your hands shook because you felt I had judged you, because you had been judged before. I would later come to discover that you shook from withdrawal. I felt I had no choice but to treat you equally. And so, I had you send a friend request to my Facebook account, so that you could get access to the group that I used for course updates and the sharing of assignments. I knew you would automatically gain access to my own personal timeline. I knew that you would gain access to the daily Baldwin quotes I curated—since the day Trump was elected to office—and I knew you would also be able to observe posts that address my queerness, my gender nonbinaryness, my Asianness, my mixed-race-ness, my pro-Blackness. But as I accepted the friend request I instructed you to send me, I held my stomach in a tight little ball, a metaphor for the fetal position I rolled myself into when I was unsure whether my father would hit me or strike me with silence, and hoped that you would ignore my posts and just do your work. Or never return.

It was the first time I'd ever hoped a student would not return. The guilt was a lead anchor in my foot. But so was my fear of what was beneath the skin that announced to the world who you would become. You handed in a single assignment, an essay about your brother dying of a heroin overdose, twenty years after being incarcerated.

But that is still not the trouble.

The trouble begins on October 23, 2017, seven days after you've been given access to my Facebook timeline and twenty-one days after the Weinstein story goes live in the *New Yorker*.

The trouble begins with a Baldwin quote: "I'd like to say that when I say 'white' I'm not talking about the color of anybody's skin. It's a curious country, a curious civilization, that thinks of it as race. I don't believe any of that. White people are imagined. White people are white only because they want to be white."

The trouble begins with a student comment to a Baldwin quote: "I'm sick and tired of your nonsense and your racial articles."

After a few hours, I delete your comment, and I add a post to the course's Facebook group wall—a disclaimer that my personal timeline is curated based on my personal beliefs, which have nothing to do with the course. I add that I expect students to respect student-instructor boundaries, and that students are free to unfollow my timeline if any of my posts bother them in any way.

Enabling students to have access to my own timeline is something I'm often questioned about, and many respond with anger when I insist on sticking with my decision. For the rare student who gets up in arms about my politically leaning posts (and by this I mean that I share articles that address politically charged but very real incidents), there are hundreds of queer, POC, trans, Dreamer, immigrant, and other marginalized students who feel, at a time so necessary, a kind of comfort in knowing where I stand, and whose rights matter to me. And I largely insist on not censoring myself from my students with these bodies in mind.

To my disclaimer post on the course's wall, you immediately respond: "Dialogue only when appropriate, right?"

I close Facebook and hope that will be the end of it. Just in case, I email my dean around eleven o'clock that night, attaching the story assignment about your brother, and explain what's just happened. By the time I am ready for bed, the dean has set up a meeting for the following morning. By the time I awake the next morning, you have unleashed weaponized hate via a Facebook message, the thing your body had set off within me, but that I didn't have the words to name:

> I just wanted to apologize if I made you feel like you weren't free to discuss how you feel about any subject with me or any other student. I'm not going to pretend that your prospective (*sic*) on race is anything less than insane (look, we live in what is more or less a police state— American has been a few steps short of pushing people into cattlecars— which I have a rather strong and personal opinion on such matters, as the reason that my grandfather ended up in a Siberian prison as I mentioned earlier—he, a soldier who earned Germany's highest honor, the Iron Cross, during WWI, surrendered to Russian troops? That's laughable until you consider the circumstances—camp after being told that his options were to fight in WWII or he could take my family to the camps—by the Gestapo, no less . . . it's no joke that they used to come to people's doors at 3 a.m. [funny how American police do the same thing], the way my mother tells the story chills your soul [if you ever want to know plenty of other insane stories about WWII Germany, feel free to buy me a beer, I am unfortunately heir to a whole legacy of such knowledge as well as it's (*sic*) brutal consequences and legacy]—is because he got drunk and went the fuck off about prisoners in cattle-cars . . . I didn't have to be a rocket scientist as a kid to put two and two together when my mother told me the circumstances of his forced enlistment) and we've always had jackasses burning books (which, I might point out, isn't too far removed from the censorship of dialogue you conducted by removing what I posted earlier—which, however long-winded it was, was not wrong; of course, none of it was appropriate for the classroom dialogue, your posts or my commentary). Anyhow, we live in a police state, and one thing that has proved effective time and again in oppressive regimes (look closely at history as it happened, not as whatever is the popular narrative happens to be) is to divide people.

Don't get it twisted, I'm a White supremacist (meaning I hold no truck with interracial sex, I don't believe that races are equal, nor do I believe that people of any race can peacefully coexist in close proximity; I am from the streets and the penitentiary, and the reality of it is that once you start mixing people of such disparate beliefs and values, all that you end up with is violence and hatred, which doesn't do anyone any good; better if you leave each to their own . . . believe my knowledge of this, I know exactly what a fragile thing peace between the races is when we are forced into close proximity with one another . . . even on the calmest prison unit, rape is a fact of life amongst every race other than Whites—and that's because homosexuality is an offense punishable by death amongst White convicts and White homosexuals are shunned—and someone is always getting stabbed) and you can look me up in the NCIC [National Crime Information Center] if you ever want to know exactly who and what I am—you don't wear the tattoos that I do without having the hands that are quite literally washed in blood (please don't take anything I say in a threatening manner, as I am certainly not dangerous to women, children, or any man that doesn't offer me a threat . . . and my skin is generally quite thick, despite the impassioned nature of my commentary earlier). But, as I was saying, divisive politics only serve the interests of those who would be our masters (and it's the oldest trick in the world to elevate a select group of people, often by race, and place them over a client body; look at your history books if you don't believe me). I'm not a friend of the police and make no apologies for their behavior. But I'm also not going to pretend that how you talk about White people is anything less than offensive and ignorant. Nor do I think that the world is so small that it belongs to one race. But make no mistake about it, you're not going to make me feel fucked up about who I am or my pride and identity as an Aryan man who fights to his dying breath to defend his people. Nor are you going to force me out of character in relations to you or anyone else who is not my people . . . I carry myself in a dignified and respectful manner in all things (do not mistake me for some ignorant thug who walks around in a fog of hatred and self-delusion; I have done many harsh and brutal things in my life, but only when required to by dire circumstance, and never lightly or dictated by fear . . . I don't hate or fear different people, only acknowledge that we are different and that some things will never be solved by expecting us to live together or trying to force us to be the same). So I politely bid you to acknowledge that we are not the same, that I will not accept attacks towards my race nor will I participate in one-sided dialogue (speaking as an individual, I will gladly discuss any matter as long as it is meaningful and carried out in a respectful fashion), and that respect and learning should be the dynamic upon which we should interact.

I'm a White supremacist
I hold no truck with interracial sex
I don't believe that races are equal
Once you start mixing people of such disparate beliefs and values, all
    you end up with is violence and hatred
Even on the calmest prison unit, rape is a fact of life amongst every
    race other than Whites
Homosexuality is an offense punishable by death
You don't wear the tattoos that I do without having the hands that are
    quite literally washed in blood
I am certainly not dangerous to women, children, or any man that
    doesn't offer me a threat
You're not going to make me feel fucked up about who I am
an Aryan man who fights to his dying breath to defend his people

I spoon a little too long with my fluffy dog covered in white curly tendrils. I scrub my face. I spin my electric toothbrush into little vibrating circles around my teeth. I dress myself. I drink coffee next to my spouse while he casually checks up on me through breaks in watching Rockets highlights. Like a ticker tape, a sentence thrumming louder than the hours it takes between the time the alarm sounds and I walk out the door. *Today is the day I may die.*

    Guns blazing, you blast me against the wall, then the students, then yourself.

    You slip through the door just as class begins, you snatch me from the room. I am never heard from again.

    A rape. Or the worst of all: not knowing what horror lies waiting for me, just that it's like nothing I could hope to imagine. I dare not. I don't want to taint the purity of hope with the poison of his words and the violence coating my skin.

Before I walk out the door, I text my therapist and a few friends. I tell my partner to keep his phone close to him. I don't tell my partner why I've done this until later. That I am texting people in case something happens to me. In case I am shot, or kidnapped, or raped, or assaulted.

I walk the twelve minutes from my house to campus. It is a beautiful fall day, wisps of white streaking the sky. I want to pull it from above me and drape it around me until my body vanishes.

My steps are brisk. I wear my shades to avoid eye contact with strangers. I question whether you know where I live, whether you're hiding in the shadows between the skinny city towers, the darkness large enough for you to conceal yourself just long enough to catch me off guard.

The minutes are quick, but they feel interminable when I don't know what lies ahead of me, how far your erasure of me will travel. I am struck by how little an instructor can know a student.

In the dean's office, I sit across from one dean—a middle-aged white woman wedded to an Asian husband, framed pictures of three mixed-race children scattered across her mahogany desk. Next to me sits another dean, one whom I've never met—an older Black man. I try to read him your message, but his boredom takes the wind out of my chest, as he listens nonchalantly while reading the new emails that have popped up on his phone.

Well, it's all on you what happens at this point, he says, his words scattering in the air above me like fruit flies.

I could say that you'd violated the Code of Conduct. He tells me that the message, although problematic, just is not *threatening enough* to do more.

Those two words hang suspended in the air above me.

I stop listening. I wonder what would have been threatening enough to remove you from my classroom, what would have made this circumstance not *all on me*.

I tell him that I am queer and that you wrote you believe homosexuals should be punished by death. I tell him that I am not white and that you believe in white supremacy and an Aryan nation. I tell him that you believe racial mixing should be abolished, that you know I am mixed race. I tell him that I feel you are unstable, that you are possibly addicted to chemical substances, that you were agitated by the loss of your brother.

At some point, I give up. The other dean offers to keep the police on call. I wonder how many men would need to shoot students in order for a warning to be taken seriously. I wonder whether there would ever be a number to answer this question. I wonder how much evidence of a student's instability would be necessary to mark one as worthy enough to be removed from the classroom.

The door to the classroom locks when shut. My class starts that day with a call from the police, from a former student, who reminds me how to reach them on the phone inside the classroom. I shut the door, dissatisfied until I hear the little lock click us into a bubble of safety after every person has entered the room. The students look concerned, but they don't ask questions. Later, they would tell me that they suspected it had to do with that guy who wrote that thing on the class group page on Facebook.

You never show up.

In the middle of the afternoon, you send me a message that arrives just underneath the message where you threatened my body and my existence. It's another excuse for missing class.

I don't respond.

Two days later, I discover a ray of hope: I could remove you for lack of attendance, a rare moment of power in an otherwise powerless situation. I knock my mouse against the table, thwack-thwack-thwack, afraid. I click the checkbox to withdraw you.

I wait two more days.

I email you, copying the chair and one of the deans, explaining in as reasonable an electronic tone as I can manage, that you have been dropped for lack of attendance; nothing can be done about it. You could take it up with the administration if you have questions or concerns. You respond with appreciation that I'd been so respectful about our differences of opinions.

I don't respond. I don't say that I've learned from over ten years of therapy how to de-escalate a situation when a person is projecting his or her own baggage on you, that I've learned this from having two narcissistic parents, two parents who betrayed any boundary I would hope to hold for myself. I don't tell you that I already know what it means to believe that I could die. You aren't the first. You won't be the last.

What I do instead is block all the social media accounts associated with you that I can find, including the Twitter account with the handle, *Violence is the only answer*. I imagine that if I had escalated the situation enough to provoke you, if I had "offered you a threat," that a snapshot of your Twitter handle would be the first thing to grace the media outlet headline. I imagine that mine would be a screenshot of my timeline with a litany of my Baldwin quotes, my queer, nonbinary, nonwhite face the little thumbnail in the upper left-hand corner.

> I imagine one of the reasons people cling to their hates so stubbornly is because they sense, once hate is gone, they will be forced to deal with pain. —Baldwin
>
> One must say Yes to life and embrace it wherever it is found—and it is found in terrible places; nevertheless, there it is. —Baldwin

Notes

1. Section 5150 of the California Welfare and Institutions Code authorizes a qualified officer or clinician to involuntarily confine a person suspected to have a mental disorder that makes them a danger to themselves, a danger to others, or gravely disabled.

2. The Reichsadler is the heraldic eagle used in modern coats of arms of Germany, including that of the Third Reich.

Reference

Caruth, Cathy. 1995. *Trauma: Explorations in Memory*. 1st ed. Baltimore: Johns Hopkins University Press.

PRAISE TO OUR SCHOOL WE LOVE SO DEAR—OR MAYBE NOT

Status Quo and Safe Spaces in High School

Hayley Zablotsky

It was never my plan to work in education, but there I was, marching up to the front doors of an enormous public Texas high school. The real stuffed buffalo in a glass case greeted me just inside the front doors. *Go Buffs!*

This was undeniably new territory for me. I didn't even go to a "normal" high school—instead, my free-spirited mom had me in and out of various "alternative" schools throughout my childhood. *My* high school butted up against a forest and had a graduating class of twenty-eight students. This might be a good time to mention that I'm from the foothills of Northern California, where people both push boundaries *and* raise picture-perfect nuclear families—something I have yet to fully understand.

I moved to Texas for college. Though I am a straight white woman from an upper-middle-class family, I didn't always fit in at the private Texas university that had captured me with a prestigious scholarship. I was a vegetarian in the land of beef. A doubter in a churchgoing province. A feminist. But I found good people and good friends nonetheless, and I decided to remain in Texas after graduation for this job at the high school.

On my first day of work, I knew I was in for an eye-opening experience. The school was located in an industrial suburban area and had almost three thousand students. The majority of students were Latinx, and many were undocumented. Most of the students were on the free lunch program. Several had parents in prison and babies of their own.

I was the new college and career adviser for the students, which I found rather ironic considering I had no clue what I was doing in my own life.

I'd just graduated with a BA in writing with a minor in women's and gender studies—useless fields of study according to almost everyone I knew. My opinion of the *real world* so far was mediocre. I missed college. During those four years, I'd found a way to make my differences work, found fulfillment in *not* fully fitting in. I'd genuinely loved my classes and what I'd learned, and I missed my eclectic friends, who had scattered across the country. Nonetheless, I *was* excited for my first job at this high school.

I quickly discovered that this new job was all about rules. The high school's administration ran a tight ship. There were seemingly hundreds of rules to learn—and enforce. I was, after all, an authority figure for the first time in my life.

I got stuck almost immediately on the student dress code.

The dress code rules were a murky and dangerous abyss. I knew that I was authorized (and expected) to haphazardly shout, "Pull your pants up!" but I really felt that I had better things to do with my time.

Since that was the only dress code rule I clearly understood, I sometimes asked my students for clarification about the other, more elusive policies. One student was particularly adamant about the situation. She pulled up a chair next to my desk.

"Look," she said. "Look at my shirt. I can wear this because I have small boobs." She was wearing a T-shirt with a scoop neck. "But my friend wore basically the same shirt one time and got dress-coded."

Dress-coded was an official term at the high school (v., "to be singled out and punished based on clothing the school deems inappropriate").

"Just because she has bigger boobs and there was a little cleavage."

So just because of her body shape, this student had to miss class time to go change into an oversize jersey or whatever more *appropriate*—and highly conspicuous—shirt was found in the principal's office. Not only was this student deprived of some of her education that day, but she was also publicly and privately shamed for the shape of her body.

I could hear the disgust in my student's voice as she told the story, and I was glad for her anger. She was starting to push back.

Most of my other students did not think to push back. They knew the norms and rules and didn't question them. They played their parts in the grand system of gender expectations and accepted the limits placed on them. They knew how to enact their femininity and masculinity, and they knew the consequences that came from deviating. And perhaps the worst part of it was that they didn't even *know* that they *knew*. It was ingrained and innate and absolutely never acknowledged.

The girls wore more makeup than I'd ever seen before in my life. Their eyebrows were flat angular rectangles that only belonged on cartoon villains. Their eyelashes were giraffe length. I wondered how early they had to wake up to do their makeup. How much sleep they literally lost over it. How much money they spent on it. How severe the social repercussions would be if they *didn't* wear it. I knew for a fact that they had more important things to worry about, because they often told me about their responsibilities. Many had to care for younger siblings (or their own children) and help financially support their families with fast-food jobs that left dark circles under their eyes, visible even through all the makeup.

And the boys. Oh, the boys. The boys knew that being academic and respectful isn't manly or cool. The boys knew that they could get away with groping a girl in the cafeteria; punishment would be minimal and girls would still want them. The boys knew they could cuss out their (usually female) teachers and be rewarded with half a day at home. The boys knew that starting a fight in the hall would bring them fame and glory. The boys knew that they *had* to hit on me but certainly didn't need to listen to my instructions.

"Hey, miss," they'd say. "You got a boyfriend?"

"Hey, miss. How old are you?"

"Hey, miss. Dannnnng, you look good today."

(All female teachers in Texas are addressed exclusively as "miss." Yes, I have thoughts about this).

They knew they were entitled to talk to me this way. They'd always been allowed to do this. *Boys will be boys, after all.*

These behaviors are undeniably problematic, but it doesn't seem fair to hold the students fully responsible. These are learned behaviors—taught and learned better than algebra, World War II history, and verb conjugations.

In her works, including her essay "Performative Acts and Gender Constitution: An Essay in Phenomenology and Feminist Theory," Judith Butler discusses how we *act out* our gender. She explains gender as an act that is repeated, ritualized, and public. She says, "The act that one does, the act that one performs, is, in a sense, an act that has been going on before one arrived on the scene" (1988, 526).

This means that my students didn't make the rules. However, they did quite a good job of keeping the operation running.

Butler goes on to explain that gender is performative in the sense that it is something we *do* with a constant audience's eyes on us. However, it isn't *theatrical*. There is no stage, no curtain call, no intermission. It is real.

In the safety of the theater, where there is a clear distinction between play and reality, we might be permitted to deviate from our prescribed gender roles or any number of other social rules and norms. Indeed, the high school administration had a grand time at the mediocre spring musical *Gypsy* (which is about perhaps the most famous striptease artist of all time), successfully suspending their dress-code beliefs for a night. Anything can happen in the theater. But when we act out gender in the real world, we are not allowed the same freedom to transgress.

Butler says that such transgression would be perceived as dangerous and detrimental to our tidy little reality. Those who do not properly act out their prescribed gender face consequences.

Butler elaborates, "The body becomes its gender through a series of acts which are renewed, revised, and consolidated through time" (1988, 523). By the time I met them, my high school students had almost eighteen years of renewing, revising, and consolidating—but they didn't realize it. Butler explores this contradictory phenomenon of how we so intently embody and enforce these gender expectations while at the same time seemingly give no thought to their necessity or even existence: "Gender is, thus, a construction that regularly conceals its genesis. The tacit collective agreement to perform, produce, and sustain discrete and polar genders as cultural fictions is obscured by the credibility of its own production. The authors of gender become entranced by their own fictions whereby the construction compels one's belief in its necessity and naturalness" (522).

Butler acknowledges that "on some level" we may understand what is happening. We may know gender is "socially compelled" (1988, 528). It is not something we regularly acknowledge, and maybe some people don't know that they know. But we must know at least a little. At least sometimes. At least some of us. We must because we have people like my angry student, fired up in her scoop-necked T-shirt about the dress code.

Whether the students realize it or not, school is one of the most influential agents of socialization. In kindergarten, girls learn to play with baby dolls and dress up in pretty princess gowns. In elementary school, the boys hear, "Don't be such a girl! Stop crying!" after falling down on the soccer field. In middle school, everyone learns the secretive and shameful nature of sex (especially in states with abstinence-only sex education).

By high school, these kids have a good grasp of the Way Things Are. Schools teach obedience and respect for authority, but I wonder if that's what they really should be teaching. It needs to occur to students that the Way Things Are isn't necessarily the way things *should* be. Authority figures are not inherently right or good. We are allowed to disagree.

Butler calls gender an "innovative affair" (1988, 531). Maybe we should teach high schoolers to innovate or at the very least give them permission to *try*. As it stands, students are not equipped to challenge the status quo, and they are not encouraged to ever question authority.

And it's no wonder. The faculty members at the high school also accept and perpetuate the Way Things Are. Either they don't see the problems or they choose to look the other way.

I don't want to give the impression that my coworkers are terrible, close-minded people because they aren't. Many of them are lovely, intelligent people. Though my immediate coworkers—the guidance counselors—are middle-class white women, the school does have some racial diversity among the teachers and administration. But they, too, were raised in this system and are part of the institution. They are comfortable enough and likely don't see the need for disruption or subversion.

And I don't mean to exonerate myself from any of this; I am also part of the system and in many ways complicit in day-to-day life. I was, however, used to having an environment—college and particularly my gender studies courses—where we would honestly and critically talk about problems. Even among the more conservative cohort in college, discussion was open. We would unpack our differences. Brainstorm solutions. We acknowledged and processed things that most people don't want to talk about: power imbalances, discrimination, sexual harassment and violence, gender norms, fluidity, bodies, and the complexities of liking the color pink.

By the second week of working in that high school, I realized that we don't talk about *any* of these things in the real world, and we certainly don't encourage high school students to learn about or explore these issues. This didn't come as a shock, but it was disappointing nonetheless.

College was a bubble, and the bubble had popped.

Meanwhile, I was busy advising my students on their postgraduation plans and helping them reach their goals, whether it was college, trade school, the military, or something else. Once the kids realized that I was young and generally nice, they came to see me for other reasons. They liked popping in my office to tell me good news, to ask for advice, or to see if there were Starbursts in my candy bowl.

"Miss, do you know why I'm so happy today?" One of my frequent-flyer students bounced into my office.

"No, tell me," I said.

"I have a date to homecoming!"

"Oh, amazing! Boyfriend? Girlfriend?"

And she grinned—a little stunned, I think—and nodded.

"Girlfriend," she said, almost confidentially. Then she hugged me. I realized I might have been the first person to not assume.

And then I noticed that something was starting to happen. Students started to open up to me, confide in me. They realized that I wouldn't treat them any differently if they were gay. If they were pregnant. If they were undocumented. If they identified as male but sometimes liked to wear makeup.

It really became clear to me one day after a long talk with a junior. We'd talked for at least an hour in my office about his career goals, fears about the future, abusive family dynamics, and best death-metal band name ideas.

He hesitated in my office doorway before leaving.

"By the way . . . could you, um, use feminine pronouns for me, please?"

She seemed uncomfortable but determined to ask this of me. The request was clearly well rehearsed but rarely spoken aloud.

"Of course," I said. "Thanks for telling me."

It was an intense and enormous moment. It shouldn't have been. But it was.

A few minutes after she left, one of my coworkers skittered across the hall to my office.

"He wants to be a *girl*, doesn't he?" she giggled. She'd overheard, since my office door was open.

I wasn't sure whether my student meant for that to be confidential, so I let my coworker's question go unanswered. What I wanted to say was, "No, she identifies as female, and it's really not that big of a deal. Go back to your office and eat more of your crunchy snacks." But, for confidentiality reasons, I didn't say that. And also, maybe I'm not as brave as I'd like to think.

Here are some facts: I was new and I was young. This was my first job out of college. The school was old, and it seemed likely that the status quo probably hadn't changed much since it first opened. Many of my coworkers were at least middle-aged and set in their ways.

I'm not offering these facts as excuses or as reasons to not be brave, but I am presenting them as part of the equation. It isn't easy to implement ideals and change minds. That certainly isn't a reason to quit trying, but the magnitude of tradition was more overwhelming than I'd expected.

It frustrated me. Sometimes I felt like a hypocrite, willfully complicit in what I knew was a close-minded and staunchly heteronormative institution. But I needed a job, and I (perhaps somewhat defensively) reasoned that it would be acceptable to bend a little. But as long as people *need jobs*, how are we ever going to change the world?

To my surprise, a few of my coworkers started to pay attention by the end of the school year. I certainly hadn't led a revolution, but I'd spoken up at lunch or in the hallways.

It's not okay to say *hermaphrodite*—try *intersex* instead.

Maybe it's time to lay off the Caitlyn Jenner jokes?

Yes, those pronouns in that email signature are there for a reason.

Of course I'm a feminist! Yeah, I said the *F* word.

More importantly, I focused on my interactions with the students. It mattered that I talked about the merits of high-heeled suede boots with one of the boys. It mattered that I didn't assume the girls had lower math scores on their SATs. It mattered that I sat with a crying student and said, "I believe you," over and over.

I operated within the system, but I carved out a space. I could run my personal office the way I wanted. I could be an ally. I could listen. I could validate. I could push back.

I couldn't change the whole institution—well, at least not in one school year—but I could create my own safe place within it. And I could hope that my kids and my coworkers would join me.

Reference

Butler, Judith. 1988. "Performative Acts and Gender Constitution: An Essay in Phenomenology and Feminist Theory." *Theatre Journal* 40 (4): 519–31. https://doi.org/10.2307/3207893.

LOVE THE KILLJOY

Justine Parkin

I hadn't set out to teach a course on feminism.

For my second year teaching at a philosophy-based high school, I had initially wanted to lean more into the critical theory and German philosophy part of my academic background. While I had been engaged with feminist thinking for a while, it had long felt so personal to me that I failed to find ways to integrate it with my academic interests, save for, perhaps, overarching critiques of what it is to be a woman in academia.

Thankfully, in graduate school, my introduction into the field of feminist science studies made me realize that what I had been aiming for when writing about political theory or ecology was indisputably intertwined with feminist theory as well. As a white woman living with a chronic pain condition, I was moved by texts like Mel Y. Chen's *Animacies*, which immerses a theory of biopolitics within a personal narrative of illness and bodily toxicity. Chen's text is a precise exercise in the kind of academic scholarship I had perhaps imagined, but not yet dared. Yet I worried that as a new teacher, the personal connection I had to the field might translate into a weak teaching experience. Moreover, having taught an environmental philosophy course the year prior, I worried that teaching feminist theory just after would paint me as "too soft," unlike the other philosophy teachers at the school, who were predominantly men and were teaching on punishment, Marx, or chaos theory. That year, we'd spent a good amount of time comparing ecofeminism and deep ecology and I'd peppered all my current research in feminist science studies throughout. To follow environmental philosophy with a course on feminist theory would be only too obvious, I feared. And for anyone who doesn't know, high schoolers are some of the fiercest (and best) critics.

But that summer before the year began, I read bell hooks's book *All about Love*. I was moved. Her charge in a related essay that love is "the heart of feminism" got me thinking. Love, of course, is not exclusive to feminism. What hooks means, I think, is that love is an ethic that must motivate a feminist's actions. Building an ethics of love predicated on respect, vulnerability, and mutuality, she suggests, is both the prerequisite to *and* the practice of upending sexist, racist, and hetero-normative cycles of domination. I realized my fears in being seen as "too soft" or "too feminine" were precisely the prejudices against feminist thinking that I had long wanted to overcome myself. And given the political climate in which we currently live and to which high schoolers especially are so attuned (though I've found that we adults often fail to give them such credit), I figured a turn toward feminism and an attempt to cultivate an ethics of love through feminist thought was in order, as much for the students as it would be for me. It's the trite truths like love, I reasoned, that remain most unquestioned, for we would all seem to tacitly agree on what they mean. But lest anyone (by which I mean the strong-willed, passionate, and searching students) think that I was unaware of my own ambivalence or reservations about being "the feminist teacher," I named the course Feminist Killjoys: Feminist Theory and Practice. *Hey*, I hoped to be saying, *I know what I'm doing here.* Except I really didn't.

It's easy to be a feminist killjoy in a high school. Even if you're a teacher, like me. It's just that you have to compete with other kinds of killjoys: the apologist historian killjoy, the grammar killjoy, the liberal gun owner killjoy, the social justice killjoy, the "racism-sexism-isn't-a-thing-anymore" killjoy—and here I'm talking mostly about the kids. The small, private high school in West Los Angeles where I teach is composed of an eclectic bunch of students. A few come from solidly middle-class backgrounds, like me, while many are from one of the two very different poles of the socioeconomic ladder—and the divide is often very clear. Some see themselves as having mastered the discourses of politics and social justice such that they can now critique and think beyond them, emboldened by the pervasive tone of internet trolls, as it were; others are still coming to understand the depth of many of history's horrors and create themselves as political thinkers today, initiating themselves into a political world that remains remote for some of them and yet so personal for others. They are all quite adept at gathering a host of pithy historical facts but may struggle, as we all do, in piecing together large chunks of information (while recognizing invariable slants of perspective) and certainly succumb to the mill of online information often fed to us secondhand. Today's teens are growing up in a world where to stand out is to be provocative or the very the first to do something, no matter how strange—all the better to do both if you can. They are all killjoys from the start, though of deeply contrasting and often conflicting kinds.

In *Living a Feminist Life*, Sara Ahmed (2017) rescues and reclaims the figure of the feminist killjoy—the willfully disobedient person who chooses to disrupt, to stand in the way, to drive nonconfrontational situations into uncomfortable territory. I had suspected that some of the first questions my students would ask would be about the ubiquitous figure of the "angry feminist." About this, I was correct. So I began the year invoking Ahmed's figure of the feminist killjoy, hoping to help correct popular criticisms of "the angry feminist" (though we also read Audre Lorde's [1984] essay "The Uses of Anger" lest they believe that anger is totally unjustified). I offered Roxanne Gay's (2014) concept of the "bad feminist" to suggest that feminism doesn't just reveal itself in one stripe and that feminists are just as messy and confused and figuring things out as the rest of us. I had a mix of students: the already-convinced girls; the students who thought my class would be "easy" because the discourse and debates in the field were already "so obvious"; the boys who just wanted to argue; and the lone, fiercely antifeminist *movement* student (but not, I might add, antifeminist himself) who drove useful wedges in our conversations, propelling us into discussions that served as perfect microcosms of debates happening today.

In all, though, we were mostly a class of reluctant feminists, me included. In spite of my studies, I wanted to be seen as a "serious scholar," and the stories I had heard from many women academics made me afraid that any lean toward feminism would position me firmly (and solely) within the bounds of feminist theory, not philosophy or political theory or environmental studies, which felt equally close to me. This all in spite of the fact that, in academia, feminist thinking is so clearly entangled with questions of power and politics that it's often impossible to separate them; yet I was afraid that the still-inchoate thinking of my students might not be able to accommodate such nuance. As a student, I also had the great luxury of not only being sympathetic toward a field of study but a sympathetic *critic* of it as well—like that moment when you finally understand what Foucault is talking about when he writes of, say, epistemes and biopower and, in that same moment, finally comprehend all the criticisms of Foucault as well so you can now engage in more nuanced debates with your peers. Yet outside academia, I realized that the dynamic structure of the field and the thoughtful criticisms of it were not as clear to an outside observer. I'd have to start from the beginning, not jump right in where my own studies had left off. And furthermore, as a teacher, I had come to the firm realization that theory is far more than semantic squabbling among academics; when theory is in action and you see its effects on real students, you realize the massive import of how we choose to speak, act, and respond in the classroom.

The first part of the class, then, was perhaps more for myself than for them. I had to first convince *myself* that feminist killjoys were worth reclaiming. I had structured my curriculum around identifying and subsequently shattering three central "myths" about women—namely, myths of women's intellectual inferiority (mind/rationality); myths about women's bodies and identities (body/sexuality/gender); and myths about women's emotional capacities and their expected role in relational life (love). Throughout the year, we sifted through Audre Lorde's work so we could discuss race and pain and sexuality and difference; we considered Simone de Beauvoir's categorization of women as "the second sex" and Judith Butler's theory on the performativity of gender; we talked bodies and birth control and the legacy of Freudian diagnoses of hysteria in the medical treatment of women even today. Those students who arrived in class already convinced of certain truths were shaken into asking new questions. Those who were perhaps dismissive of central ideas to begin with came to slowly incorporate a new lexicon into their speech.

But all the lofty ideas I had about the narrative arc of the course fell apart quickly as we had to contend early on with the confirmation of Brett Kavanaugh to the US Supreme Court, the continuing ride of the #MeToo movement, Donald Trump's comments on abortion at his State of the Union address, Jordan Peterson, YouTubers I'd never heard of, and everything in between. I felt that I scarcely had the answers to anything. And I soon realized that I wavered even in my purpose in teaching this course. Was I trying to convert them? Because a class with students and teachers all thinking the same would have meant I had truly failed as both a teacher and a scholar. Was I merely trying to convince them that feminism had something to say that they didn't already know? I suppose that was my ultimate goal: to make them at least consider feminist thinking with an intellectual seriousness and, with that, to realize that the questions feminist theorists ask are some of the same ones they often ask themselves. But faced with a constantly shifting classroom environment, formed from the changing moods and concerns of the students in it, and an even more oscillating sense of my own purpose, I quickly came to lament my decision to teach this course at all.

We got to bell hooks's texts on love at the end of the year. By that point, a part of me wished I had begun the year with her. She had, after all, inspired me to teach the course to begin with and her words were freshest in my mind. But with all my already persistent worries about being "the feminist teacher," I figured it would be altogether too soft to begin the course with something as mushy and curious as love. So I relegated it to the end, figuring we'd spend those last months dissecting the repetitive tropes of romance in film and television and that, by then, they'd finally be comfortable enough to relay all their relationship questions because I'd finally have their trust—and more, by that point I'd have them convinced.

Needless to say, I was only partly correct. It's true, we had probing conversations about gendered dynamics in popular media. We questioned what kinds of human laws govern relational life and diagnosed the coarse effects of lying. We wondered why self-love is often the hardest kind of love to practice. We considered shifting definitions of love throughout Western society, from classical antiquity (love of knowledge) to Freudian psychoanalysis (love as self-preservation) to hooks's more modern conception of love as an action, a verb, a willing dedication. They sometimes thoughtfully shared their woes regarding love and loving. I remember many of the young women sharing thoughts and fears similar to my own: that to love as a woman is so expected that many of them had neglected love or pretended it didn't matter.

It was my favorite part of the year. But I still couldn't shake the feeling that I had perhaps failed them. That I'd only hardened their prejudice *against* feminism. That they had realized that feminism (and I) did not have all the answers. That my rallying around love was merely a last-minute decision because I was out of ideas and out of energy.

But it was during this time that I thought back to a discussion we had around midyear. A new student from my history class had joined second semester. Before I had started teaching there, he had apparently done a critical presentation on the feminist movement, easily pegging himself as the antifeminist student. My conversations with him were often tough for me. I vacillated between being teacherly and being downright terse and unforgiving. Yet I found him to be one of the most thoughtful, kind, and philosophical students with whom I had ever spoken. We quickly developed a habit of getting into discussions at the end of our classes that often took us well into the next period. I realized that perhaps there was something *I* had to learn.

During one class, we were discussing theories about the presumed differences in brain chemistry between men and women. Most students were quick to throw out the oft-cited theory that women's brains were more person-oriented and men's more object-oriented (the empathizing-systemizing theory). Ridiculous, they thought, to make such simple distinctions.

At one point, my new student chimed in, asking whether this theory might explain why men were more intrigued than women by certain, shall we say, sexual objects. Or as he put it, "Does this explain why guys are more into porn and dick pics?" It was said with all the specificity and quiet vulgarity I'd come to love about high school students. The class erupted in laughter. Given that I'd had this group of students for over a semester now, I knew the laughter was directed equally toward his comment and him. As I'm sure even my student would have admitted, the question was definitely funny, in that perfectly inappropriate and yet beautifully timed way. But it was also sincere. *What serious scholar would ask that question? But also, what serious scholar hasn't theorized out of the mundane, the merely anecdotal?* I immediately began worrying about how he might be feeling, remembering full well the pain of a peer's laughter.

"Hey," I interjected, hoping it would come off as appropriately stern yet not overly punitive, "at least he deigned to ask the question." The laughter slowly faded away.

"You're right," another student responded, more quickly than I had anticipated. "It makes me think about the way that porn usually portrays women in passive positions and men in more dominating ones." He was sincere in his tone and calm in his demeanor. Class ended shortly after this exchange, but the tone of the class and the interactions among students palpably changed in those final moments of class. They were all less judgmental and more open.

We never really solved the question that day about how to interpret the differences (or lack thereof) between male and female brains. But I think we came close to establishing a relational environment built not on domination, pressure, and shame but instead on vulnerability, honesty, and trust—and perhaps also a healthy dose of laughter. Thinking back to this moment (and the many others it reminded me of), I wondered whether perhaps I had not entirely failed in my goals for this class. It's just that the real work of feminist thinking came not in the advocacy of a particular position over another but in the practice of listening, of hearing each other as willful, wondering, loving beings.

I'm not sure how far I got in convincing my students about the prejudices against feminism, nor am I sure I was able to persuade them that they themselves were already feminists. What I hoped they would recognize was that they became feminists because they dared to ask the questions. For Ahmed also writes, "To be a feminist is to stay a student" (2017, 11). It is to ask questions, to be firm, to interrupt. It is to then answer the questions by asking new ones—to be gentle yet to still disrupt. Finding myself on the other side of the room in an academic setting, I realized that teaching feminist theory is inherently performative; it cannot be just about surveying a field. It is about practicing feminist pedagogy, for feminism is truly a practice, an undertaking, an asking. As a teacher of feminist theory, I had to remain a student, to continue coming up against what I did not know, to recognize how "bad" of a feminist I truly was.

In spite of all our inciting conversations and shared laughter, it wasn't a perfect course. If I did it again, I'd likely teach it quite differently. Perhaps with a little less naïveté about how high schoolers think and fewer attachments to following my syllabus so strictly. But by the end of the year, I realized my failures were acceptable because though a teacher, I had, as a feminist should, remained a student.

References

Ahmed, Sara. 2017. *Living a Feminist Life*. Durham, NC: Duke University Press

Gay, Roxanne. 2014. *Bad Feminist: Essays*. New York: Harper Perennial.

hooks, bell. 2018. *All about Love: New Visions*. New York: HarperCollins.

Lorde, Audre. 1984. "The Uses of Anger: Women Responding to Racism." In *Sister Outsider: Essays and Speeches*, 124–133. Freedom, CA: Crossing.

Part 4

HEALTH AND MEDICINE

ACTS OF DEFIANCE

The Power of Anger and Sadness
in the Workplace

Rose Al Abosy

A friend working as an analyst at an investment bank in New York once showed me an email thread she was on with some coworkers. She had asked a question, and a coworker of hers had responded by providing a trite definition rather than an answer. She emailed back, "This isn't an exercise in reading comprehension," and restated her question. A simple act of defiance, but I found it revolutionary. I too had experienced people assuming my inferiority and boldly revealing those assumptions by talking down to me. As a queer woman of color, I always perceived undercurrents of misogyny and racism in these situations, but there was no way to be sure. Maybe, given time, I could defend my case, but with the moment fleeting, I never knew how I should respond and, bogged down by uncertainty, often wouldn't respond at all.

At the time, I was working as a research technician in a lab at the Dana-Farber Cancer Institute, a Harvard-affiliated hospital and research center. Bench science is demanding work, conducted in close collaboration with only a handful of people. Each step of an experiment can take hours of precise work, and data collection represents the culmination of diligent labor conducted across weeks or months. I often worked twelve-plus-hour days and came in on weekends; the living systems we studied didn't care what day it was. Planning is paramount and mistakes are costly with regard to both time and money. Producing interpretable data requires exacting standards of yourself and your teammates. This high-pressure environment is, of course, not exempt from the oppression that is built into the larger structure of our world.

My experiences as a researcher were similar in many ways to my friend's experiences as an analyst. The day I read that email thread, I mentioned the story to both a friend of mine from high school and one of my colleagues. The high school friend, who was completing a master's degree at the time, was ecstatic. We both knew exactly how frustrating that moment must have been, and for her to have come up with a response so clear, blunt, and intoxicatingly confident made us both hopeful that we too would figure out a way to do so as our professional careers developed. We tangibly felt the importance of fighting back, for ourselves and for others who looked like us. My colleague, a physician who also found this moment relatable, challenged our interpretation. She asked what that email response actually accomplished. She wondered whether the energy expended biting back was worth the effort, and whether holding on to that anger was healthy in the long run. A woman who had encountered discrimination at work for years longer than my friends and I had met the situation with more hesitation than we did. I was curious as to why that was, and whether there was anything to learn from that difference.

I think about this email thread often, as a case study to ask how I want to respond in the face of subtle microaggressions and overt discrimination. I consider myself a feminist. As I continue to move up the societal rungs of power, I am constantly interrogating myself and my peers what that feminism should look like, and what it purports to accomplish. This process of interrogation, influenced in large part by both my academic studies and my lived experiences, has left me feeling that my rigorous understanding of how power flows through the unjust structures of our world has not actually prepared me to know how to change the flow. Audre Lorde (1984, 110) warned us about the limitations of the master's tools, but despite my best efforts, I find myself trying to combat my own oppression with rudimentary approaches, poorly sharpened sticks whittled on the fly. "Living a feminist life," then, to invoke the title of Sara Ahmed's (2017) book on this subject, has meant observing, listening, learning, and sharing what I've learned with others around me, as we work to optimize our tools and strategies against our oppression.

This process began for me with anger. After graduating college and moving to a new city, I found myself with no support system and scarce tools to build one. As I was still mired in a racist, sexist world, anger was my rallying cry. Shortly after beginning my job in June, someone asked my supervisor whether she had hired a new female employee and then complained that this employee's shorts were "distracting the male graduate students" on our floor. My supervisor told me about this for transparency's sake, and assured me that my shorts were an entirely appropriate length for the workplace. Still, I felt scrutinized. Within the week, word spread around the lab, and a coworker jokingly commented that perhaps that initial comment had been made about another person on our floor. The person he was referring to was a sixteen-year-old girl, still in high school, working to get lab experience for her college applications. I was livid. It was one thing that I had to navigate comments about my body in the workplace, but it was quite another to ask that of a teenager. It was wildly inappropriate to have sexualized her for the sake of a punch line, especially given the power dynamics of the situation.

The next time we were working on an experiment together, I felt it necessary to discuss that comment. Another lab member who overheard the conversation joined in. I relied on language I had used in my gender studies classes, invoking the relationship between age and ability to consent, which turned the conversation into an academic debate. As the initial commenter started putting up more resistance, critiquing how the teen-ager dressed and behaved, I began delivering rebuttals with increasing fury. When he ended the conversation by asking that we agree to disagree, I shut my mouth and went back to work, even more furious at having been silenced.

The whole experience had made me feel powerless, and agreeing to disagree did not assuage the impact of that comment. He, too, was uncomfortable, and we worked in relative silence for the rest of the experiment. Ahmed describes this perfectly when she writes, "Feminists do kill joy in a certain sense: they disturb the very fantasy that happiness can be found in certain places" (2010, 2). That discussion was a powerful reminder that people like me have not historically been in spaces like that and, to this day, often aren't. The very structure of the room was not built to hold me, and pushing against it made me feel like the problem. In the meantime, as similar incidents occurred, how folks around me responded to my anger gave me information on their politics and priorities. Those who stood up for me, or showed solidarity through an offer of emotional labor, were people I forged bonds with. In a very real sense, my anger helped me begin to form a community that I could rely on for care.

Being angry all the time was exhausting. My job was already hard. Unpacking each event with extended conversation was time consuming, distracted me from my work, and made it difficult to collaborate with people on projects. At some point, I could no longer tell whether my goal was educating others about their problematic behavior or working toward making my environment marginally more hospitable. Regardless, I didn't seem to be accomplishing either. Ahmed speaks on this when she comments that "feminist emotions are mediated and opaque; they are sites of struggle, and we must persist in struggling with them" (2010, 4). I felt that my anger was a display of hope that things could be different, but it wasn't clear that it was actually changing my circumstances. One co-worker even told me that my academic work in gender theory had primed me to see and respond to these issues. I was dismissed as merely overreacting. I feel the power of these feminist emotions, but I am still struggling with them.

This is perhaps why my colleague felt so reluctant to agree with the fact that I saw power in my friend's comment about "reading comprehension." She too had experienced this dismissal of her anger and, therefore, had found her anger fruitless to hold on to. However, my friend, even with hindsight, says that she would do nothing differently. She wanted to be listened to. Through her bluntness, she hoped to address the issue, hold people accountable, and get back to the task at hand. We both saw that it wasn't that simple. Jokingly, she referenced a TV show in which a character says, "If you keep screaming your name, it forces the assailant to acknowledge you as a human" (Brock 2014). In the face of dehumanization, anger at least makes you feel heard. I was, and am, stuck in the middle between these two perspectives. It shouldn't be my responsibility to analyze and optimize my behavior to navigate the hurtful ignorance of others, but it is.

With all of this in mind, I started expressing my anger more privately. What was once hope for change slowly mutated into despondency, and I internalized my anger until I couldn't anymore. After one particularly shocking incident in which experiments I had planned and managed for weeks were referred to flippantly as "bitch work," I scheduled a small group meeting with my supervisors. Once they were all in the room, I started to cry. Despite how embarrassing this felt at the time, it also helped solidify my community. People who saw the taxing nature of what I was experiencing could relate and meet me with compassion. It also felt like a step forward. This time, I at least got an apology. No longer did I believe I could singlehandedly solve the problem of oppression in the workplace, but I was motivated to at least change how people treated me.

I changed my strategy. I began to rely on emotions to resolve conflicts, centering the hurt that a comment had caused in order to avoid discussion about whether it was actually offensive. Arguably, this was more productive, as it prevented our workflows from being derailed by debate. However, although I eventually communicated my emotions with words rather than tears, I feared that I would again be easily dismissed. Additionally, there continued to be a profound lack of consequences for any of this hurtful behavior. Ahmed writes that "you can feel a force most directly when you attempt to resist it" (2010, 5). Mounting a resistance made me painfully aware of how often I was being hurt. I was expected to do the work of advocating for myself, and the additional work of healing myself, but it seemed nothing could stop it from happening. If anything, mobilizing my emotions in an attempt to humanize myself to others exhausted me further.

Was I supposed to ignore all of this, try not to be as affected by it as I was? Or was it important to speak out against it and fight back? Was there any way to fight without getting hurt? Relying again on my support network, I found that many of my coworkers had reached a similar inflection point. They had to find ways to be *in* this space without being *of* this space. One spoke on how he had become cold and aloof at work out of self-preservation after experiencing overt racial discrimination. He had decided that the lab wasn't going to be the cornerstone of his community and made the active decision to invest his energy elsewhere. Another coworker echoed this sentiment as she described prioritizing her family because giving to them reenergized her in a way that work could not. They relied on different support networks but had in some ways stopped openly fighting against the racism and sexism they were experiencing firsthand. It was impossible to do so while continuing to survive the exhausting structural demands made of them. On the other hand, my anger and sadness, the same emotions that made me so visible and vulnerable, were how I had gained their support in the first place.

Audre Lorde once said, "My anger has meant pain to me but it has also meant survival, and before I give it up, I'm going to be sure that there is something at least as powerful to replace it on the road to clarity" (1984, 141). Anger and sadness were profound tools I had fashioned in my first attempts to live a feminist life outside college. Indeed, they represented a daily practicing of feminism that in many ways was more radical than the feminism I more comfortably practiced as a student surrounded by a community of like-minded students. I didn't necessarily see that at first. Upon leaving Dana-Farber, I felt overwhelmingly frustrated. I had expended so much emotional energy, so much anger, so much sadness, so much time playing things over in my head to figure out how to improve, with very little direct payoff. My efforts felt wasted, and that sense was compounded with shame for having been disruptive at all. I considered this practicing of feminism inefficient, unproductive, and inadequate; it didn't change my circumstances fast enough, or perhaps at all.

From that frustration, I came to understand that practicing feminism does not operate by those capitalist values. Ahmed claims that "there can be joy in killing joy" (2010, 8), and I see now that there were small joys. I can easily say that people who would otherwise not have been exposed to these ideas are now familiar with them because of me. Coworkers of mine who are women and people of color told me directly that my presence and willingness to talk bluntly about these issues changed the entire culture of the lab and made it a more comfortable place for them to work. I gained practice in dealing with these issues while navigating professionalism, and I am beginning to trust in my readings of these situations, as well as my resiliency. I have a community now that can hold me even when the walls of the room I'm in cannot.

These are the experiences, opinions, and tensions I'm trying to learn from. Anger and sadness are why I survived that workplace. Each person in my support network came with a novel perspective on how they best managed similar issues. I remain mindful that people's identities affect what balance is best for them and how easily they can attain that homeostasis. I also know that this is just what I've seen and heard in the first two years out of college. I try to have compassion for what I've done while thinking about what I would do differently knowing what I know now. I imagine my thoughts on feminism in the workplace will mature as I do.

As I begin medical school, I realize I am still working to find my own balance, one that hopefully includes clearer boundaries and more active self-preservation. I am constantly reminded by my communities that to struggle presents an image of hope to those around me. I need energy reserved as I learn to pick my battles, but more importantly, I think about how Lorde refers to caring for herself as an "act of political warfare" (1988, 104). Oppression is a distraction meant to tear you down. Often, the most profound resistance is prioritizing yourself.

References

Ahmed, Sara. 2010. "Feminist Killjoys (and Other Willful Subjects)." *Scholar and Feminist Online* 8, no. 3 (Summer): 1–8. http://sfonline.barnard.edu/polyphonic/ahmed_01 .htm.

Brock, Tricia, dir. 2014. *Silicon Valley.* Season 1, episode 3, "Articles of Incorporation." Aired April 20, 2014. HBO.

Lorde, Audre. 1984. *Sister Outsider: Essays and Speeches.* Berkeley: Crossing.

——. 1988. *A Burst of Light and Other Essays.* Ithaca, NY: Firebrand.

#MYBIRTHTOO

The Patriarchy of the Modern Obstetric System

Savannah Medley Taylor

At the age of twenty, thirty-eight weeks pregnant, I went to my obstetrician's office for a checkup, thinking everything was fine and that I was still a week out from my due date. Once there, however, I was told to head to the hospital for an induction due to pregnancy-induced hypertension. When I asked whether I had any other options, the answer was no. When I expressed to my nurses that I was in pain, I was told, at one centimeter dilated, "Get an epidural before anything gets worse." At the end of my labor, as I was pushing my daughter, my obstetrician asked me multiple times whether she could perform an episiotomy. I repeatedly said no. Forty-five minutes into pushing, she said, "I think I should do an episiotomy," and she did. My reply was, "I don't even care anymore."

Since then, I have certified as and worked for two years as a doula. The term *doula* is derived from the Greek language, meaning "female servant," and a birth doula is present with birthing people during pregnancy, labor, and the postpartum period. Through my journey as a doula, I have learned that in fact there were other options at each of the moments of my labor. There are alternatives to induction. Pain is normal during labor, and there are many ways to manage it without resorting to an epidural. While I accept responsibility for my decisions, I maintain that the fundamental nature of my labor was rooted in an attitude of convenience for providers, as well as the medicalization of birth. Instead of helping me cope with labor, those in positions of power over an uneducated and naïve young mother sought to manage and corral it. At the end of my birth, I was ecstatic, overcome with love for my daughter. But shortly after, I walked away feeling damaged, as if something had been traumatically taken from me. I realized, after much soul searching, that it was my power.

My daughter's birth inspired me to delve into the realm of birth work, which would later transform my feminism. As a young mother, pregnancy overtook me, confused me, and dismantled me. But through it, birth, motherhood, and the process of finding a new identity taught me an entirely new form of feminism. I viewed and continue to view my birth experience as traumatic. I do not believe that I was given options, or that I gave proper consent. I believe that I was an easy target for the powers that be of obstetric care, and from this experience, I have found a passion and voice for revolutionary birth. I now view birth as an inherently feminist act. In its true form, undisturbed and left to its own devices, birth laughs in the face of the systems of power that try to make female, nonbinary, and trans-identifying bodies small and quiet. Birth is true power.

Becoming a mother has dramatically expanded my idea of what it means to be a feminist. Before my daughter, I was anxious that motherhood would relegate me to a Cinderella style of living. But through my personal experience and my work as a doula, I have seen the truly feminist nature of childbearing and childrearing, and the ways birth and the intimate events of caretaking break down binaries at every corner. Birth work as feminism dismantles the dichotomies of public and private, the personal and the political, and the individual and collective. It is my hope, as a doula, to bring feminism to the forefront of conversations surrounding birth.

The obstetric model of maternity care, which perceives pregnancy, birth, and the postpartum period as medical events requiring observation, management, and intervention, as well as requiring the birth to occur in a hospital facility, creates and propels the prevailing mindsets surrounding birth in American society. While obstetric care provides critical management for specialty cases of pregnancy that require heightened observation, it is fundamentally rooted in patriarchal normativity—a system of personal and political governance that sees nonmale people as inherently less than, creating a value base that normalizes the objectification and oppression of the nonmale person. Author Jennifer Block writes in her book *Pushed: The Painful Truth about Childbirth and Modern Maternity Care*, "What they [pregnant people] don't understand is that obstetricians are surgeons, and they know pathology, but they really suck at wellness. They are trained to sew up a tear, but not to prevent one" (2008, 176). Obstetrics views birth as a weakness, a medical event to be managed. This is one example of patriarchal normativity, showing how it creates a toxic environment in birth culture, where birthing people submit to their physicians and providers in the name of safety and necessity. This rhetoric, as noted by Block, is coercive, as it chips away at the power held by birthing people during pregnancy and childbirth, all under the guise of safety. Obstetrics mistrusts birthing people, instead making itself the pinnacle of power and authority on the childbirth experience, claiming to "know best"—to know even more than the person to whom birth truly belongs.

Since the Me Too era, the exposition of sexual assault and corrupt power has been at the forefront of social conversation. However, while Me Too was used by celebrities and common people alike, it did not attend to birthing bodies, who experience oppression at the hands of those who are entrusted to protect them during one of the most vulnerable times of their lives. Consent—central to the Me Too movement—is also key to understanding birthing. Providers often fail to properly inform birthing people of their rights, options, and risks when it comes to interventions, both necessary and unnecessary, during the birthing process. Consent, as I describe it in terms of my own experience, is rarely secured.

Furthermore, the concept of informed consent, while valuable insofar as it provides the birthing person with information regarding the risks and benefits of procedures, is still rooted in the power dynamics of the patriarchy. Providers often present informed consent as a statement, as in, "I am going to do X. Are you okay with that?" This is obstetric assault, plain and simple. It does not fully provide an analysis of the pros and cons of a procedure, such as a cervical exam, and it assumes that the birthing person will submit to the procedure, either presently or in the future. There is no real option to say no. Even when interventions seem like a choice, the choice is often an ultimatum, assumption, or flat-out lie.

The idea that obstetric care is the ultimate authority on decisions about the birthing body, as opposed to the birthing body being the authority on determining what care is acceptable for pregnancy and birth, showcases that the behavioral methodology of obstetrics is a product of rape culture. Therefore, I choose the title "#MyBirthToo" in order to expose the realities of obstetric violence. This term is my own, but I am not the first to speak to the necessity of a Me Too–style movement. In fact, many of my birthing siblings have spoken truth to power, and the movement of criticizing the obstetric model of care is not new by any means. However, I have chosen the term #MyBirthToo to describe the mass instances of violence against birthing people.

We live in a society that functions in dichotomies: feminine versus masculine, public versus private, personal versus political, black versus white. These dichotomies help us make sense of things in the world by placing their essences in easily understood categories. These categories, then, define our understanding of what it means to be human. They define our very being. However, these dichotomies also work to create power systems that suppress the impact of certain types of labor and oppress the humanity of certain types of individuals. Birth and birth work are political acts that have often been subverted into categories with the intent of minimizing their revolutionary impact. Adrienne Rich writes in *Of Woman*

Born: Motherhood as Experience and Institution, "Probably there is nothing in human nature more resonant with charges than the flow of energy between two biologically alike bodies, one of which has lain in amniotic bliss inside the other, one of which has labored to give birth to the other" (1986, 225).

The essays in the present book speak to the conditions that shape a different kind of labor—that of the workplace. Yet I argue that the work that occurs during pregnancy, inside a birthing person, is the foundational work of society building. Within the pregnant body, the future of the human essence is built. Birthing people break their own bodies, deconstruct their own selves, to give rise to the future of revolution. What once was a human being becomes a superhuman being, a keeper of the secrets of the universe that stem from sexual connection and orgasmic creation. To be filled with an unborn life is to be filled with the same dust of stars that makes up the cosmos. However, when pregnancy is in question in the liberal capitalist society, it is rendered the work of the private, the person, the woman, the body, but not the work of the public, the political, the man, and the mind. These are false dichotomies. The truth is that pregnancy and birth are actions that break down all barriers of dichotomies, revolutionizing our understanding not only of what it means to be a political subject in society but also what it means to be human.

The act of birth also creates a future political subject—someone who will be molded by their entrance into society, the way we were all molded by our entrance into the world. For this very reason, it is impossible to separate birth from the political sphere. The unfolding of a birth is revolution in action. The birthing body, covered in blood, spilt of fluid, reaches a point where it is as close to life as it is to death, and with each moment, it comes closer to changing the foundational makeup of the universe and the future of political society. It is no surprise that childbirth is part of the foundation of the patriarchy. Rich writes, "There is nothing revolutionary whatsoever about the control of women's bodies by men. The woman's body is the terrain on which patriarchy is erected" (1986, 55). It is no different with birth. In deploying fear and the paternalistic "we know best" rhetoric, the obstetric model of care has become an arm of the patriarchal machine, claiming the biology of birth to be a weakness, as opposed to the beautiful strength it is. At this point, one might note the fact that the majority of obstetricians are, in fact, women; however, they still practice within the patriarchal system, regardless of how they identify.

Furthermore, birth creates parents. Parenting consists of more than the mundane acts of caretaking mixed with love (even though that alone is fairly remarkable). Parenting is a political act. Parents create normative assumptions about reality and transfer this understanding to their children. Understandings of race, gender, the environment, and all other political subjects are formed at home and then further realized and developed at various sites outside the home. The domestic and the public, while distinct, depend on each other; the "public" cannot live without the births that occur in "private."

Our modern medical system attempts to silence the roars of birth, clean up the blood of the vagina, dull the sensations of oxytocin with drugs, and surgically moderate physiological birth. Birthing bodies are compelled to be as quiet and small as possible. In birth, the birthing person is placed in the factory of a birthing machine that aims to hasten the normal functions of the body by synthesizing hormones and claiming the superiority of their efficiency.

For after all, modernity fetishizes efficiency above all else. The birth is to be quiet, with a controlled ejection of the neonate. The birthing person may not push on their own terms but must wait for the all-knowing gatekeeper of birth to arrive to give instructions on when to push. For after all, trust in female, trans, and nonbinary bodies has never been fully recognized by patriarchal society. Pain is something to be feared and dulled, and the birthing person is confined to a bed barely large enough to fit a body swollen with the life of pregnancy. For after all, our liberal society has never taken too kindly to rebelling in spaces not deemed acceptable. If the birthing person is a person of color, the chance of death is higher in the United States than in any other "developed" country. For after all, hatred of Black bodies is systemic in US history. Obstetric assault is a symptom of a larger illness, the illness of the patriarchy. Simply by needing to "manage" labor, "control" pain, and "monitor" birthing people, instead of submitting to their authority, trusting their intuition, and following their cues on how to birth, we are escalating a system of deep violence against birthing people.

Unfortunately, instances of coercion at the hands of the obstetric system are severely underreported. In part, these instances go unreported due to a lack of awareness of what constitutes obstetric violence. Many of these assaults are not viewed as such—even by the birthing people themselves—because they are so normalized as part of routine care by the obstetric system that they are seen as beneficial to the birthing person, instead of what they truly are: deep and systemic violent acts. However, while there is a lack of quantifiable data surrounding instances of obstetric sexual assault, qualitative evidence does exist, within the stories of birthing people, me included. As no definition of obstetric violence exists in American statute, we must rely on what we know to be true about attitudes surrounding birthing bodies in American culture. We must listen to these stories from survivors and learn from them, adjusting our standards of care and our options provided to childbearing people.

There are birth workers who exist outside the umbrella of obstetric care. They ride the wave between the medical aspects of childbirth and the realm of childbirth that encompasses the mental, emotional, and spiritual components of humanity beyond the physical experience. They go by many names: doulas, birth keepers, birth attendants, childbirth educators, and even midwives (licensed and unlicensed). These workers, and I am one of them, care for birthing, breast- or chestfeeding, and postpartum bodies in intimate ways, often in a parallel relationship to medical providers.

The work of a doula is political and revolutionary. We are agents of change and connectivity in the birth world. Immediately after my daughter's birth, I became deeply on fire for the power of childbirth, and this fire has turned into an uncontrollable blaze. As a doula, I am present with birthing people from pregnancy to postpartum. I am not responsible for the medical parts of birth, such as blood pressure or fetal heart rate. But I do hold in my hand the secrets and sacred aspects of bringing new life into the universe. With each birth, I cherish the elements of humanity beyond the physical aspects of one's body and hold them carefully within my heart, providing deep reverence for the power of childbirth. Doulas as figures in maternity care statistically improve birth outcomes in many ways, such as by reducing reliance on pain medication, shortening labor times, decreasing interventions, and decreasing instances of cesarean rates; in short, the birthing person has a much more positive birthing experience. Any instance of holding space for birth in its true form—regardless of medical intervention—rebels against the notion that birth does not truly belong to the birthing person but instead to medicine. Every act of true doula work undoes oppression and resists the norms of patriarchy within obstetrics.

A 2014 survey of doulas, childbirth educators, and labor and delivery nurses found that 90 percent of them had witnessed a care provider violate some type of consent during the childbirth process. This survey found that "respondents in all three maternity support roles indicated that it was relatively common for care providers to engage in procedures without giving a woman a choice or time to consider it. Overall, 61.9% indicated that they had witnessed this occasionally or often, compared to 35.2% that saw this occur rarely or never. Nurses were more likely to witness this often (31.8%) than doulas (25.3%) or childbirth educators (28.2%)" (Roth et al. 2014, 38).

Those who work with birthing people have a chance to speak truth to power. In a 2018 Vice article titled "There Is a Hidden Epidemic of Doctors Abusing Women in Labor, Doulas Say," the author interviews a birth doula, Mychal Balazs, who explains the nature of obstetric violence perpetrated against birthing people. This piece describes why Balazs feels that lack of consent in particular is overlooked as a maternity care issue and is one of the primary reasons for birth-related trauma. Balazs is most disturbed by a practice called "manual tearing," which she says she sees often in Los Angeles hospitals. In contrast to an episiotomy, which involves a surgical cut to enlarge the vaginal opening, this practice involves care providers stretching and tearing a patient's perineum with their hands, even when the patient has not received an epidural, causing intense pain (Tucker 2018).

As a certified doula, I have witnessed my own share of obstetric violence. I walk a fine line where I must protect the autonomy of the birthing person whom I am hired to serve but also must stay inside a "scope of practice," allowing providers to perform medical procedures when they and my client deem necessary. I cannot make medical decisions for my clients or provide them with medical advice because I do not have the knowledge or training, nor do I want to be a medical provider. However, by virtue of my training, my humanity, and my very lack of authority held over others in the birth room, I am qualified to identify abuse.

In my years attending births, I have witnessed birthing people experience the penultimate level of power, with providers primarily acting hands-off, allowing birth to be the natural and normal event that it typically is. I have also witnessed medical intervention in serious situations, where I leave the hospital grateful for modern medicine. However, what I witness often in the cracks between these scenarios is violence perpetrated by actors within the obstetric system.

In many births, I have heard providers state, "Hold her down. She is pushing wrong"; "I am ready to deliver your baby. Your options are cesarean or a vacuum assisted delivery"; "It is time for an epidural." I have seen providers insert their hands into a vagina, touch breasts, and perform procedures without giving as much as a warning to their patient. I have seen doctors rupture a birthing person's amniotic sac because labor is not moving "fast enough" and fail to receive any type of consent. I have had to ask, "Are you okay with that touch right now?" I have heard providers say, "I am going to check you. Okay . . . just my fingers," and then proceed to insert their hands into a vagina and perform an aggressive cervical exam.

These invasive practices are more often done, in my experience, when the birthing person has consented to an epidural. Once the birthing body is contained in a way that makes labor quieter and more manageable, the obstetric system often views the body as one whose consent is not required. By contrast, when the birthing person is engaging in an unmedicated birth or demands the providers be hands-off, which often requires birthing people to be advocates during labor, doing battle for their desires, labor is less often interrupted and abused. Any type of coercion, manipulation, failure to inform, pressure, or physical touch during childbirth that is not specifically asked for is a form of violence. It is a means of control and manipulation, done in order to enhance the comfort of providers who are unsure of the abilities of the birthing body to naturally birth a child.

The United States spends more money on interventions during pregnancy than any other country in the world, according to the book *Policy and Politics in Nursing and Health Care* by Diana Mason, Judith Leavitt, and Mary Chaffee (2012), but we continue to have the poorest outcomes of maternal mortality among any developed country. The insidious nature of the patriarchy within pregnancy care directly causes dehumanization of birthing bodies and fails to value the lives of birthing people. If you have nonwhite skin and you give birth in America, you are three times more likely to die during childbirth. Furthermore, all people are more likely to die in childbirth today than they were two decades ago, according to the *Harvard Health Blog*'s post "A Soaring Maternal Mortality Rate: What Does It Mean for You?" (Shah 2018).

I contend that the increase in maternal mortality rates and the abuse perpetrated during births are correlated; they are intertwined factors in a violent practice of stripping birthing bodies of their authority and autonomy during birth and the postpartum period. The patriarchy of obstetric care has deep side effects that are even more disparate for people of color and other marginalized groups. In order to fix this broken system, we must reconceptualize our view of birth and parenting as the revolutionary acts that they truly are.

References

Block, Jennifer. 2008. *Pushed: The Painful Truth about Childbirth and Modern Maternity Care*. Cambridge, MA: Da Capo, 2008.

Mason, Diana J., Judith K. Leavitt, and Mary W. Chaffee. 2012. *Policy and Politics in Nursing and Health Care*. 6th ed. Burlington, MA: Jones and Bartlett.

Rich, Adrienne. 1986. *Of Woman Born: Motherhood as Experience and Institution*. New York: W. W. Norton.

Roth, Louise Marie, Nicole Heidbreder, Megan M. Henley, Marla Marek, Miriam Naiman-Sessions, Jennifer Torres, and Christine H. Morton. 2014. *Maternity Support Survey: A Report on the Cross-National Survey of Doulas, Childbirth Educators and Labor and Delivery Nurses in the United States and Canada*. https://maternitysurvey.files .wordpress.com/2014/07/mss-report-5-1-14-final.pdf.

Shah, Neel. 2018. "A Soaring Maternal Mortality Rate: What Does It Mean for You?" *Harvard Health Blog*, October 16, 2018. https://www.health.harvard.edu/blog/a -soaring-maternal-mortality-rate-what-does-it-mean-for-you-2018101614914.

Tucker, Sarah Yahr. 2018. "There Is a Hidden Epidemic of Doctors Abusing Women in Labor, Doulas Say." Vice, May 8, 2018. https://www.vice.com/en/article/evqew7 /obstetric-violence-doulas-abuse-giving-birth.

NAVIGATING FEMINISM AND VULNERABILITY IN THE MEDICAL WORKPLACE

Lily Pierce

My first psychiatry intake interview as a medical intern was in a tiny conference room at the end of the hall inside a Veterans Administration hospital unit. The walls were lined with chairs, and the patient sat on one side of the room while I sat across from him on the other. The attending psychiatrist was at a desk by the single window, which I was later to discover was consistently obstructed by blinds, emphasizing that being present in this space separated you from the natural light of the world outside. I had reviewed the outline of the intake interview before coming in that day, but I quickly discovered that knowing the topics to cover in a conversation did not make it easier to ask sensitive questions.

It was only a few days into my psychiatry rotation, a part of my medical school training, and my job was to explore this new patient's personal background experiences as a means of evaluating how best to help him during his time in the hospital. After I finished the interview, the attending psychiatrist sympathetically said to me, "It's hard not to be good at something." He had very quickly picked up on how uncomfortable I felt trying to navigate asking someone whether they had ever considered taking their own life or to tell me the details of how their loved one had passed away. However, mixed into that uneasiness about asking sensitive questions was frustration about the lack of clarity surrounding my role as a medical student and young woman in this new environment. I felt quite removed from these patients whom I was trying so hard to connect with, and being another gender and age felt like an automatic disadvantage.

Three weeks of my intensive psychiatry rotation were at a VA hospital in Chicago that mainly treats older male patients, and I was the sole medical student in a small subsection of the hospital. The attending psychiatrist and I worked with patients transitioning to more stable homes and jobs while battling substance use disorders, mood disorders, and PTSD. I was consistently the only woman in a group of men quite different from me—I am white, college educated, and working on a professional degree; I have stable romantic and family relationships, and I have no substance addictions to speak of. Despite these strengths, I found myself preoccupied with figuring out how to be authoritative yet approachable, helpful but not overly friendly, and knowledgeable but not alienating, to the point where my approach to patient encounters was inconsistent and unsure.

Even now, after I have moved on from this rotation, I find I am still constantly trying to figure out what it means to be a feminist in this unique workplace. When I first stepped into this medical rotation in psychiatry, I naïvely thought that gender should not affect the care that I provide and that if I could just figure out how to remove it from the relationship, I would be a more effective medical student and therefore physician. I thought it was most effective to make its influence, in that respect, disappear. And as I shall explore in this essay, drawing on Judith Butler's essay on violence, mourning, and loss, I have found that sometimes it is in fact possible to at least partially and momentarily disregard gender, focusing instead on a common experience of loss.

At other times, however, gender is very operative. As I continue to find myself in new situations in the medical field, I am reminded of how public perceptions of gender can be very influential, both for patients and for health-care providers. Historically, for example, health care has relied on a paternalistic model in which doctors do not respect patients' wishes. However, that is gradually changing as health-care moves to a more patient-centered practice, thanks in part to feminism. For example, during my most recent rotation on pediatrics, on our morning rounds, we would stop in front of each room to talk about any overnight events and plans for the patient that day. My attending psychiatrist would always lean into the patient's room and ask the patient or patient's parent if they were interested in joining us for our discussion. She would include them by making sure they heard the full presentation on the patient and followed up to make sure that they understood what was going on. Even before I stepped into the hospital for clerkships, our classroom sessions continually emphasized instances in which certain patient encounters, such as choosing contraceptive methods, or more complex situations, such as cancer treatment or surgery options, should be shaped around what the patient prefers and is able to work with in his or her day-to-day life.

This example could be seen as one in which women are able to find power in claiming the gendered characteristics that have historically been associated with us, such as caring and empathy. In other words, these traits are no longer associated with a lack of power but rather with more mainstream and even valorized medical practices. That, in turn, is leading to occasions in which women in medicine are able to assert ourselves without being seen as "overbearing" or "unrightfully taking over the situation." Ever so slowly, some of the gendered binaries that have long characterized medicine are breaking down.

Vulnerability: When Gender Takes a Backseat

The VA rotation has shown me the significance of embracing my own vulnerability in professional settings, something that I do not pretend to have mastered yet. By stepping into the role of prospective health-care provider, I originally felt that my job was both to show a lack of vulnerability and to express how capable I was because, as a woman, not only did I think I needed to understand a veteran patient's violent experiences and hardships in the community and military, but I felt that I had to compensate for not embodying the gender that traditionally took on these obligations in the first place. What I have discovered, however, is that sometimes gender takes a backseat in patient interaction, especially when it comes to connection through grief and loss.

Butler's recent work on vulnerability has given me a way to think through this common experience of vulnerability. In her essay "Violence, Mourning, and Politics" (2004), she makes the point that public grieving can be selective and personal. Whom do we choose to grieve and why? What does public mourning say about the person grieving and the person being grieved? Though grief can be intimate and solitary, Butler also remarks on the community that can be formed in sharing loss. At the VA hospital, I saw the potential in this coming together in a somewhat public place around the common experience of loss. Some of these veterans have had unique and violent experiences, but their recoveries have brought them together in the hospital. They have been physically and emotionally close to the dehumanization that can occur when people are killed in times of war. They have experienced how dehumanization can be a defense mechanism when coping with violence and loss in the name of patriotism.

However, Butler also concentrates on the lack of public acknowledgment of the deaths of people who are not from the United States or who do not fit the traditional gender or sexuality mold and therefore find themselves on the wrong side of a war or other kinds of violence. She says, "We have to ask about the conditions under which a grievable life is established and maintained, and through what logic of exclusion, what practice of effacement and denominalization" (2004, 38). Whose lives are considered worthy of public mourning, and what does this say about our personal and publicly held conceptions of life? Why should or shouldn't gender and sexuality influence that?

Butler also discusses the relationality of grief and discrimination in the context of vulnerability and intimacy and with the understanding that although some experiences are not exactly the same, they can still be connected through the common feelings that shape something such as loss. My experiences with this in the hospital were not about gender's influence or power; rather, they were about connection and openness. While I sometimes couldn't empathize with the specifics of a patient's life story, the themes of losing a loved one or feelings of failure were not so far away that I couldn't reach into my own experiences for empathy. What may have begun as an uncomfortable encounter at the beginning of my rotation evolved into a sense of personal connection with my patients as time went by. In turn, that personal connection allowed me to feel some measure of authority in responding to their needs, replacing my earlier insecurities that I was too different from my patients to truly understand. However, this was not a seamless transition, and I spent a lot of time reviewing the patients' charts and trying to connect with them during casual conversation in order to learn about what was going on in their lives.

During this short rotation, I witnessed a variety of reactions and coping mechanisms used by the patients in their attempts to deal with loss. This loss was often not just about a loved one but also about a loss of personal identity, of who this patient once was or who he had hoped to become. It was during these times that my own predisposition toward gender roles in social interactions was turned on its head. These older male veterans were so free in expressing their emotions to me and my attending psychiatrist, and I was startled by the sense of confidence and openness they felt in our presence. They spoke candidly about very personal and difficult experiences and did not shy away from the tears or visible uneasiness that came with them. The first time a patient got teary was when he recounted during a session with us the details of a personal assault that he had experienced in the military. I originally thought I would be uncomfortable with patients stepping out of bounds of the traditional gender roles, but instead I saw a strength in his ability to stay in touch with difficult emotions. I personally find it hard to open up about difficult times to people I don't know well, even those with the best of intentions. Yet this patient was showing his deepest vulnerabilities because he wanted to move forward from the trials and tribulations that led him to this psychiatric unit.

In her essay, Butler explains, "When one loses, one is also faced with something enigmatic: something is hiding in the loss, something is lost within the recesses of loss" (2004, 21–22). Though many of these patients were genuine during our conversations about their struggles, I slowly came to realize that some also had long-standing losses and confounding personality and substance abuse disorders that suggested an engrained personal loss that forever changed them. These men are veterans, and some of them have suffered physical and sexual trauma in the military that was originally dealt with by using drugs or relying on unhealthy relationships until that was all they knew as a means of support. Sometimes pride or narcissism gets in the way of recovering from such a deep loss; other times the patients may not even be interested in treating that loss and instead are looking for ways to save money and feed their addictions. This eye-opening realization in the context of my relatively sheltered life was another aspect of these patients' situations that was hard to process and know how to respond to. I struggled with the recognition that not every patient actually wanted help.

Gender as Cultural Norm

This rotation has helped me gain perspective on aspects of society that influence health care in ways that I hadn't considered before. One of the reasons why I chose to study gender in college is that I am fascinated by how intertwined gender and sexuality are in so many aspects of society. They infiltrate public perceptions of people, job opportunities, behavioral and coping mechanisms, and even brief interactions with strangers. I had been interested in pursuing a career in medicine early, and I was able to personalize my minor so as to integrate science and biology into my courses. The classes that I enjoyed the most during my undergraduate career were my gender studies courses—especially two, the Politics of Reproduction and the Biology of Gender—where my interests could more transparently intersect. Now I find myself enjoying the challenge of building on that educational foundation and discovering how feminism can play a role in medical specialties that are not traditionally considered to be related to gender, such as the psychiatry work I was involved in at the VA hospital.

Even though gender could seem almost irrelevant at times throughout my rotation, there were other moments when it was very much front and center in patient encounters. This was especially the case in group settings where gender was repeatedly acknowledged. During these sessions with groups of patients, my outward appearance was what patients were taking in, and it felt like the driving force in their developing impression of me. In the same essay in which she posits vulnerability as a common human condition, Butler also attends to the ongoing reproduction of gendered norms that get in the way of this common vulnerability. For example, sitting among a group of men for a session, I felt vulnerable and exposed because of my professional dress and feminine style choices. "At the most intimate levels, we are social . . . ," Butler says, "constituted in the cultural norms that precede and exceed us, given over to a set of cultural norms and a field of power that condition us fundamentally" (2004, 45). I present myself to the patients both in a group setting and individually, and they present themselves to me based on their impressions of my public persona. But what is interesting to me is that Butler points out that I cannot fully know myself or completely comprehend my perceived differences because a part of me is made up of compiled interpretations of the patients I interact with and vice versa for the patients as they openly struggle with their grief and addictions. I can only attempt to manage my understanding of my own social persona, and this management becomes most possible when my gender stands out to me as both an obstruction to connection and an opportunity to present myself as a strong and self-assured woman.

I would attend the unit's community meetings and behavioral therapy sessions multiple times a week. These sessions were helpful for the patients and, despite my uneasiness about managing my gendered presence, they were also enlightening for me. However, at least once a week, patients would be in the middle of telling a story or making a comment and would suddenly pause to apologize for using a swear word or some other sort of foul language. I was continually baffled. I couldn't care less if they swore, and it frustrated me that my presence as a young woman was enough to suggest that I would be offended. "We have a *lady here*!" a facilitator once exclaimed when one of the patients actually did use a curse word. These comments told me that they were acting differently in my presence, when I longed to blend in and simply watch the natural progression of these meetings. I would always brush these acknowledgments off as if they didn't affect me, and perhaps with time I would have been able to manage them in a way that didn't automatically set up that expectation. But as a new medical student in a new environment, I knew I already had many perceived differences to overcome and no reputation but the one they could put together from their first impression of me.

Toward the end of my time in this subsection of the hospital, I started to feel more comfortable in my role as a medical student, and with that, how my gender shaped my interactions as well as how to sometimes transcend gender. Instead of trying to compensate for a difference, I let it be present freely in one-on-one interviews in which I led the conversation by trying to guide their impression of me. I felt that patients followed my lead by interacting with me as a person instead of making assumptions based on my appearance. The reality is that people do not fall into a certain category of public grieving or decision-making based on their gender; instead, these reactions are a complex mixture of experiences, particular to each individual even as they are shaped by larger conditions. Coming to terms with this reality has been difficult in practice, as I still catch myself quickly categorizing based on outward appearances or actions. I feel fortunate to be able to acknowledge and actively try to move past this for myself and for others.

Reference

Butler, Judith. 2004. "Violence, Mourning, and Politics." In *Precarious Life: The Powers of Violence and Loss*, 19–49. New York: Verso.

Part 5
MEDIA

WHERE ARE THE QUEER POLITICS?

#MeToo, Robin Wright, and Celebrity PR Work

Samuel Naimi

On October 15, 2017, actress Alyssa Milano prompted a nationwide grappling with sexual harassment and assault with a single tweet: "If all the women who have been sexually harassed or assaulted wrote 'Me too' as a status, we might give people a sense of the magnitude of the problem." Over the course of twenty-four hours, Facebook confirmed that the hashtag #MeToo had been reposted on its platform by over 4.7 million individuals around the world (Khomami 2017). Even more, CBS News (2017) reported that more than 45 percent of US citizens are friends with someone who posted a message on social media including the phrase "me too." During this alarming yet critically expository moment in feminist history, the contentious issues of sexual harassment and sexual assault gained more central standing in mainstream discourse as survivors publicly came forward about their experiences with sexual violence. These distressing stories served to confirm that the United States has been, and very much still is, afflicted by an epidemic, one that harms women and queer people at a systemic level. In fact, Milano did not coin the phrase or start the movement; it began a decade earlier, in 2007, when activist Tarana Burke founded a movement called MeToo to raise awareness about sexual violence.[1]

Within weeks of Milano's tweet, men, too, began to come forward about their experiences with sexual assault and sexual harassment. A particular story from a high-profile queer man that shook the public to its core emerged fourteen days after Milano initiated her call to arms. On October 29, 2017, *Rent* actor Anthony Rapp, vis-à-vis a BuzzFeed News exposé, publicly shared the allegation that Kevin Spacey of *House of Cards* attempted to assault him at a private party when Rapp was only fourteen years old (Vary 2017). Although Rapp had tangentially shared this information in a 2001 Q&A with the *Advocate* (*Advocate* Staff 2001), Spacey's name was redacted during publication and the story buried. In response to Rapp's claims the second time around, though, Spacey took to Twitter, not to apologize for his inappropriate behavior but rather to unexpectedly come out as queer: "I have loved and had romantic encounters with men throughout my life, and I choose now to live as a gay man. I want to deal with this honestly and openly and that starts with examining my own behavior" (2017).

Spacey's handling of his purported sexual misconduct proved highly problematic for several reasons: not only did he fallaciously position queerness as a sexual foible that one may appropriate whenever he or she chooses, but he also trivialized the lived experiences of survivors, in this instance the trauma he inflicted on teenage Rapp. Actor Zachary Quinto shined light on these nuances of Spacey's coming out the day after BuzzFeed News disseminated Rapp's story: "It is deeply sad and troubling that this is how Kevin Spacey has chosen to come out. not by standing up as a point of pride—in the light of his many awards and accomplishments—thus inspiring tens of thousands of struggling LGBTQ kids around the world. but as a calculated manipulation to deflect attention from the very serious accusation that he attempted to molest one" (2017). As Quinto notes in his critique, Spacey unbecomingly redirected the spotlight of this scandal to focus on his sexual orientation instead of directly addressing the more important issue at hand: sexual assault.

While Quinto's response to these circumstances was empathetic toward survivors and rightfully critical of Spacey's coming-out rhetoric, his tweet, as well as a majority of celebrity responses to this scandal, missed a key opportunity during Me Too to make known the intersection of sexual violence with the queer community. More specifically, many celebrities missed the chance to establish a separate facet within Me Too that distinctly focused on LGBTQ+ issues. During this never-before-seen conjuncture of sexual assault awareness, queer identity, and celebrity status, those with cultural influence failed to extricate queerness from the shadows of heteronormativity. What would have behooved celebrities to elucidate, in addition, is the fact that queer desires—and attacks on these desires—are just as legitimate and complex as the desires of cisgender and heterosexual people. By only addressing the tip of the iceberg, Quinto and other celebrities indirectly suggested that queerness did not merit the same critical attention as did sexual violence, despite both subjects having played substantive roles in Rapp's story. As with the omission of Spacey's name from the *Advocate* story, queerness once again became secondary to more socially recognized topics during the explosion of Me Too. This problematic relegation of queerness during a rather progressive period in feminist history was one that troubled me as the effects of Rapp's allegations slowly unfolded within the entertainment industry.

At the incipiency of the Me Too movement, I was working as an executive assistant at a celebrity public relations firm located in the heart of Los Angeles. I had recently graduated from Cornell University as a Feminist, Gender, and Sexuality Studies (FGSS) Program major, a degree that afforded me a critical eye toward deconstructing social norms and understanding how popular culture is deeply intertwined with our everyday ideological beliefs. As a recent graduate new to entertainment, I eagerly worked under the auspices of two executive publicists with various clients throughout the film and television industry. For over a year, I liaised between my firm and its clients for red-carpet events, press requests, and anything and everything pertaining to these personae's public appearances. The most engaging, and also most frustrating, experience I had with a client occurred with an actress also from *House of Cards*: Robin Wright, known on-screen as Frances Underwood's indomitable wife, Claire Underwood.

As I will delineate throughout this chapter, working with Wright during Spacey's Me Too episode sparked for me an ethical dilemma. Wright's overall handling of her former costar's accusations of sexual assault contrasted with the feminist foundation I had gained throughout my time as an FGSS major. At the same time, the larger structures involved with celebrity status placed Wright at several disconcerting impasses that hindered her ability, and my ability, to change the cultural narrative regarding Spacey, Me Too, and queerness. This painful incapacity to use fame for positive change, let alone constructive dialogue, showed me the flaws ingrained within the political landscape that constitutes celebrity PR. Along these lines, Wright's lackluster response to her coworker's scandal, as well as her lack of support for the queer community within her response, problematized my belief in the subversive power of popular culture.

My identities as a queer (liberationist) and an intersectional feminist ignited within me a critical discomfort while I worked as a public relations executive assistant. This discomfort, albeit arduous, was radically transformative. I had believed as an undergraduate student with little experience in the workforce that my own values would never be compromised in an office setting. My gender studies degree had guided me along the path of social awareness and feminist inclusivity, to the point that I had developed a deep confidence in my ability to navigate the professional world in an ethically sound manner. This confidence, however, did not mesh well with my work experiences under Wright and her publicist. Even more, my academic expertise in media studies enabled me to critique but not to change the hegemonic structures within celebrity PR that encouraged Wright's prolonged silence.

A brief analysis of Wright's public persona before Rapp and Spacey's Me Too episode will contextualize my exploration of her problematic politics while I served as her publicist's assistant. As costar to Spacey in *House of Cards*, Wright earned $80,000 less than Spacey per episode for the show's first three seasons (*Variety* Staff 2016). Upon discovering the discrepancy between the two stars' salaries, Wright, a politically active feminist, demanded from Netflix that her salary be commensurate with Spacey's and took to the media to publicize the gender pay gap. As she detailed in an interview with the Rockefeller Foundation (Konerman 2016), Wright had threatened to go public regarding this fiscal discrepancy; thus, Netflix quickly adjusted her salary and Wright began earning the same as her male costar. Following the publication of this interview, the news of Wright's win on the *House of Cards* set spread through the media like wildfire and ignited a widespread discussion concerning equal pay between men and women in Hollywood.

In addition to her fight for equal pay, Wright's charitable pajama line exemplifies her public feminist persona. In 2014, she launched Pour Les Femmes, a socially conscious sleepwear line whose profits assist women living in the Democratic Republic of the Congo. Wright explained to *Vogue* that after learning about the atrocities faced by women in this country, specifically the sexual violence inflicted on them during and after their civil war, she was in utter shock: "I was just gobsmacked" (Newbold 2018). She recounted that after meeting with victims of rape in the Congo and witnessing their everyday tribulations, she felt it was her obligation as a celebrity to share these women's stories: "[These women] said: 'We need you to be our voice.' . . . Now, I use it" (Newbold 2018). I acknowledge the problematic invocation of "voice" here, but that is beyond the scope of this essay. What I wish to emphasize is that in this situation, Wright used her celebrity influence to highlight a social injustice abroad that she deemed unconscionable.

This ability to confidently address social ills, however, was much less apparent when Rapp and the LGBTQ+ community required support in Wright's home country during the proliferation of Me Too. As I will recount, the powerful structures and allegiances associated with celebrity status, ones that likely discouraged Wright from using her voice as a political tool, undermined her feminist politics. Working so closely to this event and seeing the potential for change go unfulfilled made me critically reevaluate my ability to effect change at this site.

As assistant to Wright's publicist in late 2017, I gleaned early on during the Spacey scandal that Wright and her public relations team had decided to evade contact with the media. For one, the actress never publicly addressed her knowledge of or her opinions on the situation at hand, even though she had received many requests for interviews since the day Rapp published his allegations. In fact, it took Wright eight months to break her silence in an exclusive interview with

Today (2018). In this sense, the PR strategy to respond to Spacey's unbecoming behavior—behavior that had allegedly been transpiring for decades (Melas 2017)—raised many questions about which I can only speculate: What were the unspoken rules at play within the entertainment industry that catalyzed, or perhaps pressured, Wright to remain silent? What does the discrepancy between Wright's outspokenness abroad and her silence in the United States signify about the current iteration of the feminist movement in America? What impressions did Wright's silence confer on the queer community during such a critical moment in intersectional feminist history? These were the questions I asked myself as I began to reevaluate the trajectory of my postgraduate life as a twenty-three-year-old millennial striving to keep my politics and my values compatible with my professional life. Although Wright was likely pushed and pulled in several directions, perhaps by superiors at Netflix or professional allegiances inseparable from Spacey's, the fact that a woman of her celebrity status did not address Spacey's alleged assault troubled me greatly. Wright's silence elucidated the complexities of intersectional feminist practice when the political becomes intertwined with the (mass) cultural.

From my vantage point, Wright's reserve symbolically reinforced the historical silencing inflicted on the queer community by means of heteronormative policing, comparable to the silencing enforced by the *Advocate* in publishing Rapp's Q&A in 2001. At the same time, if I was to consider the possibility that Wright did not have full control over her response to Spacey's apologia, her quiescence communicated a rather disappointing fact: those with celebrity status are still subject to a sociopolitical hierarchy. In other words, despite Wright's position as a culturally powerful feminist, evidenced by her prior social justice efforts, she failed to influence conversations during Me Too when her longtime colleague became the subject of intense public scrutiny. Unlike her character Claire Underwood, who could defy Spacey on-screen without repercussion, Wright could not exert comparable power when the scripts were set aside and the threat of injustice loomed in front of her.

As a queer employee, I found it very hard to turn a blind eye to Wright's silence. Furthermore, as someone who had studied the intersections of feminism and queer theory with mass representation, I had learned that celebrity figures such as Wright possess the cultural capital to effect ideological shifts—they could be powerful allies to marginalized groups even if they themselves did not identify as such (for example, as queer). During the circumstances of Me Too, I perceived Wright to therefore have the unique ability to give a voice to underrepresented communities, in this case (queer) survivors of sexual harassment and assault. As an LGBTQ+ ally within the majority class party, majority race party, and majority sexuality party, Wright without a doubt could have had a great deal of influence on the Me Too movement by injecting a queer consciousness into public discourse. In doing so, she could have helped move queer people out of the shadows of a society that deems their experiences an afterthought, thus conveying to the public the fact that assaults on queer people merit the same attention as those inflicted on cisgender and heterosexual people. When she did finally come out of the shadows, she defended herself with politically neutral rhetoric to circumvent the media's desire for an insider's perspective on Spacey. As she argued in her first, exclusive interview with *Today*, "Kevin and I knew each other between action and cut and in-between setups, where we would giggle. . . . I didn't know the man" (2018). Despite having had a working relationship with Spacey for over twenty years,[2] one that included extensive off-camera publicity, Wright denied knowing Spacey beyond a professional capacity.

I believe that, given the opportunity, I could have sparked a more nuanced conversation within Wright's PR team as its members quickly determined her response to Spacey's confession. This change could have found support, even if minor, from my expertise in subjects congruent with the Me Too movement such as gender, sexuality, and feminism. For example, I believe if I had been able to invoke the subjects of queerness and cultural representation in a discussion with Wright or her publicist, we could have segued into a conversation about the significance of Wright addressing the scandal beyond her personal relationship with Spacey. The current politics surrounding sexual harassment and queerness had never before existed at such a widely recognized conjuncture; as such, I wanted to articulate to the team how a response from Wright about LGBTQ+ identity could align with her history of feminist advocacy and still be neutral toward Spacey, if she were to support a minority community in crisis.

As the executive assistant on this client's team, I certainly did not expect to spearhead the campaign; nonetheless, I was sincerely, and perhaps naïvely, surprised that I was delegated the backmost seat during the brainstorming and reactive processes of the whole ordeal. I could have helped Wright's team better approach the cultural conversation by helping them deconstruct the false, implicit ideas Spacey was feeding to the public about the twenty-first-century queer experience. Similar to Quinto's critique of Spacey's tweet, I felt that my academic expertise could have influenced the cultural narrative; this time around, though, I had hoped to more prominently extend representation to the LGBTQ+ community. Nonetheless, Wright's ultimate actions spoke louder than her (lack of) words. Rapp seemingly did not make the cut. The queer community did not make the cut.

Wright finally made her first public appearance four weeks after Rapp's exposé went viral. On November 11, 2017, Wright held an informational session on her Pour Les Femmes pajama line at the Nordstrom store in the Century City mall, located in the heart of central Los Angeles near Beverly Hills. As the executive assistant on this campaign, I was specifically responsible for planning the details of Wright's surreptitious arrival to the building; ensuring, alongside my supervisor, that all media present were explicitly prohibited from broaching the subject of Spacey; and liaising between the Nordstrom advertising team and my office to create Wright's schedule for the day. The UK outlet the *Daily Mail* picked up on the problematic nature of Wright's return to publicity and fittingly titled its coverage of the event as follows: "Smiling Robin Wright Maintains Her Silence on Kevin Spacey Sex Abuse Scandal as She Promotes Her Pajama Line" (Wright 2017). This title affirms that Wright's silence had not been forgotten or read as culturally insignificant. In fact, the *Daily Mail*'s tone suggests that Wright's silence was perceived by the media as inadequate. Why was such an outspoken proponent for women's equality suddenly taking a step back? Were there conversations and decisions transpiring behind closed doors in which even Wright herself could not participate? The facade that Spacey's scandal was no longer relevant disturbed me. Even more, questions such as these challenged me to further consider the systemic factors compelling Wright toward silence. These were also questions that gradually prompted me to change the trajectory of my professional journey.

Amid the hustle and bustle of Wright's return to publicity, I witnessed the harsh effects Me Too catalyzed within the world of entertainment PR. These effects served to further push me away from the industry. I vividly recollect a period during which more and more high-profile figures within entertainment were outed as predatory. My email inbox would flood with *Deadline* and *Variety* "breaking news" alerts every morning, coughing up the name of yet another individual whom my executive coworkers had previously admired. Like kernels under heat, these names popped up relentlessly, and the senior executives with whom I worked eagerly consumed these stories with an insatiable appetite for scandal. Much as Wright ignored her prerogative to speak up for victims and for the LGBTQ+ community, my new coworkers were more interested in the spectacle of the media outing yet another predatory man than in the stories of the people who suffered from these misogynistic and homophobic actions. In this sense, the culture within this PR office aligned more with a whodunit narrative than with one empathetic toward survivors.

A particular discussion that transpired between me and several executives in the office aptly represents the change in dynamics within entertainment during the era of Me Too. In February 2018, Ryan Seacrest was accused of sexually harassing his longtime stylist over the course of multiple years (Holloway 2018). I immediately began thinking about the consequences the alleged assaults must have had for this woman. How would this stylist's exposé in *Variety*, like Rapp's exposé, be read by audiences during this explosive Me Too movement? On which facets of the story would people focus when engaging with this piece? The employees with whom I interacted, however, had different questions in mind when discussing the situation. As the employee at the lowest notch of the totem pole within this group, I was put in the position of having to listen to these executives patronizingly convince me Seacrest was guilty. The integral focus of the conversation—or rather the debate—was about the perpetrator's irrefutable guilt, rather than the survivor's trauma or the plausibility that Seacrest was being falsely slandered. I was distressed that the trajectory of engagements like these within my PR office was so accusatory and malicious, rather than empathetic and critical.

I also witnessed entertainment office culture shift during the wake of Me Too through the way publicists began to interact with their male clients. I remember hearing publicists anxiously call their clients in order to "prep" them for what they thought would be inevitable: allegations of sexual harassment. Day after day, publicists could be heard throughout the hallway warning their clients to memorize precautionary media strategies if an accusation were to come to light. This looming fear within the office seemed misguided; not only did I feel it was problematic to preemptively bolster men's defenses against assault rather than seek the truth, but it also appeared that the image of the predatory male was being perpetuated as the normative trope within the Hollywood scene. My experiences living through Me Too surrounded by such anxiety prompted me to leave the world of celebrity PR once and for all. At the conclusion of Wright's campaign for the final season of *House of Cards*, I resigned from my assistant position.

I recall often hearing the words of scholar Audre Lorde echo in my mind as I contemplated quitting: "There is no hierarchy of oppression" (1984, 139). This erudite phrase reflected my inner turmoil while working in PR: Wright, by avoiding publicity during Spacey's problematic coming-out moment, did the very opposite of Lorde's teachings, minimizing queer assault experiences as if they were not important markers of injustice and oppression. Moreover, witnessing publicists alleviate their own anxieties about male clients by preparing them for pseudo-feminist battle catalyzed much disconcertment. In this fashion, my feminist studies degree truly became a serendipitous undergirding, one that ultimately allowed me to make the best decision possible for my career without compromising my own values and beliefs. Resignation liberated me from intense cognitive dissonance and afforded me the chance to stay true to my feminist underpinnings.

My feminist education taught me that it is wholly acceptable to prioritize one's ethics and politics when engaging with a problematic workplace. While I relished my position to critically assess the propagation of Me Too while working behind the scenes in entertainment, the hierarchy of power within my PR office proved too overpowering for me as a beginning employee to take on by myself. I had gradually realized throughout my work in PR that my perspective was painfully secondary to the supervisor's and to the client's. It pained me to watch Wright largely disregard the problematic denouement of Spacey's career; I knew that her performative silence would affect the public's interpretations of how society should handle sexual violence and that she was missing an opportunity to expand the ambit of the Me Too movement to include the LGBT+ community.

Throughout the mental tug-of-war I experienced at the end of Wright's *House of Cards* campaign, I also considered what a change in professional scenery might look like for me after leaving public relations. The unsettling politics I witnessed during the Me Too movement prompted me to consider a new career path. During my period of introspection, I realized that my feminist education had actually ingrained in me a skill integral to other employment settings: the skill of empathy. It dawned on me that my discomfort in entertainment was a rather overt sign that I was better suited for a career in which I could help people, rather than cover up for them. Learning about feminism, social identities, and inequality as an FGSS major had instilled in me a fruitful ability to empathize with other people, despite whatever background they may have. In this vein, I applied to graduate programs in social work psychology to pursue my new goal of working as a psychotherapist.

Three years later, I now hold a master's degree in social work from the University of Southern California and have two years of clinical experience under my belt. I have successfully found a way to harness my passion for feminist inquiry to help others live more honest lives. After interning as a student-therapist for homeless LGBTQ+ youths and for undergraduate and graduate students in Los Angeles, I feel that same fire that was lit within me after Cornell, now reignited and as powerful as ever. I aspire to open my own private practice with my new degree so that I may use psychoanalysis and feminist theory to treat LGBTQ+ adults. My FGSS education instilled in me a radical plasticity that allows me to transform critical discomfort into positive change, and to critique the (cultural) world around me through the adoption of an intersectional perspective. This academic foundation has also set the path for me to flourish and forever grow in my identity as a queer person. To reference Lorde once again, the power of feminism gives me the energy for genuine change within our world (1978, 59).

Notes

1. In fact, there has been much criticism of the current Me Too movement for ignoring the work of Tarana Burke, who is African American.

2. Spacey and Wright met when they worked together on the 1998 film *Hurlyburly*.

References

Advocate Staff. 2001. "Music for Boys . . . and Everyone Else." *Advocate*, June 1, 2001. https://www.advocate.com/news/2001/06/01/music-boys%E2%80%A6and -everyone-else.

CBS News. 2017. "More than 12M 'Me Too' Facebook Posts, Comments, Reactions in 24 Hours." October 17, 2017. https://www.cbsnews.com/news/metoo-more-than-12 -million-facebook-posts-comments-reactions-24-hours.

Holloway, Daniel. 2018. "Ryan Seacrest's E! Stylist Reveals Abuse and Harassment Allegations (EXCLUSIVE)." *Variety*, February 27, 2018. https://variety.com/2018/tv/news /ryan-seacrest-sexual-abuse-allegations-stylist-details-1202710460.

Khomami, Nadia. 2017. "#MeToo: How a Hashtag Became a Rallying Cry against Sexual Harassment." *Guardian*, October 20, 2017. https://www.theguardian.com/world /2017/oct/20/women-worldwide-use-hashtag-metoo-against-sexual-harassment.

Konerman, Jennifer. 2016. "Robin Wright Threatened to Go Public If She Didn't Get Equal Pay on 'House of Cards.'" *Hollywood Reporter*, May 17, 2016. https://www.holly woodreporter.com/news/Wright-wright-threatened-go-public-895270.

Lorde, Audre. 1978. *Uses of the Erotic: The Erotic as Power*. Freedom, CA: Crossing.

——. 1984. *Sister Outsider: Essays and Speeches*. Trumansburg, NY: Crossing.

Melas, Chloe. 2017. "'House of Cards' Employees Allege Sexual Harassment, Assault by Kevin Spacey." CNNMoney, November 3, 2017. https://money.cnn.com/2017/11/02 /media/house-of-cards-kevin-spacey-harassment/index.html.

Milano, Alyssa (@Alyssa_Milano). 2017. Twitter post, October 15, 1:21 p.m. https:// twitter.com/Alyssa_Milano/status/919659438700670976.

Newbold, Alice. 2018. "Robin Wright's Sleepwear Brand Has a Conscious Caveat." *Vogue*, December 1, 2018. https://www.vogue.co.uk/gallery/robin-wright-sleepwear-brand -pour-les-femmes.

Quinto, Zachary (@ZacharyQuinto). 2017. Twitter post, October 30, 2017, 9:42 a.m. https://twitter.com/ZacharyQuinto/status/925040235066679296.

Spacey, Kevin (@KevinSpacey). 2017. Twitter post, October 29, 2017, 9:00 p.m. https:// twitter.com/KevinSpacey/status/924848412842971136.

Today. 2018. "Wright Talks about Kevin Spacey on TODAY: 'I Didn't Know the Man.'" Interview by Savannah Guthrie. NBC, July 9, 2018.

Variety Staff. 2016. "'House of Cards' Star Robin Wright Demanded Equal Pay with Kevin Spacey." *Variety*, May 18, 2016. https://variety.com/2016/tv/news/Wright-wright -equal-pay-kevin-spacey-house-of-cards-1201777927.

Vary, Adam. 2017. "Actor Anthony Rapp: Kevin Spacey Made a Sexual Advance toward Me When I Was 14." BuzzFeed News, October 29, 2017. https://www.buzzfeednews .com/article/adambvary/anthony-rapp-kevin-spacey-made-sexual-advance-when -i-was-14.

Wright, Tracy. 2017. "Smiling Robin Wright Maintains Her Silence on Kevin Spacey Sex Abuse Scandal as She Promotes Her Pajama Line." *Daily Mail*, November 14, 2017. https://www.dailymail.co.uk/tvshowbiz/article-5073965/Wright-Wright -celebrates-launch-pajama-line-LA.html.

THE IMMANENCE OF SOCIAL MEDIA LABOR?

The Struggle to Find a Feminist Dwelling

Sadaf Ferdowsi

In the glittering lobby of a high-rise office building, a cart I had piled high with snacks, sodas, and coffee crashed to the ground as I tried to wheel it onto the elevator. Plastic bags holding cartons of creamer and soy milk, boxes of K-Cups, and lone bananas scattered all over the tiled floor. I ignored the gazes of everyone and everyone mercifully ignored me as I scrambled to reload the cart and disappear. Inside the elevator, my reflection stared at me. I wondered whether this was how people knew me now: frizzy dark hair, ill-fitting office clothes, and a snack cart stacked precariously. I was going through a phase where I found metaphors in everything. The toppling cart was just another quotidian representation of the instability of adulthood, the futility of work-life balance, the reality of my life.

"It's not you, it's neoliberalism," my reflection tried to comfort me.

This was in February 2019, and I was a temp for a tech company in downtown Chicago. The tech company had grown exponentially in a short time and was spread out on two floors with separate elevator banks. I spent most of my shifts pushing the snack cart back and forth between them. The year before, I had moved back to my hometown to be with my dad, driving him to his doctor's appointments and routinely burning dinner, but in the year we were together, he retired, sold and packed up the house, and moved to a condo we had found in a warmer state.

I was back in Chicago and this part-time job, coordinated over a few LinkedIn messages, was a welcome relief from sending résumés all day and hearing nothing back. The elevator chimed and the doors slid open. In the kitchen, I refilled the drawers, layering the granola bars and packages of almonds in tidy rows. I organized chips by bag color in a basket I had found abandoned in the storage room. The company had fresh fruit shipped to the office, which I arranged and rearranged into orderly displays. I enjoyed this because it reminded me of my mother and the other women in my family. Growing up, my parents and I spent my school vacations in their home country, Iran, and these childhood trips meant elaborate displays of fruit. My aunts, cousins, and grandma would emerge from the kitchen, saying they remembered my favorites, and proffer gleaming crystal bowls, dangerously overflowing but perfectly balanced with plums, cherries, and apricots.

I arranged the apples and the oranges and thought of my aunt in her sunbathed living room, my grandma on her balcony, my mother in her own home four hours away. The tech company was on the thirtieth story, with floor-to-ceiling windows overlooking the Chicago River, the dark water a stark contrast to the Loop's iridescent skyscrapers. With the river behind me, I thought about how we were all in our own corners incorporating "little beauties" in our work. I had done the same when I was an administrative assistant in my first year out of college, back when my office clothes had fit and I'd go to the corner grocery and pick the fruit myself.

Wiping down the countertops was my last task to finish before resuming my post at the front desk. There, I would look for spare moments to work on my other job, as the volunteer social media coordinator for a feminist documentary, in charge of updating the film's different accounts. As I finished the cleaning, I resisted the urge to check my phone, which was becoming harder and harder to ignore. The notifications, which I knew were about the film's social media, had paused, but they kept distracting me. I often found myself predicting the contents of emails and rehearsing their replies; I thought about the social media posts I'd type out at the front desk and which ones I'd do on the elevator ride down.

While the social media position had sounded easy enough, described in a few lines in an email ad with four exclamation marks, it actually required countless hours of labor that was invisible or undervalued. As I waited for the elevator, restocked Cokes in the fridges, or trudged through the snow to the train stop in the mornings and back home in the evenings, checking and rechecking social media on my phone, a word would float into my consciousness, more so than it had when I was in college: immanence.

My first encounter with gender theory was reading "House and Home: Feminist Variations on a Theme," by Iris Marion Young, an experience that I can only describe as revelatory. I was in my second year in college and deeply vexed over an ill-chosen major, but reading Young's essay offered more than consolation: it was transformative. Young affirmed what I had observed my whole life, that speeches given over kitchen tables were equally as important as the ones in public squares and that bowls of fruits were sites of power too. While reading Young's essay on immanence and transcendence, the invisible labor of women, and the values and violence of home, I decided this was the discourse that I wanted to belong to: "women's work," and the ongoing labor of an invisible and vulnerable workforce more broadly, was just as worthy of scholarship as the existing (read: male, privileged) canon.

In my part-time and volunteer roles, I often found myself revisiting the ideas in "House and Home." More specifically, I came to connect my role building and maintaining the film's social media with the labor and upkeep required to sustain public and private space: essential work that is rarely recognized and disproportionately falls to women and other marginalized groups. In this essay, I explore these parallels and demonstrate how Young's discussion on immanent labor enriches our understanding of digital spaces and contemporary everyday life.

Additionally, I will incorporate key points from "A Semiotics of the Public/ Private Distinction" by Susan Gal, a scholar whose work is integral to my perspective on gender and space. With both Young's and Gal's work, I hope to convey that the invisible, undervalued, and cyclical labor that predominantly falls to women in public and private spaces is also replicated and reenacted in social media contexts. In other words, similar disparities involving gender and labor continually recur online. Finally, I demonstrate that my part-time and volunteer experiences conducting this labor have helped shape deeper and more nuanced understandings of their work and my relationship to feminism more broadly.

Three major points from "House and Home" inform my personal experiences. The first point is that the home, the site for dwelling, is a complex space. Young relies on a feminist genealogy from Luce Irigaray to bell hooks to demonstrate how the home can be simultaneously a safe and a dangerous place. For example, idyllic and apolitical depictions of domesticity often obscure the violence behind closed doors. That being said, homes can still be reclaimed as zones to build meaningful worlds and create sites of resistance against dominant power structures (Young 2005, 124). In this way, social media as a space operates similarly to the home—it can be a crucial zone for connection, self-expression, and resistance but can also incite violence both on- and off-line.

The second point from Young's essay emerges in her critique of Martin Heidegger's implicit sexism in his understanding of dwelling and building. For Heidegger, dwelling is a man's mode of being, based on the ability to establish and express an individual subjectivity. However, to dwell first requires building, which Heidegger breaks down into two types of work: construction and preservation.

While he goes into detail on construction—the ability to erect structures to reflect one's identity, routines, rituals, and sense of history, he writes very little on preservation, which Young calls a "curious abandonment" (2005, 125). Unlike construction, preservation entails labor such as cultivating the soil, maintaining historical documents, and other work that does not necessarily leave a structure behind or encourage individual subjectivity. Because men were predominantly the builders and women were the preservers in Heidegger's time, Young suggests that his overemphasis on construction was linked to this gender dynamic while demonstrating how women's work is always already undervalued or goes unnoticed in patriarchal spaces.

Finally, Young incorporates Simone de Beauvoir's distinction between "transcendence" and "immanence" to further develop her point on women's labor (Young 2005, 137). On the simplest level, transcendent labor is work that is future oriented and travels on a teleological arc. For example, transcendence includes "building a house, organizing a strike, writing a book, winning a battle," and other endeavors that contribute to human affairs or one's sense of self, such as graduating from college with a gender studies degree (Young 2005, 137). Conversely, immanent labor is the work of women in the home that requires constant maintenance to sustain life. With this type of labor, women can never move on an upward trajectory because the laundry, cooking, and cleaning are never done: they require constant repetitions and cyclical routines.

Young quotes Beauvoir as saying that the housewife "wears herself out, marking time: she makes nothing, simply perpetuates the present (451)" (Young 2005, 137). By wearing herself out, she cannot build or express an individual subjectivity. While I expected this immanence labor as a part-time assistant, I was surprised to see it emerge with my role in social media, a position I had happily accepted for its feminism and stance on gender equality.

In March 2019, the documentary was close to the finish line. The director, producers, and editors—who primarily identified as women—had worked on this documentary for years. Independent filmmaking, especially for documentaries, is another one of those precarious industries where funding is limited and unpredictable and relies on unpaid labor to keep costs down. Our social media team was exclusively women, and we knew every dollar mattered for the fundraiser we were helping to launch at the end of the month. While the four months of planning (which meant nonstop emailing and coordinating, growing followers, and creating content) paid off and we exceeded our fund-raising goal within seventy-two hours of the Kickstarter launch, we were immediately back in our virtual "war room"—as one of the producers called it—trying to post and tag and engage our way to our goal.

In the mornings before and after the Kickstarter launch, on the train ride to work from 7:20 to 8:15, I would read through the multiple emails that had arrived overnight—brief dispatches from the director and producers on the improvised posts to add to our daily schedule. On the occasions I didn't nap on the Brown Line, I would get a head start on retweeting and commenting on Twitter posts; I checked in with my teammate who managed the Instagram account to align our content. While we referred to ourselves as social media coordinators, we juggled the tasks of copywriters and graphic designers, marketers and brand ambassadors, secretaries and junior executives. There was always a status to update, an article to share, or an influencer to research. The work never seemed to end. Before bed each night, around one in the morning, I scheduled Facebook posts for the day ahead, making a mental note on what was needed the rest of the week. Because we were an all-women team who put in countless hours of unpaid labor, I wanted to see whether the gender disparities of social media work occurred beyond this fund-raising experience.

What I found in some quick research was not surprising: the majority of social media labor is conducted by women, and furthermore, we are underpaid for our work. Based on PayScale data reported in a 2018 *Wired* article, "between 70 and 80 percent of social media workers self-identify as women" (Hempel). Self-reported information from Built In Chicago, an online site for Chicago startups and tech companies, showed that the average salary for men was $73,167 whereas the average salary for women was $63,168 (accessed in 2021). It is important to remember this data may not account for the many others who are not hired as full-time employees but brought on as independent contractors or volunteers.

As the weeks went on and we strove to meet the stretch goal, I was feeling more overwhelmed by the constant duties that social media required despite my ongoing goal of bringing more feminism into the world. In my attempt to do something transcendent, I had fallen into an immanent trap.

Just as Young's discussion of women, preservation, and immanent labor identifies parallels in my experiences with social media, Gal's "Semiotics of the Public/Private Distinction" works as a key theoretical framework to understand how immanence operates and replicates in public, private, and digital space. Like many scholars of gender theory, Gal believes that the boundary lines that demarcate "public" from "private" are not rigid; instead, they are fluid, subjective, and constantly renegotiated based on context. As an example, Gal demonstrates that although a house may be considered "private space," distinctions between public and private are continually re-created and reinscribed, even within the space of the home. The living room and entryway are more public than the master bedroom or bathroom; the dining room is more public than the kitchen; and, when applicable, the servant quarters are sequestered away in a seemingly invisible private. These distinctions are reproduced not only spatially but also temporally. You can take someone aside at a work party and whisper a secret, which temporarily creates a private within a broader public (Gal 2002, 82).

With this understanding, we see how the public-private distinction is replicated and recalibrated across seemingly infinite contexts. Gal helps illustrate this with the concept of the fractal, "a single pattern [that] recurs inside itself—is self-similar—often with multiple nestings" (2002, 81). For example, while the tech company was considered public space, there were private spaces nestled within it, such as the kitchen areas or the storage room, which can continually recur across myriad contexts: labeled lunches in the fridge versus the unspoken fair-game rule of food left on the countertops. With a background in linguistic anthropology and semiotics, Gal also points out that it is not just the fractals that continually recur in public and private space, it is the *idea* of this distinction (the metadiscourse of the public-private dichotomy) that is also reproduced and replicated.

When it comes to social media as a space, the complexity of these nestings and fractals becomes more apparent. For example, how would we even attempt to categorize social media? Is it a public or private space? Many of us have "public" profiles, yet we still manage our "privacy" settings—which we know do not preclude social media workers from accessing and monitoring our content. Furthermore, we have public profiles and private messages, personae that are documented and curated on timelines, and transient ones that go away on Snapchat. (A trend from my younger sister's generation: publicly posting screenshots of private messages, which is an interesting way this fractal distinction can recur from public to private and private to public.)

Private moments such as children's birthdays, engagements, weddings, and births are celebrated with the greater public of our online friends, and commerce is conducted online when personal connections are leveraged to make sales (usually but not exclusively spearheaded by women in multilevel marketing companies or through influencing). Whether it's public, private, neither, or both, social media has certainly become another zone where one can build worlds (assuming they have an internet connection). Moreover, the complex ways "public" and "private" operate on social media illustrate Gal's ideas on fractals recurring and reproducing in different spaces.

As a space to build and dwell in a world, social media, ironically enough, extends Young's critique of Heidegger's distinction between construction and preservation online. We talk about "building" an online presence, but it turns out the construction of social media *is* preservation. It's the record of our posts, the memories we preserve that we don't delete, that form our online selves. The immanent labor and preservation that primarily falls to women and unpaid workers builds out social media and creates dwellings for individuals, communities, and initiatives for feminism and film.

I had sunk to a new low. The social media posts kept piling up and my part-time contract with the snack cart was coming to an end. I kept sending out résumés, retooling my small list of experiences and accomplishments that I was beginning to resent the more I reworked it. I hadn't paid my portion of the rent for the seven months I'd been in Chicago and was living entirely off my boyfriend. I felt like a feminist failure.

My relationship to feminism slipped in other ways. When a coworker told me she loved Sheryl Sandberg, I did not make a comment about the corporatization of feminism and bit the insides of my lips instead. The tech company had a women's group and they asked whether I could help with the programming for International Women's Day. It was the first time I brought up my background in gender studies to my boss.

"We can't be too feminist," she quickly advised.

"Totally understood," I replied.

But it wasn't. I was becoming increasingly confused about what feminism even was and what it meant to me. I was receiving similar advice from the documentary team. For certain posts, I sometimes received emails or was reminded in meetings that "we don't want to be . . . too angry, you know?"

The women's group had a meeting later that day, and I rolled chairs from other parts of the office into the large conference room.

"So everyone can have a seat at the table," I joked. At the front desk, I worked on a PowerPoint presentation on inspirational women and watched the meeting through the glass of the conference room.

Even within feminist spaces, I saw immanence all around me. I felt caught in constant reproductions and renegotiations of immanent labor and the uneasy balances between being passionate but not angry, realistic but not negative, feminist but not too feminist. But it wasn't the capital-*P* patriarchy that had put me in this position. It was me. I was the one who couldn't find a job, I was the one who chose to volunteer for the film. Did it enrich my life or ruin it when I took stock of my day and saw it was immanence all the way down? Could I even "be" a feminist at this point, when I had learned all the lessons on transcendence and individual subjectivity and wasn't able to live them?

It had been nine years since my revelatory experience reading Young and Gal, which I thought about often—being nineteen years old and home for winter break; the plush white carpet in the basement; the long stretches of time for reading and schoolwork—all taken-for-granted fixtures of a previous life. I wondered, if I hadn't been so moved by gender theory, would I have reconciled with my law major and followed a more conventional arc of success?

But rereading Gal and Young as an older adult, nearly a decade since I was a college student with an unlimited meal plan, I see it was the right choice and that my work experiences, especially the immanent ones, can help shape deeper and more nuanced understandings of what feminism can mean. For example, expecting feminism to *do* something for me, believing that the knowledge of these ideas is valuable so long as it moves me across a teleological arc, inadvertently introduced a false privileging of transcendence over immanence, thus replicating patriarchal standards of success.

My education had taught me to challenge dichotomies, but this whole time I had trapped myself in one without noticing. As I stressed over not doing enough transcendent labor to make my feminism "worth it," I obscured *for myself* the value of immanent knowledge. Knowledge was no longer only a transcendent or teleological endeavor; instead, it could also encompass immanent labor: the cyclical routines and ongoing work that never ends when it comes to revisiting and reengaging feminism as our lives continue to change.

It is May 2019 and I've decided to keep my computer turned off for the day. I should be writing, checking social media, applying for jobs, or doing something more "productive," but the apartment is a mess. Because it reminds me of the women in my family, I decide to take care of my home. The sink is full of dishes, and then the sink is empty. The floorboards have collected dust, and now they're swept clean. I chop the onion and stir the stew. On an intellectual level, I understand this is immanent labor, but sometimes when I cook a meal for myself or clean the whole house, it feels transcendent—albeit transient, it's a form of individual subjectivity to me.

I drape bunches of grapes over a bowl of cherries and tangerines, moving them this way and that, thinking how my aunt, grandma, or mom might balance their shapes and colors. I think about how feminism is not just an idea to be grasped— it's a dwelling, too, one that requires constant organizing and reorganizing, cleaning messes and cleaning them again, and spending time on the "little beauties" that don't last forever but are meaningful just the same.

References

Built in Chicago. n.d. "Average Social Media Salary." Accessed April 25, 2020. https://www
.builtinchicago.org/salaries/marketing/social-media-manager/chicago.

Gal, Susan. 2002. "A Semiotics of the Public/Private Distinction." *differences* 13, no. 1
(Spring): 77–95.

Hempel, Jessi. 2018. "How Social Media Became a Pink Collar Job." *Wired*. https://www
.wired.com/story/how-social-media-became-a-pink-collar-job/.

Young, Iris Marion. 2005. "House and Home: Feminist Variations on a Theme." In *On
Female Body Experience: "Throwing like a Girl" and Other Essays*, 123–54. Oxford:
Oxford University Press.

FINDING "THE TROUBLE WITH NORMAL" IN JOURNALISM

Rachel Cromidas

The first time I ever saw a woman have an orgasm, it was onstage, in a half-filled theater on Chicago's Far North Side. She was teaching a class on rope bondage and explaining to us how in addition to being attracted to men and women, her sexuality included exhibitionism, masochism, and specific predicaments that required getting tied up in front of an audience. Her teaching partner used a vibrator on her while she stood, with her legs and arms restrained.

We were at Chicago's Leather Archives and Museum, a nonprofit dedicated to preserving the history of the leather community. The class was hosted by a local BDSM group for people ages eighteen to thirty-five.[1] I was with friends from school—we represented the young end of that age range—and we sat quiet and wide-eyed as the woman and her partner negotiated and analyzed a sadomasochistic role-playing scene right in front of us. I remember that people around me had notebooks out. The vibe was more reverent than raunchy, more birdwatching than burlesque show.

This is the sort of thing that happens on the weekends in large, liberal-leaning cities around the country, so frequently that it feels normal to those involved, if you know where to go looking for it. And at age twenty, studying gender at the University of Chicago, I was the kind of person who would go looking for it, even if that meant a two-hour, Saturday-night public transit ride from my apartment in Hyde Park. I was hoping that learning firsthand about others' sexual identities, and how the world viewed them, would help me understand my own place in the world. This was also the promise of my chosen undergraduate field of study, and specifically the foundational texts of queer theory.

Outside of school, my weekend nights were often booked with attending meet-ups and parties for Chicago's queer, kinky, and polyamorous communities. But my days could not have been more opposite: I was hustling to kick-start a career in journalism by freelancing for the *New York Times* and interning for a coopera-tive news outlet, and that meant attending all kinds of public school meetings, mayoral press conferences, and courtroom hearings. I'd skip classes to listen to lots of disgruntled people yell at their elected officials about public transit fund-ing and charter schools. Assignments ranged from the economic impact of Chi-cago's failed Olympic bid to the federal trial of corrupt ex-governor Rod Blagojevich, and from the blizzard that stranded hundreds of drivers on Lake Shore Drive to a package bomb threat on Chicago's synagogues.

At work, what I wanted most was to find fascinating, original stories to tell about the most seemingly ordinary subjects—organic farmers, struggling small businesses, laid-off public school teachers. It was the stuff regular, hardy midwesterners, like my (entirely white, cis, male, straight) editors, would want to read. I ended up writing about a Wisconsin mushroom grower's efforts to turn a profit, a coalition of Black small-business owners trying to revitalize Chicago's historic Bronzeville, the demise of Chicago Public Schools' only Japanese-language program, along with dozens of other articles that ran in the *New York Times* from 2010 to 2011.

I got a secret thrill out of the incongruity of my seemingly disparate public and private lives, how senseless it was to even try to explain how I could go from in-terviewing the mayor to attending an underground BDSM party in the China-town studio of a professional dominatrix in the span of a few hours—going from speaking to the most upstanding, legitimate people in our society to mingling with some of the least legible, the "freaks."

One morning, packing my day bag before heading out to cover the federal trial of disgraced police chief Jon Burge, I realized I couldn't bring the hemp rope, pocket knife, or leather collar that I planned to use at a party later that night through the courthouse security. It felt funny and little bad to go from my day job, which demanded the picture of normalcy, to my nightlife, where social capi-tal came from a willingness to wear a lot of leather and step on men.

At the same time, I was taking classes, learning from queer, feminist scholars who interrogated their personal lives through their work that the personal was political and therefore public. In Gayle Rubin's landmark essay "Thinking Sex," she defines sexuality as political, "organized into systems of power, which reward and encourage some individuals and activities, while punishing and suppressing others" (2002, 221). This resonated with me; at work, I readily knew which of my hobbies to discuss versus downplay and what aspects of my relationship with my college boyfriend to reveal and what to keep completely private, like the fact that he had another girlfriend.

In Michael Warner's *Trouble with Normal*, the social theorist argues that one of queer culture's "greatest contributions to modern life is the discovery that you can have both: intimacy and casualness; long-term commitment and sex with strangers; romantic love and perverse pleasure" (1999, 73). Reading it for the first time in my Introduction to Sexuality class, I underlined this sentence three times; that's how badly I wanted to believe it. Reading it again a decade later, I believe that I am truly capable of living it, and that scholarship like Warner's galvanized me to pursue a queer and feminist life I couldn't have imagined for myself before college.

The sociologist Tim Dean's book *Unlimited Intimacy: Reflections on the Subculture of Barebacking* rounded out my educational transformation into a queer feminist, giving me a deeper understanding of the social and political ramifications of nonnormative sexualities and deviant behavior. I was so compelled by Dean's focus on the subculture of cis, gay men who have promiscuous sex without condoms that I decided to analyze it for my undergraduate thesis.

What struck me most was that Dean copped to the sometimes participatory, sort of ethnographic nature of his research—he was barebacking too, and though not advocating for it, he was certainly not condemning it. And that was hard for even the academic press that published his book to stomach; I heard that for the first time in the University of Chicago Press's history, the board refused to publish the book without significant revisions.

I knew I was a baby queer in a long tradition of baby queers getting an education in queer and feminist theory, but it didn't dawn on me until much later that I was also a baby journalist, getting a somewhat conflicting education. While I was learning from the obviously legitimate work of these distinguished academics how to tell my own story, and why that might be an increasingly important thing to do, I was also seeing how doing so could expose me to mainstream condemnation. My education in gender studies, feminism, and particularly queer studies helped me figure out who I was, but it also seemed blatantly at odds with what was required of me to succeed as a mainstream news reporter, working for veteran editors who had cut their teeth in Chicago's legendary City News Bureau.

From them I learned that when it came to the newsroom, the reporter is supposed to *never* be the story. It only made sense to keep my private life private—obviously, I wasn't going to tell my coworkers about the specific sex I was having, or the multiple people I was having it with, sometimes in the semipublic setting of a BDSM conference or a social gathering. I certainly never asked myself, *Is this a story?* when I witnessed hundreds of people from around the country pay good money to gather for a long weekend in a Chicago suburb to study suspension bondage together. Usually, I was finding stories everywhere—on bike rides to work, in line at the grocery store, in passing conversations with strangers on the train home. I kept my two lives very separate.

In my early career, I faced the sexism and favoritism one would expect from traditional, legacy newsrooms. This included being flat-out ignored by male colleagues who schmoozed with each other at the desk next to mine, invited each other out, and included each other's hot takes in their columns. I also received unwanted attention from those same male colleagues in the elevator the couple of times I wore skirts to the office. Throughout my journalism career, from my college freelance to my first jobs in New York City and a residency at the *Chicago Tribune*, I have faced unequal pay, prying comments about my gender expression and the clothes I wear, and sarcastic remarks when I am secretive about my postwork plans. I knew it was wrong, but I believed it was important to endure these microaggressions and try to blend in to get the best bylines. But as my identity as a queer woman and a feminist emerged and solidified in the years after college, I gained the confidence to push for stories that centered the voices of women, as well as LGBT people and people of color. Occasionally I succeeded in bringing my intersectional feminist point of view to the straight-white-male-dominated newsrooms I worked in, writing about a transitional home for homeless trans women and how students were trying to hold their campuses accountable for sexual assault, years before the Me Too movement hit the mainstream.

Still, I was always afraid to share anything personal about my own life for publication. It's hard to get rid of something once it's on the internet or in the paper of record. I was afraid to broadcast any signs of my own "deviance" in a place that could be accessible seemingly forever. I had learned from a favorite college course on the "sociology of deviant behavior" how societies distinguish between "normal" and "deviant," and how grave the repercussions for deviance can be for the individuals involved. Books like Erving Goffman's *Stigma: Notes on the Management of Spoiled Identity* intellectually excited me. Emotionally, however, it stressed me out to imagine the subcultures I ran in, the polyamory meetup group and the BDSM club, as examples of Goffman's "stigmaphile" space, where the stigmatized and marginalized bond, learn to celebrate the characteristics they're stigmatized for, and even come to realize that there is a more authentic way of life than the dominant culture (1963, 37).

I imagined myself to have a spoiled identity, or one that easily could be if I didn't keep it hidden. A lot of theorists I read focused on how a spoiled identity could also rob an individual of dignity in mainstream society. I didn't like the sound of that, but even more, I was worried that if I didn't hide my full self, it would be illegible. Unwritable. I figured, it's easy to speak the truth of who you are when you're straight and married, or even when you're gay and married. But when your identity is messy, changing, or just doesn't fit neatly into certain well-known boxes, your ability to connect with others or even explain yourself can start to break down quickly. And for someone who thinks of herself as a storyteller, the idea of being unable to tell that story in a clear, understandable manner was about as bad as the idea of being socially or morally spoiled.

Meanwhile, as a reader, I was already hungry for more mainstream stories about people like me. I wanted *Vogue* blogger Karley Sciortino's slut manifestos, but less sex-focused; Maria Bello's *Whatever . . . Love Is Love*, but more complicated. I wanted Stephen Elliott's 2006 *My Girlfriend Comes to the City and Beats Me Up*, which I read in queer theorist Lauren Berlant's undergraduate course Sex and Ethics. I wanted exactly that, in fact; it was the first and maybe only book I have ever read that really nailed what I was looking for, as a writer and kinkster. In his poetic almost-memoir, Elliott renders the sex life of a male masochist in unsparing detail, and it is powerfully moving. It's not pulpy, it's not undignified, and it obviously does not disqualify him from having a prolific and acclaimed career as an author, filmmaker, and literary editor. Telling his stories, and barely disguising that they are drawn from his life, did not make him *that kink guy* or *that polyamorous guy*, as Elliott worries in his introduction. (Though I wonder whether someone *not* a white man would receive the same acclaim for telling these stories, or be pigeonholed.) I had writers like Elliott from my undergraduate education to look up to. And though I was still proud of my journalistic works, I knew I wasn't living up to my goals for myself as a feminist and writer.

Throughout my journalism career, I watched closely for signs that mainstream media might be interested in hearing from a queer, polyamorous woman. I checked the blog *Polyamory in the News!* every day, where a longtime polyamorist has been documenting every instance of polyamory appearing in the media since 2005, and sometimes analyzing the stories for centering normative viewpoints. Think: couples, white people, straights, and unicorn-hunters, a.k.a. heterosexual-presenting couples who "hunt" for bisexual women to hook up with.

I had more in mind. What I wanted to read was also what I wanted to write: more-nuanced takes on ethical non-monogamy and other efforts to queer kinship, from the point of view of women like me who dated people of all genders and weren't one half of a married couple; who slept with their friends and loved their friends like family; who saw their sexuality as a jumping-off point for exploring other relationship models and, beyond that, "other worlds of interaction" that, as Warner warns, "the mass media cannot begin to comprehend" (1999, 71).

I noticed that the few stories that *were* out there, particularly on TV, seemed to always be rehashing essentially the same narrative: typically, they centered a cis, straight-appearing (and, most often, thin, white) monogamous couple. The couple would open up their relationship, and jealousy, self-discovery, and promiscuous high jinx would ensue. The news pieces usually concluded with a message of deeper love and emotional intimacy for the original couple. *Sally loves*

Mark. The twist? She loves David, too. And listen, Mark's somehow cool with it—how progressive of all of them.

I thought these stories were boring. I assumed they existed because they were easier for mainstream audiences to understand than anything I would have to say. But polyamory, and the experience of a woman whose sexual and gender identities defied categories, was messier than that. I was messier than that. I didn't think the world was ready, or that I was, either, so I never pitched a story about my own polyamorous or queer life. Furthermore, I had a professional reputation to maintain, in an industry of people who already get paid to Google each other for a living—what would they think of me if they read something about my life? After leaving the *Tribune*, I kept my focus on Chicagoist, a local news website where I was hired as an editor in 2015 and quickly promoted to editor in chief. There, I wrote, assigned, and edited the same kinds of stories that inspired me back in college: stuff about how cities and their governments work and don't. Thankfully, I finally had the autonomy to work an intersectional feminist point of view into our news coverage, and I made a special effort to find and assign stories about queer people of color doing important things in the world.

However, in 2017, the world changed, and so did mine; Donald Trump became president, and I got laid off from my job by the union-busting, Trump-supporting billionaire who owned my website. It felt like the stakes for learning to speak up, or failing to learn, were higher than ever.

On one of those viciously cold February nights in Chicago when the last thing you want to do is leave the house, I pulled together some notes on an essay about my experience trying and failing to get a copper IUD. The essay, written in my free time, covered the nuances of being a woman exploring her birth control options while dating three men. Before thinking better of it, I dashed off a pitch and emailed it to an editor at Buzzfeed Reader whom I admired. She bought the essay from me the next morning, confirming that my secret wish to sell a first-person essay about polyamory to a mainstream publication was totally reasonable. It was even professionally savvy—Buzzfeed pays freelance writers better than many of its competitors.

The essay is fact driven and vulnerable, just as I've always striven to be in my traditional hard-news reporting. And it doesn't try to simplify things, even when that means describing to readers, who include my past and future employers and my parents, what I like and dislike about unprotected sex, my infatuation with a local psych-folk musician and dogwalker, and how all of my other partners felt about these subjects. It also mentions a bloody chunk of uterine lining my gynecologist yanked out of my body when my copper IUD needed to come out. I spilled my guts.

I thought it was a feminist act on my part to put this essay out there, contributing to a thin body of work about women's experiences with the medical world as promiscuous, as polyamorous, as in an abnormal amount of uterine pain. I can even imagine some academic studying queer kinship structures or ethical non-monogamy someday to find this essay useful and cite it in an article.

In the current political climate, it feels impossible to only continue to do what feels comfortable and familiar. The essay I wrote for Buzzfeed helped me start to see a way forward in my life, as an intersectional feminist, as a queer woman, and as a journalist.

Note

1. The leather community is a generations-old queer subculture in which many participants wear leather and participate in sadomasochistic activities. BDSM typically stands for a set of nonnormative sexual practices including bondage and discipline, dominance and submission, and sadism and masochism.

References

Elliott, Stephen. 2006. *My Girlfriend Comes to the City and Beats Me Up*. Berkeley: Cleis.

Goffman, Erving. 1963. *Stigma: Notes on the Management of Spoiled Identity*. New York: Simon and Schuster.

Rubin, Gayle. 2002. "Thinking Sex: Notes for a Radical Theory of the Politics of Sexuality." In *Sexualities: Critical Concepts in Sociology,* Volume II. 220–245. Editor Ken Plummer. London and New York: Routledge.

Warner, Michael. 1999. *The Trouble with Normal: Sex, Politics, and the Ethics of Queer Life*. Cambridge, MA: Harvard University Press.

"NO PLACE TO BE, EXCEPT WITH EACH OTHER"

How Women's Studies Taught Me to Be Unionized

Reina Gattuso

There is an irony at the center of the neoliberal university: in a collection of people, students are taught to be alone. I say "taught" because this aloneness is not inevitable, and not always a fixture of the university space. It is, instead, the result of a particular model of education, in which—from the personal essay in the grueling application process to the catalog of undergraduate preprofessional organizations—individual students become both consumer and product, emerging as "bundles of self-managed flexible skills" (Urciuoli 2018, 156).

As an undergraduate at Harvard University from 2011 to 2015, I found the loneliness searing. It wasn't just a result of the looming student loan debt or ever-rising tuition, major causes of mental health crisis in American universities, particularly for low-income students. It lingered also in the class stratification of dining hall cliques; the private social clubs that throbbed with music on Friday nights; the overwhelming whiteness of the university's leadership and social norms; and the endless, internalized pressure to fill every waking hour with résumé-ready activities. In most spaces, these pressures, and the resulting loneliness, weren't politicized or historicized: they simply were, and failure to cope with them was ostensibly the result of personal insufficiency.

Luckily for my sanity, my intellectual development, and my political future, I found gender studies. I'd always been fascinated by the workings of gender and sexuality in everyday life. What was this thing called queerness, and where did it come from? Why did I feel prickly—pins and needles of arousal and fear—when men looked at me on the street? Gender studies was my path to unraveling these knots, as well as toward beginning to address the internalized supremacies of my own thinking as a white, cis, queer woman from a conservative suburb. When I first declared a joint major in comparative literature and women's, gender, and sexuality studies (WGS), I felt a nagging shame: Was studying women even a "real" discipline? While Harvard's Committee on Degrees in Studies of Women, Gender, and Sexuality had been around since the 1970s, it still wasn't a full-fledged department: its faculty and graduate students shared appointments in other departments, emphasizing that WGS couldn't be a "real" primary affiliation. Like other institutions for the study of race and queerness on Harvard's campus, the committee office was located literally underground, a spatial testimony to its marginality in the white, elite, male history of Harvard. Connecting the shame I felt in even declaring WGS to this history, and to my own internalized shame as a woman and queer person, was my first act of unlearning. From that moment onward, I was officially part of the "sanctimonious women's studies set."[1]

What I didn't know then is that gender studies would give me the scaffolding to render historical, political, and material—and thus, ultimately, to vanquish—that neoliberal collegiate loneliness. I discovered in my gender studies classrooms a set of critical tools to turn on the university itself, to begin questioning a form of education that produced students as atomized professionals, rather than unionized workers. This education took the form of class reading and professors' lectures. But mostly, it took the form of friendship with the other women and queer people (and it was majority, if not entirely, women and queer people) in my cohort.

That was my first glimmer of the feeling Vivian Gornick, writing in the 1990s, describes experiencing in the heyday of radical feminism. "To be a feminist in New York City in the early 70's—bliss was it in that dawn to be alive. Not an I-love-you in the world could touch it. There was no other place to be, except with each other" (1990, 24). It was my first glimpse of that most beautiful of relationships: the purpose-filled friendship between people getting *organized*. We supported each other through mundane classroom challenges—response papers, theses—even as we navigated the hierarchies and tensions in our own cohort, which was overwhelmingly cisgender and majority white. While the more privileged among us, including me, often made mistakes, many of us learned accountability toward one another through the practice of friendship. We became fellow travelers navigating the difficulties of college love and sex as queer people.

My senior year at Harvard, I finally became emboldened to turn my budding understanding of the structural nature of the university's malaise into public commentary and concrete action. I turned to journalism—my first taste of the power of my eventual profession—and published a series of columns in the student newspaper that analyzed the labyrinthine, hierarchical structures of undergraduate social life, exhorting other students to organize against sexual harassment, racism, and classism in their organizations. I met with students from across the university, held a strategizing session with dozens of students from various undergraduate organizations in my dorm room, and collaborated in building mechanisms for accountability within campus arts and journalism spaces. My women's studies cohort was allies throughout: we bounced ideas off each other, helped each other make connections, and unwound from it all over copious amounts of wine.

I couldn't have articulated it at the time, but that was also my first experience of what it is to be unionized. To be unionized is not just, or even primarily, to be a card-carrying member of a union. It is, at heart, a mode of thought and a means of power. It is to see oneself as a worker (for me, particularly a woman worker) in common cause with other workers, and subject to conditions that are political, historical, and thus changeable. Today, as a freelance journalist navigating an industry characterized by precarity, from the boom-and-bust cycle of online media to the ubiquity of contract work, I carry this early education with me. It affects me not only in the beats I cover (food and sex—the "care work" beat, I like to joke) but also in how I see myself and the action I hope to take to better the industry for all workers.

It would take until after college for me to really be able to articulate this glimmer of fellow feeling as a form of unionization. My education was good, but I believe the gender studies classroom in the neoliberal university is often too alienated from labor history and theory. I was never required to read Marx, so I learned materialist feminism, but I didn't understand the history of leftist thought feminist theorists drew from and were in conversation with. I learned about identity politics and the Combahee River Collective, but I didn't know that their work also fit into a history of Black socialist thought. "We are socialists because we believe that work must be organized for the collective benefit of those who do the work and create the products, and not for the profit of the bosses," the collective wrote in their statement. "We are not convinced, however, that a socialist revolution that is not also a feminist and anti-racist revolution will guarantee our liberation" (1983, 268). While my gender studies education was full of reading on the need for feminism and antiracism, I learned less about the "socialist revolution" part. This meant that while I saw myself as a woman formed by and enmeshed within interlocking, hierarchical systems, I had yet to envision myself as a woman *worker*. I heard critiques of the classism of the "lean-in" approach to women's work, but I wasn't able to see an alternative. I couldn't imagine an alternate system beyond the one in which women were atomized agents whose best hope was to negotiate raises within a flawed system.

It took completing a master's degree at New Delhi's Jawaharlal Nehru University—an educational space with a robust leftist tradition, where student politics were omnipresent and even setting classroom deadlines was an act of collective bargaining—to see myself as a worker. I had gone to Delhi for the first time as a high school student with a government scholarship for a summer of Hindi study, and returned later as an exchange student and, finally, as a master's student. Those years were a crash course in unlearning the class, racial, and colonial supremacies of the small, white world I had come from. I was indebted to the incredible political and personal generosity of my classmates and friends, who accepted me as a comrade even through my many mistakes. I was captivated by the courage of my peers. They were unionized students who relentlessly applied classroom lessons about social and economic justice to their activism and brought politics into the classroom. In an era when the Hindu Right was making increasing inroads into higher education, the atmosphere at the university was frenetic, risky, and rich.

For the first time, I truly felt that I wasn't an isolated passenger riding the university conveyor belt. I was part of a collective of students who, together, could actually drive the ship and challenge business as usual. I recall one course I took, about caste inequality, that ended up meeting only a handful of times in the semester—because most of the students were too busy organizing strikes against caste discrimination in university admissions. In this atmosphere, I realized that Harvard's lingering loneliness was political and strategic, and that the difficult, necessary work of solidarity enabled other ways to be and to live.

Now I'm a freelance journalist covering food and sex, trying to both pay rent and align my work with my values in New York City. At a basic level, gender studies has made me a more systematic thinker and a more empathic person, and thus a better journalist. I often write about marginalized histories of food and sexuality, and my research background in gender studies gives me the tools to tell stories that are conscious of social context and, I hope, informed by a diversity of voices. As a sexuality writer who produces both critical work ("What's the history of lesbian bars?") and service pieces ("What's the hottest worker-led porn?"), gender is my bread and butter.

Gender studies has also enabled me to better understand, and thus combat, the media industry's peculiar economy of feeling. Online media runs on undercompensated and precarious labor: armies of interns, "fellows" (normally postgraduates in their first or second job, with temporary, minimum- or subminimum-wage contracts), and contract workers. Meanwhile, staff roles become increasingly precarious, with ever-looming layoffs disrupting the illusion that those coveted benefits come with job security. The voracity of the online news cycle produces an atmosphere of constant productivity, driven by an unending appetite for clicks. When I entered the industry, I frequently found myself feeling "too slow": inept, sluggish, dawdling. Fellow writers were cranking out drafts like magic; what was wrong with me? The answer, of course, is that it wasn't me at all. The industry was too damn fast, the pay was too damn low, and the feeling of inadequacy functioned to persuade me to extract more labor from myself for less money. Thanks to my academic and organizing experience, I was able to recognize in the feeling the same atomization that had tainted the emotional water as an undergraduate, the same tendency to turn blame onto ourselves rather than the system.

Finally, and foremost, I've learned the importance of being, literally, unionized. The growth of both informality and leftist politics in the United States over the past couple of years has hit journalism in a big way, resulting in unprecedented unionization among freelancers. In particular, the Industrial Workers of the World's Freelance Journalists Union, which formed in 2018 and of which I'm a member, has already generated buzz (and thousands of Twitter followers, the real test of legitimacy in online media). It's also shown how direct action, even in the sometimes nebulous online space, can lead to concrete gains for workers. When Vox Media began requiring freelancers to sign contracts that prevented them from sharing rates (Benton 2019) (one of the only means of journalist-to-journalist accountability for pay equity in the industry), the union took to the tweets (IWW Freelance Journalists Union 2019b). Within two months, the contract had changed: not only was Vox now allowing freelancers to share rates, it was "happy to proactively permit such disclosure" because it "understands the important issues inherent in the rate transparency discussion" (IWW Freelance Journalists Union 2019a).

The union as a relation is often depicted as masculine, a solidarity of white, male workers whose togetherness exists within the performative idioms of patriarchy. Even Staughton Lynd's description of solidarity unionism, the framework of the IWW, describes worker solidarity in terms of the nuclear family: "In a family, when I as son, husband, or father, express love toward you, I do not do so in order to assure myself of love in return. . . . Similarly in a workplace, persons who work together form families-at-work" (2015, 24).

But for me, at best, being unionized is the feeling of feminine—of feminist—friendship. Not the solidarity of fathers and sons, but of queer people and women. It is the emotional character of a good gender studies classroom, of a group of people committed to transforming their politics and pedagogy into daily practice, of people who see their commitment to one another not as beside the point, but as the point. To become unionized is not merely to join an organization, but to undertake a process of thought, an act of transformation: the "collective" of collective action. It is not just to believe that your interests as a worker are tied to others'—it is to live the conviction that, as Gornick writes, there is nowhere and nothing to be but together.

Note

1. The feminist website Feministe (n.d.) has reclaimed this phrase, which is often used (in varying ways) to condemn feminists.

References

Benton, Joshua. 2019. "Vox Media Has Shifted Its Hiring toward Part-Timers and Contract Workers since Its Staff Unionized." Nieman Lab, May 29, 2019. https://www.niemanlab.org/2019/05/vox-media-has-shifted-its-hiring-toward-part-timers-and-contract-workers-since-its-full-time-staff-unionized.

Combahee River Collective. 1983. "The Combahee River Collective Statement." In *Home Girls: A Black Feminist Anthology*, edited by Barbara Smith, 264–274. Latham, NY: Kitchen Table Women of Color.

Feministe. n.d. Homepage. Accessed December 18, 2020. https://feministe.us/blog.

Gornick, Vivian. 1990. "Who Says We Haven't Made a Revolution?; A Feminist Takes Stock." *New York Times*, April 15, 1990, 24.

IWW Freelance Journalists Union (@IWWFJU). 2019a. "DIRECT ACTION GETS THE GOODS! From Vox's new contract: [image]." Twitter, August 16, 2019, 2:00 p.m. https://twitter.com/IWWFJU/status/1162469189187227649.

——. 2019b. "@voxmedia is trying to prevent freelancers from sharing their rates, and we won't stand for it. Send us the rates Vox websites have offered you and we'll share them here anonymously: freelancejournalists@iww.org." Twitter, June 20, 2019, 7:20 p.m. https://twitter.com/IWWFJU/status/1141893685866639360.

Lynd, Staughton. 2015. *Solidarity Unionism: Rebuilding the Labor Movement from Below*. 2nd ed. Oakland, CA: PM.

Urciuoli, Bonnie. 2018. *The Experience of Neoliberal Education*. New York: Berghahn Books.

Contributors

Rose Al Abosy graduated from the University of Chicago with degrees in biological sciences and gender and sexuality studies, researched mechanisms of resistance to immunotherapy at Dana-Farber Cancer Institute, and is currently a student at Boston University School of Medicine. They have many plants and one cat.

Rachel Cromidas is a writer and editor in Chicago. Her work has appeared in the *New York Times*, the *Wall Street Journal*, the *Chicago Tribune*, and *Buzzfeed Reader*, among many other publications.

Lauren Danzig received a BA with honors from the University of Chicago in 2011 and an MSW from the Columbia University School of Social Work in 2014. She has worked as a fundraiser for a variety of nonprofit organizations in New York City and specializes in corporate philanthropy.

Sadaf Ferdowsi received her BA from the University of Chicago and her MFA from Columbia College Chicago. She served as the assistant managing editor for the nonfiction magazine *Punctuate* from 2015 to 2020 and is currently the junior strategist and copywriter at the design agency Kaleidoscope. Her previous publications include pieces for the *Rumpus*, *Newcity*, *INTER*, and the *2nd Story* podcast.

Reina Gattuso is a feminist journalist, teacher, and organizer who lives in New York City. She was a 2015–2016 Fulbright fellow in women's studies at Jawaharlal Nehru University in New Delhi, India. She received her MA from Jawaharlal Nehru University and her BA from Harvard College.

Jael Goldfine is a freelance writer focusing on music and pop culture. She has written for *Paper* magazine, *Nylon*, *Stereogum*, the *Forward*, and Thinknum Media.

Jane Juffer is professor of English and director of Feminist, Gender, and Sexuality Studies at Cornell University. She is the author of four books, including, most recently, *Don't Use Your Words: Children's Emotions in a Networked World* (2019).

Sassafras Lowrey's books have been honored by organizations ranging from the Lambda Literary Foundation and the Dog Writers Association of America to the American Library Association. Sassafras's work has appeared in the *New York Times*, the *Rumpus*, *Catapult*, and numerous other publications. Sassafras lives and writes in Portland, Oregon, with hir partner and their menagerie of dogs and cats. Learn more at SassafrasLowrey.com.

Alissa Medina is the founder of *Fembot* magazine and a digital strategist based in Los Angeles. She received her master's in media, culture, and communications from New York University in 2017. Her writing has been featured in numerous publications, including *Bust*, *Immediacy*, and *Fembot*. You can catch her on Instagram @alissa_digital and find Fembot at fembot-mag.com.

Samuel Naimi is a writer and psychotherapist living in West Hollywood. He treats adult patients in private practice through the lens of feminist psychoanalysis. He continues to produce scholarship in the fields of feminist cultural studies and social work psychology.

Stephanie Newman is a Brooklyn-based writer and entrepreneur. She is currently working on her MFA in fiction writing from New York University. You can learn more about her work at stephanienewman.com.

Justine Parkin is a writer and educator based in Los Angeles. She has a BA in literature and philosophy from the University of California, Berkeley, and an MA in comparative literature from the University of Oregon. Her writing and research lie at the intersection of political theory, feminist science studies, and the environmental humanities.

Lily Pierce grew up in the suburbs of Chicago and went to the University of Chicago, where she majored in biology and minored in gender studies. She is currently a medical student at the University of Illinois College of Medicine, where she is in the process of completing her medical clerkships and applying to residency.

Kate Poor has supported refugees, asylum seekers, and other forcibly displaced folks in a handful of organizations focusing on the intersections of border issues and labor and housing justice in Mumbai and central Texas ever since graduating from Cornell University. She currently works at an English school and community center for refugees and asylum seekers in Austin, Texas.

Laura Ramos-Jaimes is a feminist born in Barrancabermeja, Colombia. She holds a BA in economics from the Universidad Nacional de Colombia in Bogotá and a master's degree in gender, policy, and inequalities from the London School of Economics and Political Science. She is currently a PhD student in economics at the University of Massachusetts, Amherst.

Savannah Medley Taylor graduated with a bachelor's degree in political science and philosophy in 2017 from Southwestern University and is a certified birth doula and postpartum doula. Savannah actively works to bring light to the revolutionary feminist nature of birth and breastfeeding in her Austin, Texas, community.

Addie Tsai is a queer nonbinary artist and writer of color. She teaches courses in literature, creative writing, dance, and humanities at Houston Community College. She holds an MFA from Warren Wilson College and a PhD in dance from Texas Woman's University. Addie is the author of the queer Asian young adult novel *Dear Twin*. Her writing has been published or is forthcoming in *Honey Literary*, *angstzine*, *Foglifter*, *VIDA Lit*, *Banango Street*, the *Offing*, the *Collagist*, the *Feminist Wire*, *Nat. Brut.*, and elsewhere.

Hayley Zablotsky graduated from Texas Christian University with a degree in writing and a minor in women and gender studies. Since graduation, she has worked as a college and career adviser, tutor, and freelance writer. In her spare time, she enjoys inventing new recipes (and eating the results), riding horses, and volunteering with her local animal shelter.

Index

activism on campus, 43
Adichie, Chimamanda Ngozi, 81
affective labor, 10–12; and immigrant advocacy nonprofits, 19
Ahmed, Sara, 2, 20, 23, 87–101, 126, 129, 134–36
anger, 4–5, 126, 134–138
Anzaldúa, Gloria, 4
Armbrust, Jennifer, 21, 83. *See also* feminine economy

Babcock and Laschever, Women Don't Ask, 63–64, 67
Baldwin, James, 110, 115
BDSM, 176–78
Berardi, Franco, 31
Berlant, Lauren, 180
Block, Jennifer, 140
brown, adrienne maree, 22, 37
Burke, Tarana, 157
Butler, Judith, 14, 52–53, 119–120, 149–52
Butler, Octavia, 21–22

capitalism, 9–14; in corporate feminist discourse, and attempts to represent feminism, 73, 75; and philanthropy, 49–54; in relation to nonprofits, 30–31; subversion of, 76–77
Caruth, Cathy, 106
Chicago Women's Liberation Union, 49, 54
Colombia, economic conditions, 59; colonial history, 60–61; racism against Indigenous and Black people, 65, 68; working-class femininity, 66–68
community college, 105–116
consent, in birthing, 141, 144–46
corporate feminism, 59–60, 62–64, 75, 81
Crenshaw, Kimberle, 82
criollización, in Colombia, 65, 68, 70

Dana-Farber Cancer Institute, 133
Dean, Tim, 178
de Beauvoir, Simone, 5, 170

Diels, Kelly, 83
Doulas, 138–46
Duffy, Brooke, 7–8, 11–12

Eisenstein, Zillah, 79
Elliott, Stephen, 188
entrepreneurial feminism, 79–85

Fembot magazine, 74–78
feminine economy, 21–22. *See also* Armbrust, Jennifer
"Founderitis," in nonprofit leadership structures, 36–38
Floyd, George, 5

Gal, Susan, 169–172
Gay, Ross, 29
Gay, Roxanne, 126
gender neutral bathrooms, 43
gender pay gap, 3, 15 (note), 160, 171
gig economy, 8
Goffman, Erving, 179
Gumbs, Alexis Pauline, 20
gun violence, 105–6

Halberstam, Jack, 28
Haraway, Donna, 29
Hardt, Michael, 10–11, 20
Hartmann, Heidi, 9–10
heteronormativity, and capitalism, 75–76; in the Me Too movement, 158
high school and feminist pedagogy, 117–130
Hill Collins, Patricia, 45–47. *See also* subjugated knowledge
hooks, bell, 4, 12, 69, 125, 127
House of Cards, 159–65
housing needs for migrants, 24–28; for LGBTQ youth, 44

immanent labor, 168–74. *See also* Iris Marion Young
immaterial labor, 10–11, 20
Immigration and Customs Enforcement, 22–24

Jaggar, Alison, 4, 21
journalism, 176–182

Lean-in feminism, 14, 59, 62. *See also* Sheryl
    Sandberg
Lorde, Audre, 4, 22, 81, 97, 126, 134, 137, 138,
    164–65
Lui, Rebecca, 93

Marxism, 9–11
McRobbie, Angela, 6–8, 11
Me Too movement, 141, 157–65
Migrant advocacy, 22
Milano, Alyssa, 157
Mohr, xx, Playing Big, 62–63
Moore, Darnell, 38
Moraga, Cherríe, 4
Mothering and feminism, 138–46

Negri, Antonio, 10–11, 20
Nelson, Maggie, 36
neoliberalism, 6–8, 89–101

obstetrics, 138–46
Odell, Jenny, 21

patriarchy, 9–10; and birthing, 140, 142–46;
    in Colombia, 60–61, 68; in the corporate
    workplace, 58, 83; in nonprofit management
    structures, 47; in philanthropy, 49–54
polyamory, 177–183
psychiatry, 147–53
publicity industry, for music, 90–91; for
    Hollywood celebrities, 159–65

queer politics, 157–65

racism, 30, 133–38, 146
Rapp, Anthony, 157–58
Rich, Adrienne, 141–42
Rubin, Gayle, 177

Sandberg, Sheryl, 14, 59, 62
Seacrest, Ryan, 163–64
secondary trauma, 31–32
social media work, 168–74
social work, 49–51
Solnit, Rebecca, 30
Spacey, Kevin, 157–63
subjugated knowledge, 45–48. *See also*
    Patricia Hill Collins

TEND Academy, 31–32
theory in the flesh, 4, 15
Tippett, Krista, 38
transcendent labor, 170–74

Union organizing, 14–15, 49, 54

van der Kolk, Bessel, 22
Veteran's Administration hospital,
    147–53
victim-blaming discourse, 68
vulnerability, 149–53

Warner, Michael, 178, 180
white supremacy, 106–116
workplace hazards, in nonprofits, 33–35
Wright, Robin, 159–65

Young, Iris Marion, 168–69, 172, 174

Zeisler, Andi, 81

Lightning Source UK Ltd.
Milton Keynes UK
UKHW010937191021
392187UK00013B/335

9 781501 760280